THE BUFFALO SOLDIERS

A Narrative of the Negro Cavalry in the West

THE
BUFFALO
SOLDIERS

A NARRATIVE OF
THE NEGRO CAVALRY
IN THE WEST

WILLIAM H. LECKIE

University of Oklahoma Press   :   Norman

By William H. Leckie

The Military Conquest of the Southern Plains (Norman, 1963)
*The Buffalo Soldiers: A Narrative of the Negro Cavalry in the
 West* (Norman, 1967)
Unlikely Warriors: General Benjamin Grierson and His Family
 (Norman, 1985)

LIBRARY OF CONGRESS CARD NUMBER: 67-15771

ISBN: 0-8061-1244-1

21 22 23 24 25 26

To Glorieta, Bill, Jr., and Bettie Sue

Helen,
The Troopers who
guard your Mom & Dad
are some of the best.

Larry.

FOREWORD

MY INTEREST in the American Negro soldier goes back two decades to the close of World War II. At that time I was placed in charge of two hundred Negro airmen en route to separation centers in the United States after long service in the South Pacific. A duty, which I at first regarded as onerous, became one of the most rewarding experiences of my life. Despite more than two years of arduous service and a low priority for discharge from the Army Air Corps, the men were obedient, cheerful, proud of their uniform, and altogether a credit to themselves and to their country. On the long voyage home I made many friends among them, and when our destination was reached, to a man they came by to shake my hand and express appreciation for "fair" treatment.

In the years that followed, casual reading revealed that the Negro had played a far greater role in American military history than I had ever imagined. Serious interest was aroused with my discovery that for a generation following the Civil War two regiments of Negro cavalry, the Ninth and Tenth, had served continuously on the Western frontier. An intensive search in the existing literature proved frustrating. In thousands of pages the Third, Fourth, Fifth, Sixth, and Seventh Cavalry, great regiments all, rode and fought their way to glory, but the Negro troopers were usually dismissed with a bare mention, ignored completely, or their efforts mocked. Only a handful of books and articles proved helpful, and virtually nothing was found in way of letters, diaries, or journals—not surprising in view of the fact that most of the troopers were illiterate.

It was not until I turned to the wealth of material in the military records of the National Archives that the true character and contributions of the Ninth and Tenth stood clearly revealed. For twenty-four years these regiments campaigned on the Great Plains, along the Río Grande, in New Mexico, Arizona, Colorado, and finally in the Dakotas. Their antagonists were the enemies of peace, order and settlement: warring Indians, bandits, cattle thieves, murderous gunmen, bootleggers, trespassers, and Mexican revolutionaries. All these they met many times, and with success, regardless of extremes of climate and terrain that ranged from the broken, rugged, and torrid Big Bend of Texas to the rolling plains, badlands, and subfreezing temperatures of South Dakota.

Their work was not limited to fighting. Many a frontier post arose as a result of their labors and the foundations thus were laid for future cities. Fort Sill, Oklahoma, and the thriving city of Lawton are prime examples. Scouting detachments stripped the mystery from little-known areas, located water, wood, and grass, and paved the way for eager settlers. Many a frontier official owed his life and his job to the support given him by these black men in blue, and many more farmers and ranchers slept soundly in their beds because a thin line of Negro troopers guarded them from harm.

The only obstacles the Ninth and Tenth could not overcome were those of prejudice and discrimination. These twin foes were constant enemies, ever harassing, hampering and embarrassing their efforts, and denying recognition for tasks well done. Three-quarters of a century have passed since the work of these regiments on the frontier came to a close, and their contributions still go largely unknown and unheralded. This book is an effort to tell the story of the Ninth and Tenth Cavalry, in the conviction that they deserve recognition for what they were—first-rate regiments by any standards one wishes to apply and major spearheads in the settlement of the West. It is a story of significant achievement under many handicaps, and a record in which every American can take justifiable pride.

In the research and writing of this book, I am indebted to many people. The assistance of Miss Sara Jackson of the National Archives is gratefully acknowledged, and Mrs. Anne Henry of Washington, D.C., was a tireless research assistant. Savoie Lottinville, director of the University of Oklahoma Press, has been a constant source of guidance and inspiration. Don Rickey, Jr., of the National Park Service provided information I would have otherwise overlooked. President William S. Carlson and Dean Jerome Kloucek of the University of Toledo gave every encouragement along with released time necessary to complete the manuscript. Particular thanks are due John Morgan of the University of Toledo Library, for his many courtesies and untiring efforts to secure desired material. Mrs. Josephine Soukup of Norman, Oklahoma, typed the manuscript with great skill and even greater patience.

My wife, Glorieta Leckie, assisted in the research and made possible the long periods necessary for undisturbed writing. The errors and shortcomings of this book, however, are entirely my own.

WILLIAM H. LECKIE

Toledo, Ohio

CONTENTS

ILLUSTRATIONS

Maps

Drawings

THE BUFFALO SOLDIERS

A Narrative of the Negro Cavalry in the West

THE EARLY YEARS

NEGRO TROOPS marched in the ranks of Washington's armies in the cause of independence and they served with Andrew Jackson at New Orleans in 1815 to repel the British invader, but their first large-scale employment awaited the coming of the Civil War. When Confederate batteries fired on Fort Sumter early on the morning of April 12, 1861, inaugurating four years of internecine warfare, many Negroes were eager to wear the Union blue. They found their services were neither wanted at that time nor contemplated in the future.[1]

The bitter conflict dragged on, however, and the casualty lists grew apace, and as thousands of black refugees sought sanctuary behind Union lines, sentiment began to change. On the first anniversary of Fort Sumter, General David Hunter, commanding the Department of the South, organized a Negro regiment. His effort was abortive, for it brought no joy to the hearts of Lincoln and his advisers, and the regiment was "turned off without a shilling, by order of the War Department."[2] Seven months later, however, Colonel T. W. Higginson of Massachusetts was invited to take command of the First Regiment of South Carolina Volunteers, the "first slave regiment mustered into the service of the United States."[3]

Colonel Higginson accepted the proffered command although had "an invitation reached me to take command of a regiment

[1] L. D. Reddick, "The Negro Policy of the United States Army," *The Journal of Negro History*, Vol. XXXIV, No. 1 (January, 1949), 14–15; Benjamin Quarles, *The Negro in the Civil War*, 31.
[2] Thomas Wentworth Higginson, *Army Life in a Black Regiment*, 15.
[3] *Ibid.*, 1.

of Kalmuck Tartars, it could hardly have been more unexpected."[4] This experiment, as well as others, proved successful and with the Emancipation Proclamation of January 1, 1863, enlistment of Negroes was on in earnest.[5]

The decision to use Negro troops was by no means universally popular and was little motivated, apparently, by idealism, but rather by the dictates of a grueling war. One historian of that war has written:

> This decision to use the Negro as a soldier did not necessarily grow out of any broad humanitarian resolve; it seems to have come more largely out of the dawning realization that, since the Confederates were going to kill a great many more Union soldiers before the war was over, a good many white men would escape death if a considerable percentage of those soldiers were colored.[6]

Such "dawning realization" did not come swiftly to many officers and men in the Union army in which stout opposition developed, and General Grant was forced to enjoin his subordinates that:

> It is expected that all commanders will especially exert themselves in carrying out the policy of the administration, not only in organizing colored regiments and rendering them effective, but also in removing prejudice against them.[7]

Grant's instruction may have tempered resistance somewhat, but many officers vowed never to serve with Negro troops and there was resentment and anger among rank and file. Feeling ran so high in one Ohio division that the men threatened to stack their arms and return home. Adjutant General Lorenzo Thomas felt compelled to warn that any such action would be regarded as treason and the men involved would be shot.[8]

Resistance to the use of Negro troops soon diminished. Officers discovered that a commission in a black regiment could mean

[4] *Ibid.*, 2.

[5] Quarles, *op. cit.*, 182.

[6] Bruce Catton, *This Hallowed Ground: The Story of the Union Side of the Civil War*, 222.

[7] George W. Williams, *A History of the Negro Troops in the War of the Rebellion, 1861–1865*, 108.

[8] *Ibid.*, 110.

quick promotion and no shortage of candidates developed in meeting the needs of the new organizations. Further, as the Negro proved his worth as a soldier, general though reluctant acceptance became the rule although discrimination persisted until the end of the war.[9]

And prove his worth he did. Negroes fought at Fort Wagner, South Carolina, and Milliken's Bend, Louisiana, at Baxter Springs, Kansas, and Point Lookout, Virginia, and in the slaughterhouse that was Cold Harbor. Hundreds were massacred at Fort Pillow, Tennessee, and they bled and died on scores of other battlefields, and if there was any lingering question of their merit, spirit, and courage, it should have been dispelled by their charge into the "Crater" before Petersburg on July 30, 1864.[10]

Here Union sappers tunneled under a Confederate strong point in the Petersburg defenses and mined up. The mine was exploded at dawn, blasting a huge "crater" in the Confederate line. General Ambrose Burnside, a master fumbler, failed to attack at once and the Confederates took advantage of the respite to build a new line to the rear of the "crater." The Union attack, when finally launched, was a failure and even after this became clear, Burnside ordered General Edward Ferrero's Fourth Division composed entirely of Negro infantry, to try to break the Confederate defense. They charged with great spirit and gallantry, but met a galling fire in which "hundreds of heroes carved in ebony fell." They were forced to retire, but some stood their ground until most were killed.[11]

By the end of the war nearly 180,000 Negroes had served in the Union army and taps had sounded over the bodies of 33,380 of them who had given their lives for freedom and Union. Despite the record there were many who still doubted that the Negro could

[9] James G. Randall, *The Civil War and Reconstruction*, 506–507. Negro soldiers were paid ten dollars per month for their services, while their white counterparts received thirteen dollars. There was also a difference in bonuses.

[10] Frederick Phisterer, *Statistical Record of the Armies of the United States*, 68. At Fort Pillow, Tennessee, on April 12, 1864, three hundred Negro soldiers of the Sixth United States Colored Heavy Artillery and the Second Colored Light Artillery were murdered as they sought to surrender to Confederates under General Nathan Bedford Forrest. See Dudley T. Cornish, *The Sable Arm*, 173–74.

[11] *Battles and Leaders of the Civil War*, IV, 564.

be a first-rate combat soldier, and his future in the Army of the United States remained clouded in uncertainty.[12]

On May 23–24, 1865, the Union Army staged its last great spectacle. Nearly a quarter of a million men in blue passed in grand review along Pennsylvania Avenue in the nation's capital. Swiftly then the United States reverted to its traditional policy of a small peacetime army. Within little more than a year the military establishment had been all but dismantled and the authorized strength of the army was only 54,641 officers and men—the actual strength was considerably less.[13] This was the situation in the face of a savage Indian war in the West and conditions approaching anarchy along the Mexican border.

Congress, meanwhile, had cleared up some of the uncertainty surrounding the future of the Negro in the armed forces, and, in so doing, altered the face of military tradition. By an act passed on July 28, 1866, provisions were made for the Negro to serve in the regular peacetime army. Six regiments of Negro troops were authorized, two of cavalry and four of infantry. By this legislation Congress opened a new chapter in American military history and afforded the erstwhile slave an opportunity to play a major role in the settlement of the West.[14]

Since the use of Negro troops in the peacetime army was regarded as something of an experiment, the authorizing act contained some unusual provisions. Chaplains were normally assigned to a particular post or station, but in the case of the Negro units the chaplain was assigned directly to a regiment with both spiritual and educational duties, for he was to instruct the soldiers in the rudiments of reading, writing, and arithmetic.

There were no experienced Negro officers and Congress provided that all officers of the new regiments were to be white along with a requirement that all of them must take a special examination

---

[12] Cornish, *The Sable Arm*, 288; Reddick, *loc. cit.*, 17–18.
[13] Actual strength of the army was only 38,540. *Annual Report of the Secretary of War for the Year 1866*, 3–4; William A. Ganoe, *The History of the United States Army*, 307.
[14] Major John Bigelow, Jr., Historical Sketch, Tenth United States Cavalry, 1866–1892, United States Army Commands, RG 98, NA (hereinafter cited as Bigelow, "Sketch").

before a board of experienced officers appointed by the secretary of war. Two years of active field service in the Civil War were required of all officers, with two-thirds of those holding the rank of captain or above drawn from the volunteer regiments and one-third from the Regular Army. Officers of lower rank were to be drawn exclusively from the volunteer services.[15]

Early in August, 1866, General Grant telegraphed General Philip Sheridan, commanding the Division of the Gulf, and General William T. Sherman, commanding the Military Division of the Missouri, to organize a regiment of Negro cavalry in their respective divisions. The new regiments were designated as the Ninth and Tenth United States Cavalry, and Grant recommended two officers with brilliant Civil War records to command them—Colonel Edward Hatch of Iowa and Colonel Benjamin Grierson of Illinois.[16]

Edward Hatch, a blond, blue-eyed native of Maine, had gone early to sea and then engaged in the lumber business in Pennsylvania. In 1855 he moved to Iowa and was residing there when the war came. He received appointment as a captain in the Second Iowa Cavalry in August, 1861, and in less than a year was its colonel. He took part in Grierson's famous raid of 1863, received citations for gallantry and meritorious service at the battles of Franklin and Nashville, and closed out the war as brevet major general of volunteers. Able, decisive, ambitious, and personable, he received Grant's unqualified endorsement to lead the Ninth Cavalry.[17]

Tall, swarthy, scar-faced Benjamin Grierson was a most unlikely candidate for a distinguished career as a cavalryman. Since the age of eight, when a pony kicked him in the face and left a cheek scarred permanently, he had been skittish of horses. A small-town music teacher and an ardent admirer of Abraham Lincoln,

[15] *Ibid.;* Lieutenant Grote Hutcheson, "The Ninth Regiment of Cavalry," in Theodore F. Rodenbough and William L. Haskin (eds.), *The Army of the United States,* 280.
[16] Grant to Sheridan and Sherman, August 4, 1866, SLR Relating to the Ninth and Tenth Cavalry, AGO, RG 94, NA.
[17] Francis B. Heitman, *Historical Register and Dictionary of the United States Army,* I, 510; D. Alexander Brown, *Grierson's Raid,* 61–62.

he volunteered immediately when the war came and sought a commission in the infantry. But fate decreed otherwise and when his appointment came through, he found himself a major in the Sixth Illinois Cavalry. Despite an almost complete lack of military experience and his dislike of horses, Grierson was soon promoted to colonel and was selected by General Grant in April of 1863 to lead three regiments of cavalry in a diversionary raid through Mississippi.

Grierson's six-hundred-mile, sixteen-day raid through the Confederate heartland contributed materially to Grant's successful operations around Vicksburg, led the latter to describe the raid as the most brilliant expedition of the war, and made the easygoing and tolerant Grierson a national figure. By the time of Appomattox he was a brevet major general of volunteers and had the confidence of both Grant and Sherman. Mustered out of service in April, 1866, he gave brief thought to a business career and then accepted the proffered command of the Tenth Cavalry.[18]

Hatch and Grierson wasted no time in proceeding with the organization of their regiments. The former established headquarters at Greenville, Louisiana, and the latter at Fort Leavenworth, Kansas. From the first, however, difficulty was encountered in procuring experienced officers, for many of them refused to serve with Negro troops. More than a few agreed with Brevet Major General Eugene A. Carr that Negroes simply would not make good soldiers, and took a lower rank in order to serve with a white regiment. The dashing "boy general," George A. Custer, refused a lieutenant colonelcy with the Ninth and wangled the same rank in the newly formed Seventh Cavalry—a decision that was probably a stroke of good fortune for the Ninth and launched Custer on the road to the Little Big Horn and a dubious niche in history ten years later.[19]

[18] Brigadier General Benjamin H. Grierson, *The Lights and Shadows of Life, Including Experiences and Remembrances of the War of the Rebellion,* manuscript autobiography, Illinois State Historical Society; Heitman, *op. cit.,* I, 478. Brown, *op. cit.,* contains considerable material concerning Grierson's early life.

[19] Bigelow, "Sketch"; E. D. Townsend, AAG, to Sheridan, August 3, 1866, SLR Relating to the Ninth and Tenth Cavalry, AGO; James T. King, *War Eagle: A Life of General Eugene A. Carr,* 77.

Despite possibilities for greater rank and more rapid promotion in the Negro regiments, many officers of lower rank had their feelings expressed clearly in an advertisement that appeared in the *Army and Navy Journal*:

> A first Lieutenant of Infantry (white) stationed at a very desirable post in the Department of the South desires a transfer with an officer of the same grade, on *equal* terms if in a white regiment; but if in a colored regiment, a reasonable bonus would be expected.[20]

Under such circumstances officer procurement proceeded at a snail's pace. In November Hatch complained to the Adjutant General that he had several hundred recruits on hand at Greenville, was receiving arms and horses, but still did not have a single officer present for duty. Grierson had an additional complaint. He believed that regular army officers were being assigned to white regiments and only volunteers were staffing the Negro units. If this was the policy of the government, he wrote Mrs. Grierson, "I will not remain in the army."[21]

Officer procurement was stepped up and the Ninth obtained some excellent ones, including Lieutenant Colonel Wesley Merritt and Major Albert P. Morrow, but the flow was still much too slow in Hatch's case, for recruits were pouring into the camp at Greenville. Army recruiters, with great haste and little judgment, concentrated their efforts in nearby New Orleans and vicinity and had little difficulty in enlisting the necessary numbers, for in most instances they seem to have winked at physical qualifications. Many young Negroes were eager to enlist because the army afforded an opportunity for social and economic betterment difficult to achieve in a society all but closed to them. Thirteen dollars a month was meager pay, but it was more than most could expect to earn as civilians, and when food, clothing, and shelter were added, a better life seemed assured.[22]

20 *Army and Navy Journal*, Vol. VIII (June 10, 1871), 684.

21 Grierson to Mrs. Grierson, October 6, 1866, Grierson Papers, Illinois State Historical Society; Hatch to the AG, November 4, 1866, SLR Relating to the Ninth and Tenth Cavalry, AGO.

22 Wesley Merritt was a graduate of West Point with a brilliant record in the Civil War. He received seven brevets for gallant and meritorious service and held the

For whatever reasons, they enlisted in droves. Nor were all of them from Louisiana. Kentucky contributed, among others, farmer George Gray, doomed to die of tetanus in the post hospital at Fort Clark, Texas, and laborer William Sharpe, with an Indian arrow awaiting him on the rocky banks of the Pecos River. Little Emanuel Stance, nineteen years old and scarcely five feet tall, was a native of Charleston, South Carolina, with a Medal of Honor in his future. From Virginia came Washington Wyatt who would die at the hands of persons unknown in Austin, Texas, before he reached his twenty-first birthday. And so they came, farmers, teamsters, dyers, cooks, bakers, painters, waiters, and cigar makers, to enlist for five years in the Ninth Regiment of Cavalry, USA.[23]

But they came too quickly and officers were far too few to train, discipline, and educate so many green recruits or even to keep them busy at routine tasks. The men were nearly all illiterate and filled with superstition. The wildest rumor found ready ears and provoked constant unrest, while the enforced idleness led to gambling, drinking, quarreling, and fighting. Harlots swarmed about the camp along with other undesirables. The cotton compresses in which they were quartered became overcrowded and along with rations, poorly cooked over open fires, led to illness and disease. Cholera struck in October and November, killing twenty-three men and spreading fear among the rest. Desertions became frequent and morale slid toward the vanishing point.[24]

Despite the difficulties and shaky discipline, Hatch managed

---

rank of Major General of Volunteers when the war ended. He accepted the lieutenant colonelcy of the Ninth Cavalry in July, 1866, and remained with the regiment until July, 1876, when he was appointed colonel of the Fifth Cavalry. Albert P. Morrow rose through the ranks to become a brevet colonel of the Sixth Pennsylvania Cavalry. He joined the Ninth as a major in March, 1867, and served with the regiment for fifteen years. See Heitman, *op. cit.*, 706–29.

23 Organizational Returns, Ninth Cavalry, August–September, 1867, AGO, RG 94, NA; Registers of Enlistments in the United States Army, 1798–1914, Microcopy No. 233, NA. These registers are arranged alphabetically and by year, giving the name, place of enlistment, place of birth, age, civilian occupation, and condition of service termination. As such they are a mine of information on enlisted men for the period given.

24 Organizational Returns, Ninth Cavalry, November–December, 1866; Hutcheson, *loc. cit.*, 282.

to organize all twelve companies of the regiment by February, 1867, though only eleven officers had reported for duty at that time. Rumors of impending service on the frontier were circulating among the men, and officers noted that some of their neophyte troopers were becoming surly and unruly. Rumor became fact in March when Hatch received orders transferring the regiment to Texas. Two companies, L and M, were to take station at Brownsville on the Río Grande while the remaining ten companies were to encamp near San Antonio and undergo further training.

Marching orders had come much too soon. Hatch had little more than an ill-disciplined mob on his hands and the stage was set for violence and tragedy. En route to San Antonio mutiny flared in K company and was suppressed only with great difficulty. When the city was reached, no brass bands turned out to welcome black men in blue uniforms and friction developed quickly between troopers and citizens. Clashes with police became an almost daily occurrence. Serious trouble was only a matter of time, and it came on April 9 as too few officers strove to control their men. Mutiny broke out in A, E, and K companies, and before order was restored, young Lieutenant Seth Griffin of A received a mortal wound and Lieutenant Fred Smith of K was forced to shoot two of his troopers.[25]

Hatch placed the blame for this tragic affair on a shortage of officers, and Captain W. S. Abert, Sixth Cavalry, assigned to investigate the mutiny, sustained him, but added that many of the men were "too light, too young and have weak constitutions."[26] He might have added that among the villains in the piece were careless or indifferent recruiters who had enlisted far too many men who were unfit for military service.

Hatch appealed for more officers, pointing out that only four-

[25] Organizational Returns, Ninth Cavalry, February–April, 1867; Hatch to the AAG, District of Texas, May 14, 1867, SDLR, AGO, RG 94, NA; San Antonio *Daily Express*, May 8, 1867.

[26] Hatch to the AAG, District of Texas, May 14, 1867, SDLR, AGO; Captain W. S. Abert to the AG, June 7, 1867, *ibid*. The Ninth was not the only new regiment to face the problem of mutiny. In July, 1867, a serious outbreak occurred in the Seventh Cavalry and three troopers were shot. See Theodore R. Davis, "A Summer on the Plains," *Harper's Monthly Magazine*, Vol. XXXVI (February, 1868), 306.

teen had been present at the time of the mutiny and that little could be expected of the regiment until this shortage was corrected. The War Department responded with alacrity and within a month Hatch could report that both morale and discipline were much improved. It was none too soon, for conditions in the vast expanse of West Texas and along the Río Grande were fast becoming intolerable and troops were needed badly. Hatch received orders in May to march west and occupy Forts Stockton and Davis. Before midsummer all ten companies had reached these posts, and an untried regiment with the stain of mutiny on its standard faced the formidable task of standing guard over hundreds of miles of of raw frontier.[27]

Meanwhile, at Fort Leavenworth, Grierson struggled with problems that were, if anything, more exasperating than those of Hatch. Organization of the regiment proceeded very slowly because of lack of officers coupled with Grierson's insistence on a very high standard for enlisted men. These instructions sent to Captain L. H. Carpenter, on recruiting service in Philadelphia, were typical:

> recruit men sufficiently educated to fill the positions of Non-Commissioned Officers, Clerks and Mechanics in the regiment. You will use the greatest care in your selection of recruits . . . enlist all the superior men you can who will be a credit to the regiment.[28]

And to Colonel S. Hendrickson, recruiting in Boston, he wrote, "Endeavor to secure the best material, as the quality is more important than numbers."[29] These standards were difficult to meet and at the end of September, 1866, only one man, Private William Beauman, had arrived at Leavenworth, and he was ill with malaria.[30]

The pace of organization was so slow that Grierson found ample time to write frequently to Mrs. Grierson concerning the

27 Organizational Returns, Ninth Cavalry, May–June, 1867; Hutcheson, *loc. cit.*, 283; Hatch to the AAG, District of Texas, May 14, 1867, SDLR, AGO.
28 Grierson to Carpenter, March 5, 1867, LS, Tenth United States Cavalry, United States Army Commands, RG 98, NA.
29 Grierson to Hendrickson, June 3, 1867, *ibid.*
30 Organizational Returns, Tenth Cavalry, September, 1866, AGO, RG 94, NA.

social scene at Leavenworth and to relate with considerable relish some details of a grasshopper invasion:

> . . . they were [grasshoppers] impolite and unceremonious enough to hop up, get up or in some way make their merry way up under the hoops and skirts of the ladies who are bold enough to promenade among them. From the motions I have myself seen made by ladies walking the streets, I am of the opinion that they were being tickled almost to death by grasshoppers—in some instances wiggling was most excruciating—even enough to drive a man with a heart of stone promptly to the rescue . . . should the grasshoppers remain here very long, I have no doubt but what some Yankee will invent some new pattern for the relief of the ladies in the way of *solid drawers.*[31]

The tempo of enlistment increased slightly in the late fall and winter as additional officers reported for duty and were detailed at once on recruiting service. Early efforts had been concentrated in the states of the Upper South, but Grierson was dissatisfied with the results and most of the recruiters were shifted to northern cities such as Philadelphia, Boston, New York, and Pittsburgh.

And Grierson kept a watchful eye on the new recruits as they arrived at Leavenworth to insure that his standards were being observed. He was quick to take a careless officer to task and wrote a tart letter to Captain H. T. Davis at Memphis, Tennessee, in which he warned, "You will have to foot the bill for your rejects in the future."[32] Needless to say, the quality of Davis' enlistees improved as if by magic. The net result, however, was a continued slow pace, and as 1867 opened Grierson could report that only seven officers and eighty enlisted men had joined the regiment.[33]

Spring brought a sharp upswing in enlistments, but also increasing friction between Grierson and General William Hoffman, Third Infantry, commanding at Leavenworth. The latter, contemptuous of Negro troops and apparently of officers who served with them, contrived to make their stay at his post as uncomfortable as possible. He quartered them on low ground that became

31 Grierson to Mrs. Grierson, October 3, 1866, Grierson Papers.
32 Grierson to Davis, March 6, 1867, LS, Tenth Cavalry.
33 Organizational Returns, Tenth Cavalry, January, 1867.

13

a swamp when wet with the result that a number of troopers were soon in the hospital with pneumonia, and he ignored Grierson's pleas for a change of quarters or even to provide walkways so the men could at least keep their feet dry.[34]

Prejudiced and a master of the petty, Hoffman bombarded Grierson with complaints about untidy quarters, alleged tardiness to meals, training methods, and improper routing of correspondence. One group of Grierson's recruits, encamped along the road between Leavenworth and the city, was ordered to "get out of sight."[35] During inspection Grierson's company commanders were ordered to keep their men at least ten to fifteen yards from white troops, and the Negroes were not allowed to march in review but were ordered to remain at parade rest.[36]

Such rank discrimination led Grierson to fiery protest on the paradeground, but Hoffman refused to yield. Grierson fought back as best he could. Tolerant and genuinely fond of his men, he ordered his company commanders not to use the word "colored" in their reports—"The regiment is simply the Tenth Regiment of Cavalry, United States Army."[37] And he complained directly to Department Headquarters of "invidious distinctions between white and Negro troops" and insisted on impartial treatment for his men.[38]

Grierson received no satisfactory answers to his complaints and came to fear that the future of his regiment was endangered. He resolved to organize his companies and get them on the march "double quick." He wrote to his wife that there were "Old Fogies" in the army who wished to disband the Negro regiments and he was glad that there were few recruits at Leavenworth "for the

34 Grierson to the PA, Fort Leavenworth, February 2, 1867, LS, Tenth Cavalry; *Annual Report of the Secretary of War for the Year 1867*, 39; Organizational Returns, Tenth Cavalry, February–March, 1867.

35 Captain George T. Robinson to Grierson, June 30, 1867, Grierson Papers; Hoffman to Grierson, June 27, 1867, *ibid.*; Grierson to the PA, June 21, 1867, LS, Tenth Cavalry; Lieutenant Henry E. Alvord to the PA, April 17, 1867, LS, Tenth Cavalry.

36 Hoffman to Grierson, June 27, 1867, Grierson Papers.

37 Lieutenant Henry Alvord, Acting Adjutant, Tenth Cavalry, to Lieutenant N. D. Badger, June 18, 1867, LS, Tenth Cavalry.

38 Grierson to the AAG, Department of the Missouri, June 19, 1867, *ibid.*

powers that be to wreak their spite and wrath upon."[39] In a pro-phetic vein he continued, "Colored troops will hold their place in the Army of the United States as long as the government lasts."[40]

Another difficulty arose at Leavenworth that would plague Negro troopers for as long as they remained on the frontier—poor horses. Grierson journeyed to St. Louis to inspect a herd of fifty animals and found not a single one that was suitable for service. Many were wind-blown cripples of the Civil War and others were more than a dozen years old. Grierson began a campaign, which he was to continue for many years, to obtain decent horseflesh for the troopers of his regiment.[41]

Poor mounts did not delay Grierson's resolve to move at "double quick" to organize his regiment. A Company was out-fitted and sent west in February, and two months more were re-quired for Company B, but Company C was "armed, organized, uniformed, equipped, mounted and marched west under Captain [Edward] Byrne at this post [Leavenworth] last week in forty-eight hours after arrival of recruits from St. Louis."[42] General Hoffman took a parting shot at C Company by denying permis-sion for the laundresses to accompany it, but Byrne was equal to the occasion and told the women to walk out of the post and when out of sight to climb on the wagons.[43]

Grierson became so impatient that he did not wait for the normal complement of ninety-nine men to fill D Company, but wrote to Captain J. W. Walsh, on recruiting duty at Little Rock, Arkansas, to organize the company at Fort Gibson, Indian Ter-ritory, with the men on hand, though he cautioned Walsh to draw one hundred Spencer repeating carbines, sixteen to eighteen re-volvers for the non-commissioned officers, and all other supplies necessary for a full company. The remaining personnel could be assigned later.[44]

39 Grierson to Mrs. Grierson, May 24, 1867, Grierson Papers.
40 *Ibid.*
41 Grierson to Mrs. Grierson, April 26, 1867, *ibid.*
42 Alvord to Captain J. W. Walsh, May 23, 1867, LS, Tenth Cavalry; Organiza-tional Returns, Tenth Cavalry, February–May, 1867.
43 Mrs. Grierson to Grierson, May 21, 1867, Grierson Papers.
44 Grierson to Walsh, May 4, 1867, LS, Tenth Cavalry; Alvord to Walsh, May

Organization was thus hastened, and even greater speed could have been achieved but for the illiteracy of the men. A company was fortunate to have one man who could read and write, and he was invariably made quartermaster sergeant. Grierson soon found, however, that literacy was not an absolute prerequisite for non-commissioned rank. Most of the initial companies had illiterate first sergeants, most of whom performed well, but for many months the officers were forced to do the clerical work and delays in the organization and training of the regiment were the inevitable result. The necessity for officers and men to work closely together, however, brought future dividends in the form of more intimate relationships between officers and men than characterized other regiments of the army.[45]

Despite the difficulties, including an outbreak of cholera in June and July that took many lives, eight companies of the Tenth were in the field by the beginning of August, 1867. Companies D, E, and L were assigned to Indian Territory while the others were stationed at posts and camps along the Kansas Pacific Railroad under construction in central Kansas. Early in August, Grierson received orders to transfer his headquarters to Fort Riley, Kansas, and in a matter of hours he left Fort Leavenworth, General Hoffman, and fears for the future of his regiment behind him.[46]

At Fort Riley, Grierson welcomed the arrival of an old friend

23, 1867, *ibid*. Revolvers issued to the cavalry at this time were usually the Colt Army .44, a single-action, six-shot weapon using percussion cartridges. The Spencer carbine, standard for the cavalry until 1873, was of .56–50 caliber, with a seven-shot magazine that was inserted into the stock through a hole in the butt plate. The cartridges in the magazine were nose to tail, however, and the gun had a discouraging tendency to discharge accidentally. "Death by accidental gunshot wound" is a common entry in the Organizational Returns of both the Ninth and Tenth Cavalry until the Spencer was replaced by the Model 1873 Springfield in that year. See S. E. Whitman, *The Troopers*, 178–88. See also Larry Koller, *The Fireside Book of Guns*, 77–80.

45 Bigelow, "Sketch"; Grierson to Lieutenant Robert Gray, May 9, 1867, LS, Tenth Cavalry.

46 Organizational Returns, Tenth Cavalry, June–July, 1867. Sixteen men died of cholera in July alone. Grierson to the AG, Washington, D. C., August 7, 1867, SDLR, AGO. Fort Riley, first real home of the Tenth Cavalry, was situated on the north bank of the Kansas River at the junction of the Republican and Smoky Hill rivers. It was named for Colonel Bennett Riley, First United States Infantry, and became a permanent cavalry post in 1855. See Robert W. Frazer, *Forts of the West*, 57.

and aide of Civil War days, Lieutenant Samuel Woodward, who replaced Captain Henry Alvord as regimental adjutant, while the latter took command of Company M. For the next twenty years, without promotion, "Sandy" Woodward served the Tenth Cavalry and its colonel with singular efficiency and unfailing devotion.[47]

Organization of the remaining four companies of the regiment was completed at Riley, although it was October before Company M, the last, was ready for the field. But M enjoyed the privilege of being the first to depart for the west to the tunes of the regimental band. Music lover that he was, Grierson managed to find a few musicians and to teach some others, but no funds were available for instruments. He solved this dilemma by establishing a band fund to which the enlisted men were asked to contribute fifty cents apiece while each group of company officers donated fifty dollars.[48]

One year of history was behind the Tenth Cavalry, but the fighting qualities of officers and men were still an unknown quantity—they would not long so remain.

The movement westward of the Ninth and Tenth Cavalry in the spring and summer of 1867 marked the beginning of more than two decades of continuous service on the Great Plains and in the mountains and deserts of New Mexico and Arizona. The challenge was a formidable one. Ten years of near constant campaigning were required before the wild-riding nomads of the Southern Plains—the Comanches, Kiowas, Kiowa-Apaches, Southern Cheyennes, and Arapahoes—were defeated and pinned securely within their reservations; half again as long before peace prevailed along the tortured Río Grande frontier where Kickapoos and Lipans, Mexican bandits and revolutionaries, roamed, raided, stole, and murdered under conditions approaching anarchy. And, for just

[47] Alvord to Grierson, September 21, 1867, Grierson Papers; Woodward to Grierson, October 3, 1867, *ibid.* Woodward, a New Yorker, rose through the ranks in the Sixth Illinois Cavalry and was discharged as a major when the Civil War ended. Commissioned as a lieutenant in the Tenth Cavalry, he was not promoted to captain until 1887. See Heitman, *op. cit.*, I, 1059.

[48] Organizational Returns, Tenth Cavalry, July–October, 1867; Circular, Grierson to All Company Commanders, September 14, 1867, LS, Tenth Cavalry.

as many years, the Ninth and Tenth fought the Apaches of New Mexico and Arizona in mountain nests and on waterless, desolate desert wastes.

The duties of the regiments would not be limited to fighting Indians. Law and order were little more than a hope in the post-Civil War Southwest, and civil authorities were compelled constantly to call upon the army to assist in rounding up border scum. The region swarmed with cattle thieves as well as men who killed with little or no provocation. Petty, scheming, and sometimes murderous politicians, combined with greedy land and cattle barons, crooked government contractors, heartless Indian agents, and land-hungry homesteaders, were the source of civil broils of a scope far beyond the control of local or state authority. The result was inevitable involvement in civil affairs for the Ninth and Tenth with little hope or expectation of gratitude regardless of outcome or contribution. But in the summer of 1867, Hatch, Grierson, and their troopers rode west with no foreknowledge of the awesome tasks that awaited them, and perhaps it was just as well.

II

THE TENTH MOVES TO THE PLAINS

G RIERSON and his fledgling regiment marched westward
and straight into an Indian war of almost unprecedented
scope and violence. The coming of the Civil War and the withdrawal of federal garrisons from the Plains had given the Indians
an opportunity to reclaim lands lost to aggressive whites. The
Kiowas and Comanches had driven in the Texas frontier for many
miles, while the Cheyenne War of 1864–65 had ravaged the Central Plains. An uneasy peace had been achieved with these tribes
by the Treaty of the Little Arkansas in October, 1865, but lands
assigned them under terms of the treaty lay partly in Texas and
Kansas, and both states had refused to countenance reservations
within their borders. The result was that for more than two years
these people had no official home.[1]

This state of affairs could only mean a swift renewal of the
conflict, and the Kiowas and Comanches struck once more at
their old Texan foes while the Cheyennes grew increasingly sullen and restless. To forestall a major outbreak, General Winfield
Scott Hancock, commanding the Department of the Missouri, took
the field in April, 1867, to "overawe" or defeat any hostile redmen
he might encounter. Hancock's campaign brought disastrous results. He failed to overawe a single Indian, and he provoked a
full-scale war which he was unable to control. By the summer of
1867 Indians were running wild over the area of the Central and
Southern Plains.[2]

[1] Charles J. Kappler, *Indian Affairs: Laws and Treaties*, II, 887–95; Donald J.
Berthrong, *The Southern Cheyennes*, 238–44; *Annual Report of the Commissioner of
Indian Affairs for the Year 1868*, 35.
[2] New York *Tribune*, September 2, 1857; Berthrong, *op. cit.*, 277–87; William
H. Leckie, *The Military Conquest of the Southern Plains*, 44ff.

Cheyenne war parties, with the help of hostile Arapahoes and Sioux, took a heavy toll along the Smoky Hill River, the line of the Kansas Pacific Railroad, and brought work virtually to a halt. In mid-June General Hancock reported that every station along the road for nearly one hundred miles on either side of Fort Wallace had been attacked, some as many as four times. Nor was Fort Wallace itself immune. Four men were killed and scalped near the post early in the month, and on June 21 two teamsters hauling stone from a quarry were killed within sight of the post. Five days later a force of Cheyennes estimated at two to three hundred attacked Pond Creek Station just west of Wallace. Three hours of desperate fighting on the part of Captain Albert Barnitz and Company G, Seventh Cavalry, were required to save the station.[3]

Other hostile warriors swarmed in the vicinity of Forts Hays and Harker killing unwary trappers and travelers and running off stock. Near the latter post a gentleman from Boston, refusing to believe the Indian danger either so real or so near, persisted in searching for geological specimens along Fossil Creek. While walking along the creek bed he met an incoming settler who remarked, "You'll find my partners body a layin' down there; the Injins was in half an hour ago and tuk his scalp, and I haint had time to get him in since."[4] Interest in gathering fossils ceased then and there.

The Texas frontier and the Civilized Tribes of Indian Territory suffered heavily from Kiowa and Comanche raiders. Governor J. W. Throckmorton of Texas telegraphed Secretary of War Edwin M. Stanton that in the month of July alone 18 persons had been killed by these Indians, and that since the end of the Civil War 162 citizens had lost their lives, 43 had suffered capture, and 24 had been wounded. Cattle to the number of 30,838 had been stolen, along with nearly 4,000 horses. Captain E. L. Smith, Nineteenth Infantry, reported from Fort Arbuckle that a thou-

---

[3] *Annual Report of the Secretary of War for the Year 1867*, 33; Post Returns, Fort Wallace, June, 1867; *Harper's Weekly Magazine*, Vol. XI (July 27, 1867), 467–68.
[4] *Army and Navy Journal*, Vol. IV (July 20, 1867), 770; Post Returns, Fort Hays, June, 1867.

sand men would be required to protect the lives and property of the Civilized Tribes.[5]

An ugly and dangerous situation existed, therefore, from the Platte River on the north to the Río Grande on the south, but General William T. Sherman, commanding the vast Military Division of the Missouri, which encompassed the Great Plains, had far too few troops at his disposal to provide a solid defense for such a long frontier, and an economy-minded Congress was in no mood to provide funds to strengthen the military arm. Sherman would have to make do with such troops as he had.[6]

As a partial remedy, therefore, three companies of the Tenth, D, E, and L, were assigned to Indian Territory with the remaining nine companies taking station at camps and posts along the line of the Smoky Hill and Santa Fe routes. It marked the beginning of more than two decades of continuous frontier defense for the troopers of Benjamin Grierson.[7]

From Forts Harker, Hays, and Larned detachments fanned out to protect railroad working crews, escort stages and trains, and to scout along the Saline, Solomon, and Arkansas rivers. Initially, however, disease proved a greater enemy than marauding Indians. Epidemic cholera broke out at Harker and Hays, killing seven men in ten days among Captain George Armes' Company F, stationed at the latter post. Losses were also heavy at Fort Harker. Some lives might have been saved with proper food and nursing care, but post commanders were often reluctant to release men for such duties or to provide details to maintain proper hygiene around the military posts.[8]

[5] J. W. Throckmorton to E. M. Stanton, August 5, 1867, *Texas Indian Papers,* Vol IV, 235–36; Captain E. L. Smith to the AAG, Department of the Arkansas, February 16, 1867, LR, Office of Indian Affairs, Kiowa, NA.

[6] Sherman's resources were slender indeed. In the Department of the Missouri, comprising all of Kansas, Missouri, Indian Territory, and the Territory of New Mexico, there were only three regiments of cavalry, the Third, Seventh, and Tenth, and four regiments of infantry. See *Annual Report of the Secretary of War for the Year 1866,* 19.

[7] Organizational Returns, Tenth Cavalry, June–July, 1867.

[8] Medical History, Fort Larned, Vol. 164, Medical History of Posts, AGO, RG 94, NA; Medical History, Fort Hays, Vol. 412; George A. Armes, *Ups and Downs of an Army Officer,* 230–31.

But these were not the only hazards of tenure in a remote post hospital. At Fort Larned a large, rabid, gray wolf invaded the hospital, bit a finger off startled Corporal McGillicoddy, Third Infantry, and lacerated badly the right foot of Private Willie Mason, Company C, Tenth Cavalry, who was trying to climb the wall. Having created utter bedlam in the hospital and undoubtedly promoted some remarkably rapid recoveries, the wolf departed between the legs of a doughty sentinel who fired and understandably missed. Loping along officers' row and leaving complete demoralization in his wake, the animal paused long enough to sink his fangs into a Lieutenant Thompson before adjourning to the post haystack where a guard's bullet put an end to the raid.[9]

Rabid wolves were not uncommon on the Kansas frontier and in the summer of 1867 neither were hostile Indians. On August 1, word reached Fort Hays that a strong party of Cheyennes had attacked Campbell's Camp, thirteen miles down the railroad, killing seven men. Captain Armes, with thirty-four troopers, marched to Campbell's, found the trail, and followed it northeast to the banks of the Saline. On the morning of August 2, he turned upstream and had scouted perhaps a dozen miles when he was suddenly attacked by seventy-five to eighty warriors.

The command dismounted to fight on foot and soon found itself surrounded as more warriors continued to arrive as the fight progressed. For six hours, under a blazing sun, F Company fought off its attackers and then, with ammunition running low, the troopers mounted and shot their way through the encircling Indians. Fifteen miles of skirmishing were necessary, however, before the Cheyennes broke off the action. Armes had suffered a hip wound and Sergeant William Christy, a little ex-farmer from Pennsylvania, had been killed by a shot through the head—the first combat death in the Tenth Cavalry. Armes placed Indian casualties at six killed and an undetermined number wounded.[10]

9 Medical History, Fort Larned, Vol. 164.

10 Armes, *op. cit.,* 237; Post Returns, Fort Hays, August, 1867; Bigelow, "Sketch"; Registers of Enlistments, 1867. Christy had served only two months. He enlisted in the Tenth on June 4, 1867. Captain Armes was an able but contentious and controversial officer. His long military career was dotted with arrests and quarrels with his

Critically short of cavalry in the face of wide-scale Indian attacks, Sherman authorized Governor Samuel Crawford of Kansas to raise a force of volunteer cavalry. Designated as the Eighteenth Kansas Cavalry, the volunteers rendezvoused at Fort Harker under the command of Major Horace L. Moore. Cholera took a heavy toll before Moore received orders to transfer his four companies to Fort Hays, but they were ready for field duty by mid-August.[11]

Captain Armes, sufficiently recovered from his hip wound to return to active duty, believed that a large concentration of hostile Cheyennes was somewhere on the Solomon River and proposed to take his F Company and two companies of the Eighteenth Kansas to scout in that area. Moore, with the remaining volunteers, would scout the same stream, and if Indians were found, a union could be effected and thus enough strength concentrated to defeat any number of the warring nomads likely to be encountered.

On August 20, Armes, with forty men of F and ninety Kansans under Captain George Jenness, left Fort Hays and set out for the Solomon which was reached on the evening of the following day. That night a light was seen some distance to the east and Jenness volunteered to take a small party and investigate. It proved to be the remains of a campfire, but no Indians were seen in the vicinity. Unable to find his way back in the dark, Jenness encamped, and at daybreak returned to the Solomon and located the wagon train which was guarded by Lieutenant Price and about thirty men of the Eighteenth Kansas. Armes, meanwhile, had moved on toward Beaver Creek with the rest of the command. There was no sign of Major Moore or of units of the Seventh Cavalry which were thought to be in the area also.

Jenness and Price moved out to link up with Armes but had gone only a short distance when hundreds of howling Indians

superiors. He was dismissed from the service in June, 1870, but the dismissal was later amended to provide an honorable discharge. He returned to the Tenth Cavalry in May, 1878, and was retired in 1883. His own account of his troubles is found in his book, *Ups and Downs of an Army Officer.*

11 Marvin Garfield, "Defense of the Kansas Frontier, 1866–1867," *Kansas Historical Quarterly*, Vol. I (August, 1932), 338–39; *Annual Report of the Secretary of War for the Year 1867*, 35–36.

swarmed down upon them. Jenness formed his men into a hollow square and opened fire with Spencer repeaters. Red warriors completely surrounded the embattled Kansans, circling and firing with rifles, shotguns, and bows and arrows. One brave, mounted on a superb white horse, led a charge that was broken by the rapid-fire Spencers, but the gallant redman rode down one soldier who tried to stop him and then on through the square, escaping without a scratch, although at least fifty shots were fired at him.

Fearful that he would be overrun, Jenness began a slow movement in the direction Armes had taken, with his wounded draped over the few remaining sound animals in his command. The Indian fire proved too hot and Jenness was forced to halt and take refuge in a ravine. The Kansans had no monopoly on the fighting, however, for Armes was having his troubles as well. As he entered the valley of the Beaver, he was attacked by an overwhelming number of wild-riding Cheyennes and was also forced to take cover in a deep ravine. The fighting raged until dark and was renewed at daybreak the next morning. Not until midafternoon did the warriors draw off sufficiently to permit Armes and Jenness to unite their battered forces.

The Indians still commanded the nearby ridges, however, and shouted insults in good English. A number of them taunted, "Come out of that hole you sons of bitches and give us a fair fight." Armes obliged by making a charge and drove his tormentors for some distance, but skirmishing continued until dusk when the Indians left the field and allowed Armes to march his weary command back to Fort Hays. F Company suffered one man killed and thirteen wounded, while Jenness counted two dead and sixteen wounded. Armes placed Indian losses at fifty killed and three times that number wounded. He and Jenness believed they had been attacked by a force of eight hundred to one thousand warriors.[12]

Company F had done well for raw recruits. True, the troopers had fired too rapidly for accuracy, but they had shown no panic in the face of great odds and had charged with spirit when called

[12] Bigelow, "Sketch"; George B. Jenness, "The Battle on Beaver Creek," *Transactions of the Kansas State Historical Society*, Vol. IX (Topeka, 1906), 447–52; Armes, *op. cit.*, 242–46; Organizational Returns, Tenth Cavalry, August, 1867.

upon. Not all their lessons were learned on the battlefield. In scouting, guarding, and escort duty, in the routine of garrison life, and through the iron discipline of the frontier army, pride of self and of regiment grew. They learned, most of them, to accept danger and death as constant companions, whether from enemy bullet, arrow, or lance, or from cholera, pneumonia, "acute gastritis," and other scourges of the day. Armes no longer led a bunch of recruits after August 21, but a company of fighting men.

Capable noncommissioned officers were quick to emerge. On September 15, Sergeant Ed Davis and nine men of Company G were on guard at a railroad camp forty-five miles west of Fort Hays. Private John Randall and two civilians left camp for a hunt and were barely out of sight before they were attacked by seventy Cheyennes. Both civilians were killed almost at once, and Randall was severely wounded before he found dubious sanctuary in a hole under a railroad cut. Gleeful warriors probed the hole with lances, inflicting eleven wounds, and then tried to cave the hole in on him. Fortunately for the cornered Randall, they eventually tired of the sport and turned to attack the camp.

Sergeant Davis did not wait to receive the attack but dismounted his men and advanced to fight the enemy on foot. The Cheyennes, apparently surprised at such audacity, turned off to attack two men who came up with an ox team, but Davis, moving swiftly and shooting accurately, forced the Indians to veer off and allow the two men to reach camp in safety. Davis then mounted his little command and rode in search of Randall and his companions. The warriors were still seeking a fight, however, and returned to the attack but once again were repulsed with a loss of thirteen killed or wounded. When the Indians withdrew, Randall was located by his cries for aid and extricated from his crumbling shelter, seriously but not fatally wounded.[13]

It was about this time that the Indians gave the Negro troopers a sobriquet. Called all manner of names—"Moacs," "Brunettes," "Niggers," "Africans"—by all manner of people, they were dub-

[13] George W. Ford, formerly First Sergeant, Troop L, Tenth Cavalry, to the Editor, *Winners of the West*, Vol. III, No. 1 (November, 1925); Organizational Returns, Tenth Cavalry, September, 1867.

Emblem of the Tenth Regiment, United States Cavalry.
Courtesy National Archives

bed "buffalo soldiers" by their red antagonists. Men of the Tenth, and later of the Ninth, accepted the title and wore it proudly. Indeed, the most prominent feature of the regimental crest of the Tenth Cavalry was a buffalo.[14]

Meanwhile, events were occurring that gave the buffalo soldiers a brief but welcome respite. The federal government was making another effort at a peaceful solution to the Indian problem. In July, 1867, Congress created the Indian Peace Commission for the purpose of conferring with the warring tribes and to remove, if possible, the causes of recurring wars. The Commission met at St. Louis in August, elected N. G. Taylor, Commissioner of Indian Affairs, as president, and quickly agreed that the Indians must be placed on permanent reservations away from the roads and railroads.

[14] The origin of the term "buffalo soldier" is uncertain, although the common explanation is that the Indian saw a similarity between the hair of the Negro soldier and that of the buffalo. The buffalo was a sacred animal to the Indian, and it is unlikely that he would so name an enemy if respect were lacking. It is a fair guess that the Negro trooper understood this and thus his willingness to accept the title.

Considerable difficulties were encountered in making contact with the tribes, but arrangements were finally made to hold a council with the Southern Cheyennes and Arapahoes, Kiowas, Comanches, and Kiowa-Apaches near mid-October on Medicine Lodge Creek in Kansas. Pending the outcome of the talks, Sherman notified subordinate commanders that all offensive military operations should cease.

More than a week of talks at Medicine Lodge brought treaties with all the assembled tribes. The Comanches, Kiowas, and Kiowa-Apaches accepted a reservation of some three million acres between the Washita and Red Rivers in Indian Territory, while immediately to the north the Cheyennes and Arapahoes received in excess of four million acres. The Indians were to be provided with ample food, clothing, and other supplies and retained the right to hunt buffalo anywhere south of the Arkansas River. Resident agents would assist them in adjusting to the "white man's road." In return, the Indians agreed to keep the peace, not to molest the whites, and to stay clear of the great roads.[15]

The treaties of Medicine Lodge brought a cessation of warfare on the Central Plains and strong hopes for a permanent peace, but disturbing factors still remained. Many influential chiefs and headmen, along with their followers, had scorned the talks and their future behavior was in doubt. To the south there was no room for doubt, for bands of Kiowas and Comanches continued to make life miserable for citizens along the Texas frontier and the Civilized Tribes continued to suffer from their incursions. To make matters worse, the Senate and House fell to haggling over financial provisions of the treaties and ratification was long delayed. It was expecting too much of a nomad Indian to understand and appreciate what his more "enlightened" white brethren often failed to comprehend—the vagaries of American politics.

During the winter of 1867–68 Grierson found conditions fa-

15 *United States Statutes at Large,* Vol. XV, 17; Kappler, *op. cit.,* II, 980–89; Alfred A. Taylor, "Medicine Lodge Peace Council," *Chronicles of Oklahoma,* Vol. 2, No. 2 (June, 1924), 100–101; "Report of the Indian Peace Commissioners," *H.R. Exec. Doc. No. 97,* 40 Cong., 2 sess., 2–3. In addition to Commissioner Taylor, other members of the commission were John B. Henderson, John B. Sanborn, S. F. Tappan, General Sherman, and Brigadier Generals Harney and Terry.

vorable enough on the Kansas frontier to concentrate most of his regiment at Fort Riley, though as a precautionary measure detachments were left at railroad camps along the Kansas Pacific to protect the workers. Meanwhile, the troopers of D, E, and L in Indian Territory had seen no fighting, but there was plenty of work to keep them busy, and in November Grierson moved Troop M under Captain Henry Alvord to Fort Gibson.[16]

Kiowa and Comanche raids on the herds of the Chickasaws and Choctaws had brought these tribes to the point of open warfare. Bootleggers plied their dangerous and illicit traffic in the Territory and bands of white men stole cattle and horses with impunity. Mail carriers between Forts Gibson and Arbuckle were murdered so often that no white man could be found to accept such employment, and Indian scouts were eventually induced to ride in teams to get the mail through. And, as winter deepened, bands of Kiowas and Comanches made their camps along the Washita and with them were a number of white captives taken on raids into Texas.[17]

In such a wild and sparsely settled country there was little that four untrained troops of cavalry and a few companies of infantry could do. Distances were great and news traveled slowly. Reports of raids or the entry of elusive whisky peddlers reached the lonely little posts long after the intruders had departed. Some success was achieved in recovering white captives though ransom proved necessary.

More progress was made in rebuilding Fort Arbuckle, a duty the buffalo soldiers would repeat many times over at different locations in their long service on the Plains. Captain J. W. Walsh and Captain George T. Robinson of D and E at Arbuckle spent much of their time in training their willing and obedient troopers who soon became proficient in mounted and dismounted drill. But garrison life was often monotonous and an occasional trooper

---

[16] Organizational Returns, Tenth Cavalry, October–December, 1867; Grierson to the AG, September 30, 1867, Tenth Cavalry, LS; Alvord to Grierson, November 21, 1868, Grierson Papers.

[17] *H.R. Misc. Doc. No. 139*, 41 Cong., 2 sess., 3; Richard Henry Pratt, *Battlefield and Classroom: Four Decades With the American Indian, 1867–1904*, 22–24.

kicked over the traces. Private William Alexander of D sold his overcoat to a teamster, bought a jug of whisky from an ever-present peddler, and went on a spree. He no doubt remembered the occasion for a long time, for he was sentenced to stand on the head of a barrel from 9:00 A.M. to 4:00 P.M. each day for ten days, and to forfeit fourteen dollars of his pay.

Some of the new troopers developed a quick aversion for army life and took off without bothering to say farewell. Others deserted after a minor infraction brought instant and severe punishment, such as confinement in a barrel from reveille to retreat without relief. But one trooper at Arbuckle, charged with desertion, came to typify the growing spirit and pride that marked the men of the Tenth.

In the dead of winter, Private Filmore Roberts was detailed to carry the mail to Fort Gibson. He never reported there and was listed as a deserter. Many months later his remains were found lodged in some willows on the Canadian River several miles below the ford. Still strapped to his back was the mail pouch for which he had given his life in an attempt to cross a swollen stream and deliver it to Fort Gibson.[18]

The tempo of activity accelerated considerably at Gibson and Arbuckle early in 1868. In February, Colonel Jesse Leavenworth, appointed as agent to the Kiowas and Comanches, arrived in the Territory and established a temporary agency at Eureka Valley. He found affairs in a critical state and there was little he could do. The failure of Congress to implement the Medicine Lodge treaties left him with little to offer his insolent and restless charges and they continued to harry the North Texas frontier. In less than a month Leavenworth became fearful for his own safety and dashed off a note to Captain Walsh at Arbuckle asking for military assistance. Walsh made a forced march to Eureka Valley with D Company, but before he arrived the more belligerent Indians had left. Raids and depredations continued, and in May a Comanche war party swept down on the Wichita Agency,

18 George W. Ford, formerly First Sergeant, Troop L, Tenth Cavalry, "Winning the West," in *Winners of the West*, Vol. II, No. 1 (April, 1924); Pratt, *op. cit.*, 15–17; W. S. Nye, *Carbine and Lance*, 40–41.

some one hundred miles northwest of Arbuckle, and burned the buildings after looting them. It was enough for Leavenworth. He threw in the sponge and departed the country never to return.[19]

The troopers at Gibson and Arbuckle, while improving daily in efficiency and effectiveness, were still much too far to the east to counter quickly the raids of these wild nomads. General Philip Sheridan, Hancock's successor as commanding general of the Department of the Missouri, ordered Grierson to move his headquarters from Fort Riley to Gibson, and then to reconnoiter the country to the west with a view to establishing a post in the heart of the recently established Kiowa and Comanche reservation. Cavalry would then be in a position to observe the activities of the Indians and operate against them more effectively.

Grierson left Fort Riley on May 1 with his adjutant, Samuel Woodward, the regimental chaplain, W. M. Grimes, and nineteen troopers. He stayed at Gibson only long enough to mount E and M companies and then pushed on to Arbuckle. Late in the month he left for the west with D, E, L, and M, and a train guarded by a company of the Sixth Infantry. Torrential rains caught the column shortly after it left the post and turned the trail into a quagmire. Long stretches had to be corduroyed to get the train through and enormous balls of mud formed on the horses' hooves. The men were soaked, bedraggled, and miserable.

Eventually the rains stopped and the column reached a delightful valley in the shadow of the Wichita Mountains. After scouting along Cache and Medicine Bluff creeks, Grierson was convinced that he had found the most desirable site in the region. There was an abundance of water, timber, grass, and limestone and Grierson hastened to stake out a site for the future post. A buffalo hunt produced plenty of fresh meat and the command

---

[19] Leavenworth to the Commanding Officer, Fort Arbuckle, March 26, 1868, Office of Indian Affairs, LR, Kiowa Agency; Nye, *op. cit.*, 47–48; *Annual Report of the Secretary of War for the Year 1868*, 16. Fort Arbuckle was first situated on the Arkansas River in June, 1834, and named for Colonel Matthew Arbuckle, Seventh Infantry. It was abandoned in 1834. A second Fort Arbuckle was built on Wild Horse Creek about five miles from the Washita River in April, 1851. It was evacuated by federal troops in May, 1861, and was not reoccupied by them until November, 1866. See Frazer, *op. cit.*, 116–17.

marched on westward to Otter Creek where a band of Comanches was encountered. Grierson arranged for a council and recovered six captives after a lengthy talk. Feeling his mission accomplished, Grierson returned to Fort Arbuckle and disbanded the expedition.[20]

Need for just such a post became readily more apparent in ensuing months. In September, Captain Alvord, writing from Fort Gibson, told Grierson that the Comanches were "getting pretty wild" in Eureka Valley and Lieutenant Robert Gray of D Company had taken every buffalo soldier at Arbuckle and gone there to quiet them.[21]

But if conditions were bad along the Texas frontier and in Indian Territory, they were worse in Kansas. With the approach of summer large numbers of Kiowas, Comanches, Southern Cheyennes, and Arapahoes gathered in the vicinity of Fort Larned to receive their promised annuities, but Congress had continued to dally and agent E. W. Wynkoop had little to offer them. There were plenty of supplies of a sort, however, that lurking bootleggers were all too ready to furnish. Idle, disgruntled, and hungry redmen, with whisky in their bellies, could only spell trouble and depredations were committed near Fort Zarah and Fort Wallace in May. Late the same month, a large war party of Cheyennes attacked a band of Kaws at Council Grove, burned several buildings, and stole some cattle.[22]

With an ominous situation developing, Sheridan concentrated seven troops of the Seventh Cavalry under Brevet Brigadier General Alfred Sully at Fort Larned, while the eight troops of the Tenth still in Kansas were equally divided between Forts Hays and Wallace. Meanwhile, Congress had finally made funds available to implement the Medicine Lodge treaties, and annuities were issued to the Indians at Fort Larned during the first week of August,

20 Organizational Returns, Tenth Cavalry, May–June, 1868; "Reminiscences of John Thomas, Late of Troop 'L,' Tenth Cavalry," in *Winners of the West* (May 30, 1934); Bigelow, "Sketch"; Nye, *op. cit.,* 49–50.

21 Alvord to Grierson, September 13, 1868, Grierson Papers.

22 *Annual Report of the Commissioner of Indian Affairs for the Year 1868,* 64–66; Post Returns, Fort Wallace, May, 1868; Thomas F. Doran, "Kansas Sixty Years Ago," *Collections of the Kansas State Historical Society,* Vol. XV (1923), 491.

and, much to Sheridan's disgust, the issue included guns and ammunition.[23]

Agent Wynkoop, immediately relieved that the annuities had been issued at last, wrote to the Commissioner of Indian Affairs that the Indians were pleased and contented. There would be no trouble on the Plains at least for a time. Wynkoop could hardly have been more wrong, for even as he wrote a large Cheyenne war party struck the settlements along the Saline and Solomon rivers like a vengeful tornado. Other Cheyenne and Arapaho raiders struck a party of woodchoppers on Twin Butte Creek, killing three of them and stealing twenty-five head of stock, killed two men on Pond Creek near Fort Wallace and a herder near Fort Dodge, chased the stage to Cheyenne Wells for four miles, and attacked a wood train of thirty-five wagons at Cimarron Crossing, killing two men and running off seventy-five head of cattle. Governor Hall of Colorado reported that two hundred warriors were devastating the southern part of his state.[24]

On August 21 an angry General Sherman telegraphed the War Department that he had ordered General Sheridan to force the Indians south of the Kansas line and to kill them if necessary. If President Johnson did not agree, Sherman wished to be notified at once. Consultations between the War and Interior departments resulted in approval of Sherman's proposal, subject to the qualification that those Indians innocent of any outrages be separated from the guilty and escorted to a rendezvous at Fort Cobb in Indian Territory where agents could minister to their needs. Arrangements were made, therefore, to remove the Kiowas, Kiowa-Apaches, and Comanches while the army undertook to punish the offending Cheyennes and Arapahoes.[25]

Punishing the hostiles was not easy, for Sheridan had far too

[23] *Annual Report of the Commissioner of Indian Affairs for the Year 1868,* 68–70; Post Returns, Fort Larned, May–June, 1868; Post Returns, Fort Hays and Fort Wallace, May–June 1868; Philip H. Sheridan, *Personal Memoirs,* II, 289.

[24] United States Army, Military Division of the Missouri, *Record of Engagements with Hostile Indians Within the Military Division of the Missouri from 1868–1882,* 9–12; *Annual Report of the Commissioner of Indian Affairs for the Year 1868,* 68–70; *Annual Report of the Secretary of War for the Year 1868,* 4–5.

[25] *Sen. Exec. Doc. No. 13,* 40 Cong., 3 sess., 9–11.

few troops at hand for the task. He could muster perhaps fourteen hundred infantry for garrison and guard duty, but he had only two regiments of cavalry for field service, the Seventh and Tenth, and of the latter regiment, four troops were needed in Indian Territory. But the fuming Sheridan did his best and put every available man in the field. General Sully, at Fort Dodge, organized an expedition of nine troops of the Seventh and three companies of the Third Infantry to subdue hostiles who had been active along the Arkansas, but two weeks of campaigning south of the river garnered precious little results and he retired with Indian warriors yapping at his heels and making obscene gestures to convey their contempt.[26]

The buffalo soldiers hardly had time to cool their saddles. Detachments were necessary for constant escort to stages and trains, to protect workers at the end of track, and to scout along the Smoky Hill, Saline, and Solomon rivers. In August alone, the overworked troopers scouted more than one thousand miles searching for the flitting red raiders but made no interceptions. September was more of the same until the middle of the month. Then, Captain G. W. Graham, with thirty-six men of I Company, struck and followed a trail along the Denver road until they reached Big Sandy Creek. Here one hundred Cheyennes were waiting and engaged them in a bitter fight at close quarters. The men of I, in their first encounter and outnumbered badly, fought like cornered wildcats. When the engagement ended at nightfall, eleven Cheyennes were dead and fourteen wounded. Graham reported his loss as one man wounded and eighteen horses either killed or missing.[27]

On September 21, Captain Louis H. Carpenter and H Company left Wallace to "finish what Captain Graham had started." He found no sign of the Indians but remained in the vicinity to secure the road, and threw out scouting detachments. It was well that he did so.

[26] Sheridan, *op. cit.*, II, 297. An interesting account of the Sully expedition is found in E. S. Godfrey, "Some Reminiscences, Including an Account of General Sully's Expedition Against the Southern Plains Indians, 1868," *Cavalry Journal*, Vol. XXXVI (July, 1927), 421–23.

[27] Organizational Returns, Tenth Cavalry, September, 1868; Bigelow, "Sketch"; Post Returns, Fort Wallace, September, 1868; Medical History, Fort Wallace, Vol. 363.

Badly in need of additional cavalry, Sheridan requested Sherman to make another regiment available and meanwhile he authorized his aide, Major George A. Forsyth, to raise a force of fifty frontier scouts for immediate service. Forsyth experienced no difficulty in recruiting the necessary men at Fort Hays and Harker, arming them with Spencer repeating rifles and revolvers. Lieutenant Frederick Beecher, Third Infantry, was second in command with Dr. J. H. Mooers as surgeon. By September 5 Forsyth and his scouts were at Fort Wallace and four days later he was on the march for the town of Sheridan, thirteen miles east of Wallace, where Indians had struck a freighter's train.[28]

The trail of the raiders was followed easily, and by the evening of September 16 it had led the scouts to a small valley along the Arikaree Fork of the Republican River. Here they encamped for the night and were prepared to push on next morning. Little did they dream that several of their number would never live through another day.

Near noon on September 22, two buffalo soldiers of H Company were riding westward from Wallace with dispatches for Captain Carpenter who was then on Sandy Creek, some forty-five miles from the post. They were hailed by two bedraggled and footsore men who proved to be scouts from Forsyth's command, Jack Stilwell and Pierre Trudeau. And they bore grim news. On the morning of September 17 hundreds of Indians had struck Forsyth's camp and savage fighting had raged all day. By evening the command was in desperate straits, surrounded by hostile warriors, rations and medical supplies exhausted, and suffering from many casualties. Stilwell and Trudeau had volunteered to go to Fort Wallace for aid and had managed to make their way safely to the Denver road. Unless relief reached Forsyth soon, his entire command might be wiped out.

The two scouts then turned toward Wallace while the troopers

28 George A. Forsyth to Brevet Brigadier General C. M. McKeever, AAG, Department of the Missouri, March 31, 1869, "Report of the Organization and Operation of a Body of Scouts Enrolled and Equipped at Forts Harker and Hays, Kansas, August 24, 1868," MS, Phillips Collection, University of Oklahoma (hereinafter cited as Forsyth, "Report").

spurred their mounts on to Sandy Creek and apprised their commander of Forsyth's plight. Carpenter determined to march at once to relieve Forsyth although not a man in his command was familiar with the country to the north. He had fought with Forsyth in the Shenandoah and in the Wilderness during the Civil War, his troopers were eager for a fight, and if the situation had been described accurately, there was no time to waste.

Before dark on September 23 Carpenter had covered thirty-five miles at an alternate walk and trot with scouts thrown far out. He was on the move again at dawn next day and after covering some twenty miles reached a dry river bed. A scout of several miles upstream proved unproductive and the northward march continued. Late afternoon brought the tired but determined column to a stream flowing through a wide, grassy valley. Here a large Indian trail was found and a search soon revealed a number of Indian dead on scaffolds. The bodies were examined and in every case the cause of death was found to be a gunshot wound. One body was mounted on a platform inside a tipi wrapped in a fine buffalo robe. The corpse was not disturbed, but Carpenter did carry away a drum which he later gave to the Pennsylvania Historical Society.[29]

Early next morning as the troopers saddled up horsemen were seen in the distance, and in a few minutes five riders came into camp. One of them proved to be Jack Donovan, another of Forsyth's scouts, who had made his way to Fort Wallace and, upon finding that most of the garrison had gone in search of Forsyth, had persuaded four men to return with him. By sheer chance he had come upon Carpenter's command. Fired with an even greater sense of emergency, Carpenter took thirty of his best mounted men, a wagon loaded with hardtack, coffee, and bacon, and moved out at a gallop, with orders to the rest of the company to follow as rapidly as possible.

Eighteen miles farther north brought the advance to the Arikaree and, when movement was seen down the valley, Carpenter

29 Carpenter thought the body was that of Roman Nose, a prominent Cheyenne warrior, but apparently it was the corpse of another Cheyenne, Killed by a Bull. See George B. Grinnell, *The Fighting Cheyennes*, 280.

and his orderly, Private Reuben Waller, put their horses to a run. In minutes they were at Forsyth's side and a pitiful sight met their eyes. Six of Forsyth's command were dead, among them Lieutenant Beecher and Surgeon Mooers. Fifteen were wounded, including Forsyth who had been shot through both legs and maggots were having a field day in the wounds. The stench from dead bodies, men, and animals, was so overpowering that Carpenter's first move was to transfer the survivors a good distance away and then attend to their needs. Dr. Jenkins Fitzgerald wanted to remove one of Forsyth's legs at once, but so vehement was the latter's protest, that the good doctor could only shake his head and warn that a life was better than a leg.

Next day, September 26, Captain H. C. Bankhead, Fifth Infantry, with Graham's Troop I of the Tenth, and detachments of the Fifth and Thirty-eighth Infantry, arrived after a forced march from Fort Wallace. Carpenter and his buffalo soldiers had already done all that could be done in the field, and on the following day the united commands set out for Fort Wallace.[30]

Meanwhile, Sheridan's request to Sherman for additional cavalry brought results. Seven troops of the Fifth Cavalry were transferred from the southern states to Fort Harker and placed under the temporary command of Major William B. Royall until such time as an officer of greater rank, Brevet Major General Eugene A. Carr, could gain release from staff duties in the Department of Washington and join the regiment. The Fifth was ready for the field by October 1, and although Carr was still absent Royall left Harker on that date to search for a large war party thought to be encamped on Beaver Creek.

[30] Brevet Colonel L. H. Carpenter, "The Story of a Rescue," in *Winners of the West*, Vol. XI, No. 3 (February 28, 1934); Private Reuben Waller, formerly of Troop H, Tenth Cavalry, "Forsyth's Fight," in *Winners of the West*, Vol. II, No. 9 (August, 1925); Cyrus T. Brady, *Indian Fights and Fighters*, 102–107; Medical History, Fort Wallace, Vol. 363; Bigelow, "Sketch"; *Army and Navy Journal*, Vol. VI, No. 7 (October 3, 1868), 98; Forsyth, "Report"; Organizational Returns, Tenth Cavalry, September, 1868. Louis Henry Carpenter was a native of New Jersey who enlisted as a private when the Civil War came and rose to the rank of lieutenant colonel in the Fifth Cavalry with brevets for gallantry at the battles of Gettysburg and Winchester. He joined the Tenth Cavalry as a captain in July, 1866, and enjoyed a long and distinguished career. One of the finest officers on the frontier, he retired as a brigadier general in October, 1899. See Heitman, *op. cit.*, I, 284.

Royall searched over a wide area and then went into bivouac on Prairie Dog Creek. From this point detachments fanned out in all directions to follow trails that seemed to be everywhere. On October 14, while most of the command was so engaged, the Cheyennes hit the camp, killed one trooper, wounded another, and ran off twenty-six horses of H Company. A frustrated Royall concentrated his command and marched to Buffalo Tank on the Kansas Pacific having done little more than to provide the Cheyennes with some amusement and some excellent horses.

On October 12 General Carr reached Fort Wallace, anxious to join his regiment, and the next day he left the post escorted by Captain Carpenter, Captain Graham, and Companies H and I of the Tenth. The column marched due north for the Beaver, struck that stream on October 15, and turned downstream searching for Royall. No sign of him was found on that day nor during the next, and on the morning of October 17 Carpenter sent Lieutenant Myron Amick, with ten troopers and scout Sharp Grover who had been with Forsyth, toward Shortness Creek to look out for Indians, while the main body continued on down the Beaver. At nightfall Carpenter encamped with the stock inside a wagon corral and soon thereafter Amick returned to report that there was no sign of Royall. Grover, however, had discovered the single tracks of a running Indian pony crossing the rear of Amick's line of march—if Indians were in the vicinity, they had no doubt been warned that soldiers were near.

Carr now entertained doubt that his missing regiment was on the Beaver and considered that it was just as well to return to Fort Wallace, but early on the morning of October 18 Captain Graham volunteered to make a short search farther downstream while the rest of the command packed up for the return march. Graham, with two troopers, trotted away but had gone no more than a few hundred yards when a small party of warriors rushed to cut him off from the main body. Graham and his troopers spurred for the creek with bullets snapping past their ears while Amick and thirty men charged the Indians and drove them off.

When Graham and Amick rejoined, the whole command

moved off, crossing to the north side of the Beaver and, as they did so, some two hundred Indians came up to the south side of the stream and gunfire flamed from both sides. Carpenter was content to duel at a distance and continued his march with H on the flanks and front and I covering the rear. Shortly after midday the Indians disappeared, only to return half an hour later with hundreds of reinforcements and attacked the column on the front, flanks, and rear. Fearful of being caught in the creek bottom, Carpenter turned off and took his stand on a small knoll, and formed his wagons in the shape of a horseshoe, with the mules facing inward, while the troopers rode inside, tied their mounts, and formed outside in open order.

The Indians charged at once but were repulsed by seven-shot Spencers, leaving three of their number within fifty feet of the wagons. They then circled, firing into the wagons, but suffered additional casualties as the buffalo soldiers maintained a steady accurate fire. No longer green troops these, H and I could hold their own with any troops in the army. As the afternoon wore on, the Indians drew off and Carpenter moved down to water at the Beaver and encamped.

"Wolves" howled around the camp all night, but there were no further attacks. When morning came, the command set out for Fort Wallace which was reached on October 21. Carpenter had marched 230 miles in nine days, killed ten Indians, and wounded a larger number. His own loss was three men wounded, and only one of these, Private John Daniels of H, was seriously injured. Sheridan personally commended the buffalo soldiers of H and I and recommended Carpenter for a Medal of Honor. As for Eugene A. Carr, men with whom he had refused to serve had saved his "hair" and he was quick to correct his earlier opinion.[31]

31 Organizational Returns, Tenth Cavalry, October, 1868; Medical History, Fort Wallace, Vol. 363; Brady, *op. cit.*, 124–35; Bigelow, "Sketch"; *Annual Report of the Secretary of War for the Year 1868*, 19; War Department, Office of the Adjutant General, "The History of the Fifth United States Cavalry from March 3, 1855, to December 31, 1905," File No. 1102491 (hereinafter cited as "History of the Fifth Cavalry"), NA; James T. King, *op. cit.*, 81–85. Carr joined his regiment at Buffalo Tank a few days later and on October 25–26 fought a hot but indecisive skirmish with the Cheyennes on Beaver Creek.

Sheridan himself had not been idle. Plans were under way for a decisive campaign against the warring tribes, and by October arrangements had been completed to move the peaceful tribes to Fort Cobb so as to keep them from harm. General Sherman had appointed Brevet Major General W. B. Hazen, Sixth Infantry, to conduct the Kiowas and Comanches from Fort Larned to Cobb, but these Indians had failed to appear at the appointed time, and a fearful Hazen set out alone for Fort Cobb believing the Kiowas and Comanches might have joined forces with the hostiles.

Meanwhile, pending Hazen's arrival, Captain Alvord, commanding M Company of the Tenth at Fort Arbuckle, was ordered to Cobb to care for any Indians who might have gone there. Alvord arrived in mid-October and to his astonishment found that several hundred Indians had preceded him—sufficient to press sorely on his available supplies. After taking care of their immediate needs, Alvord organized a small scouting force from friendly Indians and a few white scouts to locate and keep him informed of the movements of the various tribes. In this way he soon learned that the main body of the Kiowas and Comanches was nearby and had not engaged in the recent hostilities, but they were sullen and restless. Alvord requested troops and Company L, of the Tenth, and E, Sixth Infantry, were sent from Fort Arbuckle. The men erected crude picket shelters for themselves and roofed several crumbling adobe structures to protect the supplies.

Hazen arrived early in November and held councils with many of the chiefs and headmen of the Kiowas and Comanches. He disliked their arrogant attitude, and when he learned later in the month that many of the Cheyennes and Arapahoes had arrived on the Washita River within easy striking distance of Fort Cobb, he sent for additional reinforcements, and Companies D and M of the Tenth were soon on hand. Hazen was now able to protect his position and, in addition, to supply Sheridan with valuable information regarding location of the hostile camps.[32]

32 Organizational Returns, Tenth Cavalry, October–November, 1868; W. B. Hazen, "Some Corrections of Custer's *Life on the Plains,*" *Chronicles of Oklahoma,* Vol. III, No. 4 (1925), 300–10; *Sen. Exec. Doc. No. 13,* 40 Cong., 3 sess., 22–23; *Annual Report of the Commissioner of Indian Affairs for the Year 1868,* 388–96;

While Alvord and Hazen dispensed supplies and forwarded information, Sheridan completed plans for a winter campaign to conquer a peace with the Cheyennes and Arapahoes. Vast stores were accumulated at Forts Dodge, Lyon, and Arbuckle and a four-pronged plan of attack devised. A "main column" was organized under Brevet Brigadier General Sully, consisting of eleven companies of the Seventh Cavalry under Lieutenant Colonel George A. Custer, five companies of infantry, and the Nineteenth Kansas Volunteer Cavalry under Governor S. J. Crawford. Acting as "beaters in," to drive the Indians into the path of the main column, were three commands. One of eight companies of cavalry and infantry under Brevet Lieutenant Colonel A. W. Evans would march east from Fort Bascom, New Mexico, a second led by General Carr would push southeast from Fort Lyon, while the third, under Brevet Brigadier General W. H. Penrose, would precede Carr from Fort Lyon and effect a junction with him on the North Canadian.[33]

The role in the winter campaign assigned to the badly scattered buffalo soldiers of the Tenth was diverse. D, L, and M remained at Fort Cobb to keep a watchful eye on the Indians assembled there, E operated out of Fort Arbuckle, A, C, H, and I guarded the Kansas frontier, while B, F, G, and K moved to Fort Lyon to join Penrose along with one troop of the Seventh Cavalry.[34]

Penrose's command, the first to take the field, left Fort Lyon on November 10 with forty-three days' rations and "Wild Bill" Hickok as a scout. Supplies thereafter would be drawn from a depot that Carr was to establish on the North Canadian. All went well at first, but five days out the command was struck by a heavy snowstorm that forced Penrose to encamp in a barren area with no wood or even buffalo chips for a fire. Twenty-five horses in the rear guard gave out in the heavy going and had to be shot. Despite bitter cold and snow, however, the command pushed

Alvord to Hazen, Sherman-Sheridan Papers, University of Oklahoma Transcript, October 30, 1868; Hazen to Sherman, November 10, 1868, in Sherman-Sheridan Papers.

[33] Sheridan, *op. cit.*, II, 309; *Annual Report of the Secretary of War for the Year 1868*, 44–45; *Sen. Exec. Doc. No. 7*, 40 Cong., 3 sess., 1.

[34] Organizational Returns, Tenth Cavalry, November, 1868.

on toward the North Canadian, its back trail littered with dead animals. On November 17 alone, fourteen horses died.

Penrose slogged on with temperatures pushing well below zero until he reached San Francisco Creek on December 6. No Indians had been seen nor were any signs of them observed. The half-frozen troopers ranged out in small scouting parties with no results except severe frostbite to themselves. The men were reduced to half rations and there was no forage for the animals. Unless Carr arrived soon, the command would be in desperate straits. Nevertheless, the buffalo soldiers remained cheerful as they rubbed frozen feet and hands and fashioned makeshift footgear from the hides of dead animals to replace boots that had fallen apart.

Carr was also having his troubles. He left Fort Lyon on December 2 in clear but cold weather. Three days later, however, a howling blizzard struck the column, froze four men to death, and caused the loss of more than two hundred head of cattle that were to supply fresh meat for both Carr and Penrose. Carr fought his way slowly through mountainous drifts, worrying increasingly about the fate of Penrose and the possibility of not being able to locate him in such weather.

These doubts were resolved on December 21 when Carr's chief scout, "Buffalo Bill" Cody, met two buffalo soldiers who were out searching for Carr. Two days later the commands were joined on the San Francisco. Penrose's troopers, reduced to quarter rations, were slowly starving and more than two hundred of their animals had starved to death. Carr established a supply depot and, after selecting about five hundred of the strongest men, set out for the Canadian which was reached on December 28. He remained there until January 7 when news came that the "main column" under Custer had struck the Cheyennes a devastating blow on the Washita and that Evans, on Christmas Day, had soundly whipped a large band of Comanches on the North Fork of Red River.[35]

---

[35] *Ibid.*, November–December, 1868; Armes, *op. cit.*, 280–86; Luke Cahill, "An Indian Campaign and Buffalo Hunting with 'Buffalo Bill,' " *The Colorado Magazine,*

Carr and Penrose had accomplished their mission, although they had not seen a single Indian. The march of their forces had prevented the Cheyennes from moving north or west and kept them firmly in the path of the principal striking force sweeping down from the north. There was nothing now for them to do but retrace a cold and weary path back to Fort Lyon, which they reached on February 19. Penrose's service with the buffalo soldiers made a lasting impression, and he penned an affectionate farewell:

FT. LYON, C. T.

MAR. 14, 1869

OFFICERS AND SOLDIERS OF THE TENTH U. S. CAVALRY:

Having been relieved from command before an opportunity was given me to promulgate an official farewell, I take occasion, through courtesy of your commanding officer, of taking leave of you.

You started from this post on an important mission under many disadvantages. Your horses were in poor condition, and you were to march, without forage, to penetrate a raw, and before unknown, country. Hardly had you started when you encountered severe storms of rain and snow, accompanied by intense cold; you were without suitable and necessary shelter for such inclement weather; your horses perished day by day, you yourselves suffering from intense cold, many with frostbitten hands and feet; but through these hardships and difficulties you pushed nobly on, undaunted, undismayed, anxious to meet the enemy.

But few commands have ever been called upon to endure more than you have, and none have more cheerfully performed their duty.

Although it was not your fortune to meet and engage the enemy, yet this movement was a part of a grand plan, emanating from that great soldier, Major-General Sheridan.

You were instrumental in compelling a large force of the enemy to make a retrograde movement, and there appears to be no doubt

---

Vol. IV, No. 4 (August, 1927); "History of the Fifth Cavalry," 181; King, *op. cit.,* 87–93. For a good account of the oft-told Battle of the Washita, see Brigadier General E. S. Godfrey, "Some Reminiscences, Including the Washita Battle, November 29, 1868," *Cavalry Journal,* Vol. XXXVII, No. 153 (October, 1928). Evans' campaign is described by C. C. Rister in "Colonel A. W. Evans' Christmas Day Indian Fight (1868)," *Chronicles of Oklahoma,* XVI (September, 1938).

that this was the identical force which Bvt. Major General Custer was thus enabled to encounter and destroy. Your efforts were therefore of material service in the winter campaign.

Had you had the opportunity I am fully assured you would have maintained in battle the honor of the flag and your regiment.

To the officers and men who so nobly stood with me in our most difficult task I extend my kindest, heartfelt thanks, and wherever you go my kindly interest shall be with you in all your undertakings. May success crown all your efforts.

Respectfully,

W. H. PENROSE

Captain and Bvt. Brig. General U.S.A.
Late Commander Indian Expedition from
Fort Lyon, C. T.[36]

Four troops of the Tenth had thus made a considerable contribution to the success of Sheridan's winter campaign, but, as Penrose pointed out, they had not been fortunate enough to meet the enemy. The four troops in Kansas could hardly complain of lack of activity and on occasion they met the enemy. A detachment of ten troopers from Captain Nicholas Nolan's A Troop, under Sergeant Augustus Wilson, scouting out of Larned, overtook a small party of hostiles on November 19 and in a twenty-mile running fight killed two of them. Late in the month the indefatigable Carpenter with H and I scoured a large area south of the Arkansas but the group was forced to return after encountering on December 4 a blizzard that permanently disabled two troopers.[37]

Late in January Carpenter was in the field again with H and I along with two companies of the Fifth Infantry under Captain Bankhead. The command searched the country between the Big Sandy and the Republican, the same area over which Carpenter had marched to Forsyth's relief. No Indians were encountered, but enough fireworks were supplied by the men themselves when a few of the buffalo soldiers tangled with white infantrymen, and Doctor

---

[36] Armes, *op. cit.,* 287–88.

[37] Organizational Returns, Tenth Cavalry, November, 1868; Post Returns, Fort Wallace, November, 1868; Medical History, Fort Wallace, Vol. 363.

Fitzgerald was obliged to amputate a trooper's arm. Captain Byrne with twenty-five men of C Company from Fort Dodge had better luck. On January 29 he overtook a party of Pawnee horse thieves, killed seven of them and wounded one. Byrne's loss was two men wounded.[38]

Meanwhile, to the south the winter campaign was coming to a successful conclusion, and this course of events served to move the whole of the Tenth Cavalry to Indian Territory. The previous year had been a difficult one. Eight troops of the regiment had scarcely been out of the saddle and the winter had been a harsh one. Many of the men had scurvy which the surgeon at Fort Wallace attributed to "hardships and privations of arduous winter scouts which were frequent with often little time intervening for purposes of recuperation . . . and a monotonous pork diet."[39] Little wonder the men looked forward to a change and the possibility of a home in a comfortable garrison for a time.

[38] *Army and Navy Journal*, VI, No. 6 (February 6, 1869), 397; Medical History, Fort Wallace, Vol. 363; Engagements and Casualties During the War of 1868–1869, Against Hostile Indians in the Department of the Missouri, SLR Relating to the Ninth and Tenth Cavalry, AGO.
[39] Medical History, Fort Wallace, Vol. 363.

General William T. Sherman, commander of the Military Division of the Missouri. (Courtesy National Archives)

Colonel Benjamin H. Grierson and party at Medicine Bluff, near Fort Sill, Oklahoma, 1869 or 1870. The photograph probably was taken by William S. Soule, who became official post photographer for Fort Sill in 1869 and held the post for six years. (Courtesy U.S. Army Artillery and Missile Center Museum, Fort Sill)

Looking down from top of Medicine Bluff Gap, with Medicine Bluff Creek at bottom. Negro soldiers, probably Tenth Cavalry, sitting and standing in center of gap. The gap, earlier known as Medicine Man's

Walk from Indian legend, later was called Cavalry Gap. Signed by Soule at lower left. (Courtesy U.S. Army Artillery and Missile Center Museum, Fort Sill)

Cavalry Gap from the north bank of Medicine Bluff Creek in 1870. The creek is in the foreground and on the opposite bank is a small white tent, with Soule signature. Tenth Cavalry buffalo soldiers are standing near the creek. Outline of gap shows at top. (Courtesy U.S. Army Artillery and Missile Center Museum, Fort Sill)

A party (probably of Grierson's Tenth Cavalry) at Medicine Bluff, near Fort Sill, about 1870. The view is along the entire escarpment face, showing Medicine Bluff Creek at the base and rounded hill at top of bluff. Probably a Soule photograph. (Courtesy U.S. Army Artillery and Missile Center Museum, Fort Sill)

Colonel Benjamin H. Grierson, commander of the Tenth Cavalry.
(Courtesy National Archives)

III

AN ARMY OF OCCUPATION

THE COLUMNS of Custer, Evans, Carr, and Penrose, in a fine display of teamwork had inflicted a severe defeat on the Cheyennes at the Washita in November. Early in December, Sheridan, accompanied by Custer and the "main column," left recently established Camp Supply and marched to the Washita. Here he turned downstream, driving before him some Kiowas under Satanta and Lone Wolf. Distrustful of these chiefs, Sheridan placed them both under arrest before reaching Fort Cobb. Here he found most of the Comanches awaiting him and, using the captive chiefs as bait, soon forced the Kiowas to come in and surrender. But the Cheyennes and Arapahoes remained out. Some wished to surrender, others were fearful of a trap, while still others were prepared to carry on the war. Many months of campaigning and negotiation were required before these proud people were on their reservation.[1]

Sheridan disliked the location of Fort Cobb. Like Fort Arbuckle, it was ill-situated with respect to the Kiowa-Comanche reservation and too far removed to afford effective protection for the Texas frontier. He desired a new post to replace both Arbuckle and Cobb. In discussing possible sites with Colonel Grierson, who had arrived from Fort Gibson, Sheridan asked about the former's reconnaissance in May to Medicine Bluff Creek. Grierson still felt this place was ideal and was ordered to visit the site once more

---

[1] Camp Supply was established on November 18, 1868, as a base of operations for troops of the "main column" in Sheridan's winter campaign. Located near the junction of the North Canadian River and Wolf Creek, it was an important post for more than a decade as a focal point for operations against the Southern Cheyennes and Arapahoes. See Frazer, *op. cit.,* 124–25.

45

to ascertain if there would be enough grass for the animals and to make a thorough inspection and report. Grierson, Hazen, a number of other officers, and journalist De B. Randolph Keim set out at once, escorted by forty buffalo soldiers of D Troop under Lieutenant William E. Doyle.

The party reached Medicine Bluff on the morning of December 29 and a daylong inspection reaffirmed Grierson's earlier impressions and delighted his companions. The clear, trickling water of Medicine Bluff and Cache creeks assured a pure and ample supply, the whole area was covered by a rich carpet of grass, wild game was seen everywhere, and the rugged beauty of the Wichita Mountains promised an abundance of building material. Grierson was back at Fort Cobb the following day, and his report to Sheridan caused the latter to decide to move immediately to the new site and to construct a permanent post there.[2]

Heavy rains delayed departure for a week and even then the long column of troops and wagons sloshed through a sea of mud and water. Swollen streams added to the difficulty and four days were required for all the troops to reach "Camp Wichita."[3] The men set to work immediately erecting temporary shelters, the troopers of the Tenth constructing their "homes" from condemned tentage, brush, and mud. Supplies expected from Arbuckle had not arrived because of the condition of the road between that post and Camp Wichita. Grierson at once sent Captain Robinson and the men of E Company to put the road in good condition. Working swiftly, the troopers threw a 135-foot-span across Beaver Creek, cleared trees and underbrush, and by the end of February supplies were flowing without difficulty between Arbuckle and the new post.[4]

Meantime, General Hazen and agent A. G. Boone, recently

2 De Benneville R. Keim, *Sheridan's Troopers on the Borders: A Winter Campaign on the Plains,* 231–32; Sheridan to Sherman, January 8, 1869, Sherman-Sheridan Papers; Organizational Returns, Tenth Cavalry, December, 1868.

3 Keim, *op. cit.,* 247–52. This name was selected because it was the site of an old Wichita Indian village.

4 Grierson to Mrs. Grierson, January 20 and January 30, 1869, Grierson Papers.

appointed, moved the Kiowas and Comanches from Fort Cobb and settled them near Camp Wichita. Sheridan lectured their chiefs for past bad behavior and, after securing their promises that they would behave themselves in the future, he released Satanta and Lone Wolf. There was still little indication that the Cheyennes were ready to take up reservation life, though contacts with the Arapahoes, indicated this tribe was ready to surrender. Sheridan assigned Custer and the Seventh Cavalry the task of rounding up these tribes and prepared to return to Fort Hays.[5]

To Grierson and the Tenth, Sheridan gave a new role. Headquarters would move from Fort Gibson to Camp Wichita, and the regiment would serve as "an army of occupation" among the Kiowas, Comanches, Southern Cheyennes, and Arapahoes as these tribes settled down to reservation life. It was not an enviable assignment as the next six years were to prove.

Grierson moved his headquarters to Camp Wichita in March. Four troops of the regiment were already there and two more were on the way. The remaining six companies were to garrison Camp Supply as rapidly as they could be moved from Kansas. From these posts, the Tenth must do its best to ride herd on thousands of wild Indians, drive out white trespassers, whisky peddlers, and horse thieves, furnish escorts for stages, supply trains, and the mail, and build an entire post from scratch.

Work began immediately on the new post. An old sawmill was dismantled at Fort Arbuckle and moved to the new site, fatigue details cut logs in the Wichita Mountains, opened rock quarries, dressed the stones, and began the construction of quarters, stables, and storehouses. The work was slowed in late March and April by a steady flow of Cheyenne and Arapahoe bands that came in, surrendered, were fed, and then escorted to Camp Supply.

[5] Custer made two expeditions from Camp Wichita against these Indians and managed to induce most of them to move toward the reservations without a fight. See George A. Custer, *Wild Life on the Plains* (St. Louis, Royal Publishing Co., c. 1891). A scholarly and interesting account of this phase of the Cheyenne campaign is in Berthrong, *op. cit.*, 334–44. Tall Bull's band of Cheyenne "irreconcilables" fled north, but they were cornered at Summit Springs, Colorado, by General Carr and defeated decisively. See George F. Price, *Across the Continent With the Fifth Cavalry.*

By early summer, however, most of this "traffic" had ended and Grierson believed there would be peace.[6]

There were others who shared Grierson's views, particularly the Society of Friends. When Ulysses S. Grant was inaugurated as president on March 4, 1869, he launched a new Indian policy. He proposed to reform the Indian Bureau, long a political hotel, where party faithful were housed without reference to qualifications. To achieve this objective, Grant called upon the religious denominations of the country to nominate candidates to supervise the agencies and in this way to bring interest and integrity into the Indian service. This plan became known as the "Quaker policy," for the most enthusiastic response came from the Society of Friends. Eager, peace-loving, and industrious Quakers were soon filling roles as agents to most of the Indian tribes, among them Lawrie Tatum for the Kiowas and Comanches and Brinton Darlington for the Southern Cheyennes and Arapahoes.

If the Indians were now to be "killed with kindness," the role of the military had to be redefined. After lengthy discussion between the Secretaries of War and Interior, it was agreed that Indians on the reservations would be under the exclusive control of their agents, who might, if the need arose, call upon the military for assistance. Indians off the reservations would normally be regarded as hostile.[7]

Grierson was in accord with the new policy and gave it his full support. He learned quickly to like and respect Agent Tatum, but he soon found that he and his regiment were in a virtual strait jacket when the reservation Indians chose to misbehave. Tatum's charges, as well as those of Darlington, gave little trouble during the remainder of 1869—on the reservations. But small bands of Kiowas and Comanches constantly left their camps and headed south across Red River to strike at the hated Texans. Here they

6 Post Returns, Fort Sill, March, 1869; Alvord to Grierson, February 14, 1869, Grierson Papers; Grierson to Mrs. Grierson, February 7, 1869, Grierson Papers; Grierson to the AAG, Department of the Missouri, April 3, 1869, SDLR Relating to the Ninth and Tenth Cavalry, AGO.

7 Loring B. Priest, *Uncle Sam's Stepchildren: The Reformation of United States Indian Policy, 1865-1887* (New Brunswick, Rutgers University Press, 1942), 44–47; *Annual Report of the Commissioner of Indian Affairs for the Year 1869*, 5.

were joined by the implacable Kwahadis from the Staked Plains, who spurned all attempts to bring them to the reservations. The fall of 1869 was thus a bloody one on the Texas frontier.[8]

For the time being at least Grierson and his troopers could continue their construction work and spend some time preparing for field duty when the need arose. There was more of the former than the latter, however, and Grierson grumbled over poor showings on the firing range and complained that discipline was only "fair." In at least one case it was somewhat less than that. In August the name of the new post was changed to Fort Sill, and Private Benjamin Kewconda of E Company celebrated the occasion by getting drunk and disorderly in an Indian camp near the post. When arrested he shouted that Grierson and all the officers of the Tenth were a "bunch of God-damned sons-of-bitches." He may or may not have changed his opinion after being "tied up."[9]

Grierson ran a "dry" post and Kewconda's escapade caused a search for the source of his inspiration. Sergeant Gibbs, of Kewconda's company, found a number of kegs of whisky buried just outside the post and ownership was traced to a couple of teamsters with a four-wagon train. Grierson had the kegs broken up and the men and wagons escorted to Van Buren, Arkansas, for trial.[10]

Early in October Grierson, and as many of his troopers as could be spared from extra duty, took their first tour of the reservation. The column consisting of the "effectives" of Companies B, D, L, and M—a total of sixty men—marched west to Otter Creek and then southwest to the North Fork of Red River. After a bit of exploration and feasting on wild game, the command moved north-

8 Grierson to Tatum, September 30, 1869, Kiowa Files, Military Relations, Indian Archives, Oklahoma State Historical Society, Oklahoma City, Oklahoma; *Annual Report for the Department of Texas, 1869*, 2.

9 Charges and Specifications Preferred Against Benjamin Kewconda, Private, E Company, Tenth Cavalry, August, 1869, LR Relating to the Ninth and Tenth Cavalry, AGO; Organizational Returns, Tenth Cavalry, August–September, 1869. Fort Sill was named for Brigadier Joshua Sill, who was killed at the Battle of Stone River, Tennessee. See Frazer, *op. cit.*, 124. When a trooper was "tied up," he was seated on the ground with knees up and feet flat with arms bound to the front. A stick was pushed across his arms and under his knees rendering him completely helpless. A piece of wood was commonly used as a gag. The normal time of such punishment was about half a day. See Whitman, *op. cit.*, 93.

10 Mrs. Grierson to Louisa Semple, November 23, 1869, Grierson Papers.

east and visited a large Comanche camp on Rainy Mountain Creek. The Indians extended a warm welcome and gave assurances of future good behavior. Grierson undoubtedly hoped the Indians were sincere. A kind man, he had no desire to war against these people unless their actions forced him to mete out such punishment. Satisfied with his first excursion, Grierson returned to Fort Sill. For officers and men it was a welcome release from the monotony of garrison duty, and a much needed acquaintance with the country in which they would operate for many years.[11]

Little else interrupted the daily routine until the end of the year when Lieutenant Doyle apparently found stimulation to equal that of Kewconda. Meeting Lieutenant T. C. Lebo of C Company and the commissary officer, Captain N. D. Badger, Doyle called them both sons-of-bitches, went to his quarters, loaded a carbine, and told Lieutenant R. H. Day that he intended to kill Badger "before I sleep." He failed to find Badger that day, but on the next morning he was still on the rampage and again accosted Lebo and offered to fight a duel. When the long-suffering Lebo refused, Doyle called him a "God-damned coward" and then fired the carbine at Captain Robert Gray who tried to mediate the dispute. Fortunately the shot went wild and post guards arrived in time to prevent further trouble. A court-martial suspended Doyle from rank and pay for six months and confined him to the post for the same period. The frontier army was no place for the sensitive or the weak at heart.[12]

Grierson's pride and joy, the regimental band, did much to soften the rough work and loneliness at Fort Sill. Evening concerts "under the stars" were keenly anticipated and much enjoyed by the officers and men. It was thus that the tune of "Auld Lang Syne" welcomed in the new year, but the notes had scarcely died away before Indian trouble rumbled in the distance.[13]

11 Post Returns, Fort Sill, October, 1869; Organizational Returns, Tenth Cavalry, October, 1869.

12 General Court Martial Orders No. 48, Headquarters, Department of the Missouri, March 29, 1870, Grierson Papers.

13 E. N. Glass, *History of the Tenth Cavalry,* 18; Alvord to Grierson, February

The regiment was ill-prepared to cope with any large-scale Indian difficulty. Death, disease, disability, and desertion had cut the total enlisted strength to fewer than eight hundred in the fall of of 1869. When the sick, men in confinement, and those on extra duty were deducted, Grierson could field not more than five hundred men. As 1870 opened, some three hundred raw recruits arrived at Fort Sill and Camp Supply to bring the regiment near to full strength, but it was many months before these men were capable soldiers.[14]

Green troopers were not the only difficulty, however. Captain Carpenter at Camp Supply with his hard-bitten veterans of H Company, voiced a common complaint in a letter to Grierson. The Tenth was "getting mean and wornout horses of the Seventh Cavalry." Some of these trail-weary nags died within days of reaching the post. Carpenter wrote, "Since our first mount in 1867 this regiment has received nothing but broken down horses and repaired equipment as I am willing to testify to as far as my knowledge goes."[15] Two years of meritorious service had failed to dull the edge of discrimination, and, in the eyes of many military authorities, the combat caliber of the buffalo soldiers remained to be proved.

Old mounts, old equipment, and untried men notwithstanding, there was a challenging task ahead as the burly Kiowa chieftain Satanta was quick to provide. Early on the afternoon of January 11, about forty miles south of Camp Supply, Satanta and a large force of Kiowa warriors stampeded a trail herd of three hundred Texas cattle. The drover, Jacob Hershfield, and fourteen cowboys were pushed back to their wagons, where the Indians took all their sugar, bacon, flour, coffee, and tobacco, as well as one hundred and fifty dollars in cash. The timely arrival and intervention of Chief Kicking Bird of the Kiowas probably saved the lives of

14, 1869, Grierson Papers. Grierson had difficulty in getting the necessary instruments and a fire at Camp Wichita destroyed some of them.

[14] Organizational Returns, Tenth Cavalry, September–January, 1869–70.

[15] Carpenter to Grierson, May 22, 1870, Grierson Papers.

Hershfield and his men. Five hours were required to round up the cattle, and Hershfield might just as well have spared himself the effort, for Satanta again stampeded the herd and none was recovered.[16]

When news of Satanta's raid reached Camp Supply, Brevet Colonel A. D. Nelson, Third Infantry, commanding the post, sent Major M. H. Kidd with A, F, I, and K companies of the Tenth to drive the Kiowas back on their reservation. On the way Kidd stopped off at the Cheyenne camp of Chief Whirlwind, who told him, "You don't have half enough men for the job." Whirlwind believed that the appearance of troops in the Kiowa camps would precipitate a war. Kidd continued on to Kicking Bird's camp, however, and here received assurances of good behavior sufficient to cause him to turn back without a fight. Kidd felt the appearance of his troopers had produced a "salutary effect" on the Kiowas.[17]

Kidd had avoided serious trouble, but as spring came and passed, rumors of war sifted steadily into Sill and Supply, and Grierson decided that a demonstration in force might be in order, but so great was the demand for detachments of the Tenth for other duties that a major concentration of the regiment proved unfeasible. White horse-thieves were a constant nuisance, and since the restrictions of the Quaker policy did not prevail in such cases, Grierson's troopers managed to make this occupation an extremely hazardous one.

On May 6 a party of thieves stole 139 mules from a government train at Bluff Creek, Indian Territory, and made for Texas with their haul. Lieutenant William Harmon with five men of M Company went in pursuit. Two days later in Montague County, Texas, Harmon overtook five men driving the mules and pressed them so hard that they abandoned one hundred of the animals near Clear Creek in Cook County. After a chase of eighteen more miles, Harmon brought his quarry to bay in a wooded ravine,

16 Jacob Hershfield to Lieutenant John Sullivan, January 11, 1870, SLR Relating to the Ninth and Tenth Cavalry, AGO.
17 Grierson to the AAG, Department of the Missouri, May 20, 1870, SLR, AGO, RG 94, NA; Brevet Colonel A. D. Nelson to the AAG, Department of the Missouri, January 18, 1870, *ibid*.

killed one of them, and captured the other four. On questioning his prisoners, Harmon learned that they were expecting three others to join them. Harmon awaited the threesome, captured them without a fight, and recovered two wagons, three horses, and four mules. He then marched to Fort Arbuckle with his prisoners, 127 government mules, 3 horses, and 2 wagons.[18]

The troopers at Camp Supply were the first to feel the annual summer upswing of Indian activity. Early in May a small party of warriors stole some stock near the post and defied all the efforts of Captain Nicholas Nolan and A Company to find them. A much stronger war party attacked a wagon train north of Supply the same month, ran off all the mules, and killed a man before Carpenter and old reliable H Company came to the rescue and drove the Indians off. On the last day of the month, thirty-five Arapahoes hit the mail station on Bear Creek about forty miles south of Fort Dodge on the Supply road, killed two privates of the Third Infantry, and inflicted eight arrow wounds on their sergeant as the little detachment fought to save the station. Major Kidd with A and K drove off the Indians and brought the critically wounded sergeant into Dodge.[19]

In June Indian war parties grew bolder. On June 8 a government train from Fort Dodge escorted by Lieutenant J. A. Bodamer and twenty-five men of F Company was attacked by one hundred hostiles. A hard-riding buffalo soldier broke through the encircling Indians and raced to Camp Supply for aid. Nolan and A Company galloped to the rescue, but when they reached the scene Bodamer had fought off the attackers and killed three of them. Corporal Freeman and Private Winchester suffered slight wounds.[20]

Most of these attacks had been made by Kiowas, but on June 11 a formidable body of war-hungry Comanches decided to test

[18] *Army and Navy Journal*, Vol. VII (May 21, 1870), 622.

[19] Post Returns, Camp Supply, May, 1870; Organizational Returns, Tenth Cavalry, May, 1870; Brevet Colonel W. G. Mitchell to General John Pope, June 6, 1870, SLR, AGO.

[20] Post Returns, Camp Supply, June, 1870; Organizational Returns, Tenth Cavalry, June, 1870.

the mettle of all the buffalo soldiers at Camp Supply. They first attempted to run off the cavalry horses, but, failing in that, they lingered long enough to skirmish for an hour with all five companies then at the post. They paid for their audacity with six dead and ten wounded, and the Comanches were never quite so curious again about the fighting qualities of the Tenth. Shortly after this fight the troopers received another boost in their morale when Lieutenant Colonel Davidson of their own regiment replaced Colonel Nelson as the new commander at Camp Supply.[21]

Grierson and his troopers at Fort Sill were having their problems as well. On June 12 an inveterate Kiowa raider, White Horse, ran off seventy-three mules from the quartermaster's corral at Sill. Captain Walsh with D and E were quick to pursue but lost the trail in a maze of fresh buffalo tracks. Other red prowlers, along with lurking white thieves, kept detachments on the move in the vicinity of the post and Tatum's agency, but these were minor annoyances compared to Kiowa and Comanche activity in Texas.[22]

In May and June war parties from these tribes struck heavily along the North Texas frontier, killing fifteen persons in Jack County alone. Fresh from his coup at the quartermaster's corral, the redoubtable White Horse crossed the Red into Texas, killed a Mr. Gottlieb Koozier, and took Mrs. Koozier and her six children as captives. In the opinion of Colonel James Oakes, Sixth Cavalry, commanding at Fort Richardson, the Kiowas were making all-out war on Texas and it "should be stopped." Oakes professed to believe that the Indian agent at Fort Sill was actually arming the Indians with late model weapons and implied that Grierson and the Tenth were doing little or nothing to stop the raids. Texas newspapers echoed these charges and vented their wrath on both Tatum and Grierson.[23]

21 Organizational Returns, Tenth Cavalry, June, 1870; Post Returns, Camp Supply, June, 1870.

22 Post Returns, Fort Sill, June, 1870; Organizational Returns, Tenth Cavalry, June, 1870; Nye, *op. cit.*, 107.

23 Oakes to the AAG, Department of Texas, September 10, 1870, SLR, AGO; Austin *Daily Journal*, May 14, 1871; Post Returns, Fort Richardson, Texas, May–June, 1870. The Indians were not so well armed as charged, and most of their

These accusations were unjustified and unfair, and General John Pope, Sheridan's successor as commanding general, Department of the Missouri, was quick to defend Grierson and his troopers, pointing out the handicap under which they worked:

> Indian reservations and the Indians upon them are wholly under the jurisdiction of the agents in charge who are alone responsible for the conduct of the Indians, and for the protection of the rights of persons and property both of the Indians and of white men on Indian reservations. The military forces on or near such Indian reservations are placed there solely to assist the Indian agents to preserve good order on the Reservations.
>
> Under no circumstances except specific orders from Department Headquarters or higher authority will any commander of troops assume jurisdiction or exercise control over reservation Indians or their agents, nor originate nor execute any act of their own volition in regard to affairs on such reservations.[24]

Within these severe limitations Grierson did what he could. All through the summer he kept patrols along the Red River, but a few troopers, no matter how alert, had little chance of intercepting red bands who could cross at dozens of places along many miles of river. More than this he could not do unless called upon by Agent Tatum. As for that harassed Quaker, he slowly lost faith in the peace policy and at length asked Grierson to station troops at the agency on issue day. This had some effect, for Tatum was able to recover thirty-seven mules White Horse had stolen and also to recover the captive Kooziers, but even this limited reliance on the military was deplored by Tatum's superiors, who had little if any understanding of conditions on or off the reservation.[25]

Raids and depredations declined as fall came on, and Grierson was able to resume construction work at Fort Sill. But there

weapons were obtained in trade with the *comancheros* of New Mexico. See J. Evetts Haley, "The Comanchero Trade," *Southwestern Historical Quarterly,* Vol. XXXVIII, No. 3 (January, 1935).

24 General Orders No. 28, Headquarters, Department of the Missouri, War Department, AGO, File No. 1305–1871, NA (hereinafter cited as File No. 1305–1871).

25 Grierson to the AAG, Department of the Missouri, August 7, 1870, SLR, AGO; Organizational Returns, Tenth Cavalry, June–August, 1870; Lawrie Tatum, *Our Red Brothers and the Peace Policy of President Ulysses S. Grant,* 42–44.

were vexing problems within the regiment. Captain Charles Cox of K Company was court-martialed for drunkenness on duty, selling government property, breach of arrest, and conduct unbecoming an officer and a gentleman. Cox was dismissed from the service, fined five hundred dollars, and sentenced to three years' imprisonment. His fate was to be made a matter of public notice and it was "deemed scandalous for an officer to associate with him."[26] Captain Graham of I, an officer with a fine combat record, was dismissed for selling government property, and tempestuous Captain Armes of F also suffered court-martial on an impressive list of charges. Captain Edward Byrne of C Company ran afoul of Grierson in an argument over the former's prerogatives as temporary commander at Fort Arbuckle and was shortly mustered out of the army.[27]

It was a time of trial for the troopers as well. Malaria swept through the ranks and this, combined with typhoid and a wretched diet, caused twelve deaths. Sergeant Frank Skidrick of I died of an accidental gunshot wound, Sergeant Boyd Daniel of L drowned in Cache Creek, and Private George Watkins of I was shot and killed by another trooper. The manner of Watkins' demise was a rare one, for the men normally got on well together. Fist fights were far more common in settling disputes, although these could be sanguinary affairs if the antagonists were wearing "drinking jewelry"—horseshoe nails bent into a ring with the head up.[28]

Despite these difficulties and the heavy demands for work details on quarters, barracks, stables, and a new stone corral, time was found for training and target practice. The role of "an army of occupation" in the first year had, on the whole, been an exasperating one. Staunch supporter of the peace policy that he was, Grierson nevertheless intended to be prepared for the worst—and there seemed every possibility of a full-scale war.

And it was well that Grierson prepared, for the Kiowas and

[26] SLR 1870 Relating to Captain Charles G. Cox, Tenth Cavalry, AGO, RG 94, NA; Organizational Returns, Tenth Cavalry, August, 1870.
[27] Organizational Returns, Tenth Cavalry, August, 1870; Grierson to Mrs. Grierson, July 30, 1870, Grierson Papers.
[28] Organizational Returns, Tenth Cavalry, October–December, 1870; Don Rickey, Jr., *Forty Miles a Day on Beans and Hay*, 57–59.

Comanches did not wait for spring to strike in Texas. They were at it again in January and in the process killed a bona fide hero, Brit Johnson, a Negro frontiersman, who had managed the recovery of a number of captives from the Comanches at great risk to himself. Johnson and three companions, hauling supplies from Weatherford to Fort Griffin, were attacked by an overwhelming force of warriors on January 24. The four men killed their horses for a breastwork and were slain only after a desperate fight. Johnson's corpse was horribly mutilated, the stomach split open, and the body of his little pet dog stuffed into it.[29]

Peaceful chiefs told Tatum that many small parties were in Texas and reports of raids came steadily into Sill. Grierson blamed part of the trouble on railroad surveying parties, whose appearance upset the Indians, but he believed a long delay in the arrival of annuities was the prime difficulty. Whatever the causes, the situation grew steadily worse and in March a thoroughly disillusioned Tatum requested Grierson to keep patrols along the Red River in an effort to stem the tide.[30]

Grierson sent L and M to the mouth of Cache Creek to scout the line of Red River, but it was a hopeless task. The entire regiment would have been insufficient to guard all the many crossings and turn back the swift-riding bands.

Meanwhile, General Sherman had been bombarded with letters, telegrams, and resolutions from Texas citizens and their legislature complaining of raids and depredations and demanding greater protection. Doubtful that conditions were as bad as painted, Sherman, nevertheless, decided to make an on-the-spot inspection. On April 28 he arrived in San Antonio, and four days later he set out for the frontier, accompanied by Inspector General Randolph B. Marcy, two other officers of his staff, and with a picked detachment of seventeen troopers of the Tenth as an escort. The little

29 J. W. Wilbarger, *Indian Depredations in Texas,* 581–82; Kenneth W. Porter, "Negroes and Indians on the Texas Frontier," *Southwestern Historical Quarterly,* LIII (October, 1949), 155–56.

30 Tatum to Enoch Hoag, March 18, 1871, Kiowa Files, Depredations; Grierson to the AAG, Department of the Missouri, September, 1871, Annual Report, Military Division of the Missouri, File No. 1305–1871; Tatum to Grierson, March 25, 1871, Kiowa Files, Depredations.

party visited Forts McKavett, Concho, and Griffin, hearing much but seeing nothing of Indian activity. On May 18 they arrived at Fort Richardson, their tour of the Texas posts completed. Sherman's doubts had not been resolved, although Inspector Marcy, who had surveyed the same region years earlier, pointed out that there were fewer people along the route than had been the case prior to the Civil War.

Sherman's doubts were soon erased. Early on the morning of the nineteenth a bloodstained teamster named Thomas Brazeale staggered into Richardson with the story of a massacre. About mid-afternoon of the previous day a war party of one hundred or more Indians had attacked a ten-wagon train on open prairie about twenty miles west of Jacksboro. According to Brazeale, seven of his eleven companions had been killed. He and four others had managed to escape into some nearby timber.

Sherman at once ordered Colonel Ranald S. Mackenzie, Fourth Cavalry, who had replaced Oakes as commanding officer at Richardson, to take every available man at the post and run down the raiders. Mackenzie was on the march at noon with one hundred and fifty men and reached the scene of the attack early in the evening during a driving rainstorm. Seven bloated and mutilated bodies were found, including one that had been chained to a wagon pole and burned to a cinder. Five dead mules were found, but forty-one others were missing. Leaving a small detachment to bury the dead, Mackenzie pushed on in an effort to overhaul the war party, but rain and mud made progress difficult.[31]

An angry Sherman set out for Fort Sill where he arrived on May 23. Wasting little time with formalities, Sherman, accompanied by Colonel Grierson, called on Lawrie Tatum and told him about the attack on the train. He then asked the horrified agent if he knew of any Indians who had recently raided in Texas. Tatum was not certain but felt sure he could find out. The Indians

[31] Post Returns, Fort Richardson, May, 1871; Extracts from Inspector General R. B. Marcy's Journal of an Inspection Tour While Accompanying the General in Chief during the Months of April, May and June, 1871, Phillips Collection, University of Oklahoma, Norman, 186–91; Sherman to Mackenzie, May 19, 1871, File No. 1305–1871; Report of Assistant Surgeon J. N. Patzki, File No. 1305–1871.

would be in for their rations in a few days and he could question them at that time.

On Saturday, May 27, the Kiowas came to the agency, and Tatum called the chiefs into his office, told them about the raid on the train, and asked if they knew who had done it. A boastful and belligerent Satanta rose immediately, berated Tatum for the many wrongs the Kiowas had suffered, accused him of cheating the Indians, and demanded guns and ammunition. He then bragged that he had led the raid and that Chiefs Satank, Eagle Heart, Big Tree, and Big Bow had accompanied him. Instructing his employees to go ahead with the rations issue, Tatum excused himself and penned a hurried note to Grierson relaying the information Satanta had given him and asking that the guilty Indians be arrested.

Tatum then went in person to see Sherman and Grierson, whom he found on the porch of the latter's headquarters. A decision was made to call a council in front of Grierson's house at which time the guilty parties would be arrested. Orders were issued swiftly to the buffalo soldiers to go to the stables, saddle, and mount. At a given signal the companies would take up designated positions to prevent escape. As an added precaution, a dozen troopers were stationed inside Grierson's house behind shuttered windows facing the porch.

Hardly had these preparations been completed when Satanta arrived. He had heard that a big Washington officer was at the post and he "wished to measure him up." Under questioning from Sherman, the chief readily admitted his part in the raid, but as he saw the former's temper rising, he first altered his story and then rose and started for his pony. Grierson's alert orderly drew his pistol immediately and ordered Satanta to sit down—an order he obeyed with alacrity. Some twenty Kiowas, among them Satank, now arrived for the council, and Sherman informed them that the guilty chiefs were under arrest and would be sent to Texas for trial. Satanta flew into a rage and clutched at the revolver under his blanket, but at this instant Sherman gave a command and the shuttered windows flew open revealing a dozen buffalo soldiers with carbines cocked and leveled. Satanta subsided at once.

THE COUNTRY
of the
BUFFALO SOLDIER

0 Miles 200

    The signal was now given to the troopers in the stables. The
gates opened and D Company, led by Lieutenant R. H. Pratt,
trotted into position in line on the left of Grierson's quarters
while Captain Carpenter and H took position on the right. Captain Robinson's E formed two detachments, with one covering
the rear of the house and the other moving to the front. For the
Indians on the porch there was no escape. Another detachment
under Lieutenant L. H. Orleman, consisting of ten men from

each of the companies, moved quietly into position across the parade ground and behind a large body of Indians who had gathered there to watch the proceedings on the porch.

At this point Lone Wolf rode up from the trader's store where he, Big Tree, and several others had been helping themselves to wares they fancied. Lone Wolf dismounted carrying two Spencer repeaters and a bow and arrows. As he advanced toward the porch, he tossed the bow and arrows to one warrior, a carbine to another, and then, with the remaining carbine at full cock, he faced General Sherman. It was a delicate moment. A shot could have made the porch a slaughter pen, but Grierson's cold courage saved the day. He grabbed Lone Wolf's carbine and at the same time shouted to interpreter Horace Jones to tell the Indians that violence would not save their chiefs. It was sound advice, and fortunately the jittery Indians accepted it and the crisis passed. Without more ado, Satanta and Satank were escorted to the guardhouse and put in irons.

A summons was sent to Big Tree and Eagle Heart, and when they failed to appear, Lieutenant Woodward, Lieutenant Pratt, and D Company were ordered to the trader's store to take them. When they reached the store, Woodward dismounted with a detail and entered to make the arrest. Big Tree was behind the counter passing out goods when he saw the troopers enter. With no waste motion he dashed to the rear of the store, pulled his blanket over his head, and plunged through the glass window. Once outside he took to his heels across a fenced field. Pratt sent his troopers at a gallop along the sides of the fence, hemmed in the flying chieftain, and forced him to surrender. In a matter of minutes he joined Satanta and Satank in the guardhouse. Eagle Heart, on his way to answer the summons, saw Big Tree's arrest and, thus forewarned, made good his escape.

Meanwhile, the Indians Orleman had been watching started to edge away and, when called upon to halt, opened fire. The only casualty was Private Edward Givins of D Company who was hit in the leg by an arrow. The troopers returned the fire, killing one Indian, but the rest escaped in a wild stampede. They were joined in a mad dash toward the Wichita Mountains by other Kiowas who had remained in their camps.

The council on the porch now drew to a close. Sherman told the chiefs that Satanta, Satank, and Big Tree would be held in arrest and that the forty-one mules from the wagon train must be returned within ten days. When the Indians assented, the troopers opened ranks and permitted them to return to their people.[32]

With the wagon train affair thus solved, Sherman left for Fort Gibson, escorted by Carpenter and a proud H Company. He had been much impressed with the post that Grierson and his men were constructing, deeming it one of the best he had ever seen.[33]

Colonel Mackenzie, whose pursuit of the raiders had bogged down in the mud, came into Sill on June 4 and made preparations to return the Indian prisoners to Jacksboro, Texas, for trial. On June 8 two wagons were driven to the guardhouse and a cursing, struggling Satank was forced into one of them, guarded by a corporal and two privates. Satanta and Big Tree climbed meekly into the second wagon with one trooper watching each of them. The column then set out on the Fort Richardson road. What followed is told simply in a letter from Grierson's young son Charles to his aunt:

Fort Sill, June 9, 1871

DEAR AUNT:

Yesterday General Mackenzie's command left here with the Indian prisoners for Texas. Satank said that he was not going to Texas at all, that he was going to kill somebody. He attempted to put his threat into execution by stabbing the corporal that was sitting in the wagon with him and he was shot in 3 or 4 places. When the soldiers were shooting at Satank, some of them shot the teamster making a long wound on the head. The other Indians made no fuss at all.

---

[32] Richard H. Pratt, "Some Indian Experiences," *Cavalry Journal*, XVI (December, 1906), 210–11; Sherman to Sheridan, May 29, 1871, File No. 1305–1871; Sherman to Townsend, May 28, 1871, File No. 1305–1871; Marcy, "Journal," 195–97; Organizational Returns, Tenth Cavalry, May, 1871; Post Returns, Fort Sill, May, 1871; Pratt, *op. cit.*, 44–46; Tatum, *op. cit.*

[33] Sherman to General Pope, May 24, 1871, SLR, AGO.

Today Captain Robinson is going to the mouth of Cache Cr. with the remainder of his company.

Affectionately yours,

C. H. GRIERSON[34]

Mackenzie got the remaining two chiefs safely to Fort Richardson where they were turned over to civil authorities for trial. Both were sentenced to hang, but pressure, largely from Quakers, including Agent Tatum, caused Governor Edmund J. Davis to commute their sentences to life imprisonment. Sherman was disgusted, for he had earlier warned that if the chiefs were set free, "no life from Kansas to the Rio Grande will be safe, and no soldier will ever again take a live prisoner."[35]

For the buffalo soldiers the capture and arrest of Satank, Satanta, and Big Tree added an exciting episode to the history of the regiment, but it was more than that. The troopers had carried out their orders with a crisp coolness and disciplined restraint. A moment's loss of nerve or an instant's "trigger-itch" could have launched a blood bath. Neither had occurred and only two maddened Kiowas had lost their lives. The climax to the wagon train affair was a tribute to the officers and men of the Tenth.

While the Kiowas captured most of the attention in the spring and early summer of 1871, the Cheyennes were also a source of concern. Kiowas constantly visited the Cheyenne camps urging war, but with the exception of a few young warriors they gained few adherents. Agent Darlington worked carefully and diligently to keep Indians at peace and Colonel Davidson co-operated fully. Rumors of war persisted, however, and in May, when more than three hundred of the Cheyennes left the reservation, it was feared they had joined the Kiowas. Davidson sent out Lieutenant Bodamer with F and K to locate the absentees, and they were found encamped on San Francisco Creek. They had not listened to the

---

[34] C. H. Grierson to Louisa Semple, June 9, 1871, Grierson Papers.

[35] Sherman to Townsend, May 28, 1871, File No. 1305–1871; Post Returns, Fort Richardson, June, 1871; Wilbarger, *op. cit.*, 563; Tatum, *op. cit.*, 122; Special Order No. 185, September 12, 1871, Headquarters, Department of Texas, File No. 1305–1871.

Kiowas, however, and Bodamer had no difficulty in persuading them to return to the reservation.[36]

The Comanches were another matter. Along with the Kiowas they had been raiding frequently in Texas, and Grierson strengthened his river patrols, but with little success. On the afternoon of May 30 a small party of prospectors was attacked by a band of thirty-five Comanches just south of Red River and within six miles of the picket post Grierson had established at the mouth of Cache Creek. John Hoxey of Macomb County, Michigan, was killed and scalped, but his companions escaped to the river and made their way to the camp on Cache Creek. Lieutenant T. J. Spencer immediately sent a courier to Fort Sill for reinforcements and then, with only twelve men of L Company, swam rain-swollen Red River and took up the pursuit. The Indians had apparently recrossed, however, and Turner lost the trail.[37]

Meanwhile, the Indian Bureau revised somewhat the peace policy. Henceforth, the military would be permitted to enter the reservations to pursue raiders and to recover stolen property, but the Tenth still operated under severe restrictions. It could not take action outside the reservation against Tatum's Indians unless in "hot pursuit" of raiders. The role of an "army of occupation" was beginning to wear a little thin with the men of the Tenth. There was enough latitude, however, for Grierson to combine with Mackenzie and his Fourth Cavalry to strike the Kiowas if they failed to return the stolen mules and to hit the Kwahadis, who had never been on the reservation and who were bringing so much woe to the Texas frontier.[38]

In July Grierson concentrated nine companies of the Tenth at Fort Sill. A and F remained at Camp Supply while C was escorting a party of Atlantic and Pacific Railroad surveyors to Santa Fe.

36 Organizational Returns, Tenth Cavalry, May, 1871; Post Returns, Camp Supply, May, 1871; Darlington to Davidson, July 10, 1871, File No. 1305–1871; Berthrong, *op. cit.*, 359–62.

37 Organizational Returns, Tenth Cavalry, May, 1871; *Army and Navy Journal*, Vol. VIII (July 1, 1871), 731.

38 Secretary Delano to Commissioner E. S. Parker, June 20, 1871, File No. 1305–1871; Grierson to the AAG, Department of the Missouri, September 21, 1871, File No. 1305–1871.

A campaign of three weeks was planned and arrangements were made for a rendezvous with Mackenzie on Otter Creek. Young Robert Grierson was much impressed with the bustle of preparations and wrote his aunt: "Papa is going out to the west end of the mountains and is going to take two cannons with him." "Papa" was taking considerably more than that—six companies of eager buffalo soldiers who thoroughly agreed with Captain Carpenter that a chance to hunt down some "feathered varmints" was going to be fun.[39]

On August 10 Grierson and Mackenzie reached camp on Otter Creek and made final plans. Five days later, in extremely hot weather, the two long columns set out, with Mackenzie moving up the Salt Fork and Grierson the North Fork of Red River, with the intention of going as far west as McClellan Creek. The march was scarcely "fun." The country was broken and rough, the streams gypsum-impregnated, and temperatures soared over one hundred degrees, causing great suffering among men and animals. And it was all for naught. On August 24 Grierson received word from Tatum that the Kiowas had returned the forty-one mules and he turned back to Fort Sill, leaving four companies at the camp on Otter Creek to await Mackenzie's return.

Mackenzie came in on September 1 thoroughly disgusted. He had not seen an Indian, much less killed one. Perhaps his effort was not entirely wasted, for he was rewarded in a different respect. The resourceful Carpenter, equal to any occasion, had a full-course dinner prepared for Mackenzie and his staff. One of Mackenzie's officers remarked that his commander was most impressed, especially with the prune pie on which he commented, "Prune pie! Prune pie! Well I'll be damned."[40]

Actually, the troopers at Sill enjoyed more excitement than those in the field. On the night of August 10 two civilians named

[39] Organizational Returns, Tenth Cavalry, July–August, 1871; Robert K. Grierson to Louisa Semple, August 3, 1871, Grierson Papers; Carpenter to Grierson, September 15, 1871, Grierson Papers.

[40] Robert G. Carter, *On the Border With Mackenzie,* 142–43; Mrs. Grierson to Charles Grierson, August 15, 1871, Grierson Papers; Post Returns, Fort Sill, August, 1871; Grierson to Mrs. Grierson, August 11, 1871, Grierson Papers; Grierson to Tatum, August 14, 1871, Kiowa Files, Military Relations.

Edwards and Neal and three troopers, all confined in the guard-house, cut a hole in the floor, dropped down into the basement, and escaped through the rear entrance. The sergeant of the guard heard the noise but ran first to the prison room, and the escapees got a start. Four of the guards started in pursuit and fired a number of shots but none took effect. A mounted detachment took up the chase, but early next morning the three errant troopers returned and gave themselves up. Edwards and Neal made good their escape.

A week later the sawmill caught fire and a bucket brigade of sixty men turned out to douse the flames. Most of the woodwork was destroyed, but repairs were made quickly and the mill was running again by the time Grierson returned from the field.

C Company had, meantime, returned from Santa Fe with a story that cast a pall over the garrison. En route, Lieutenant Robert Price, new to the company, had permitted himself to quarrel with privates York Johnson and Charles Smith. In a fit of rage Price shot both men to death. He remained in arrest in Santa Fe when the company returned to Sill, but was released in the fall and allowed to resign from the army. The affair was a shock to the regiment, for the officers and men normally enjoyed a close relationship.[41]

There was a killing of less serious nature at Fort Sill this torrid summer of 1871. Mrs. Grierson explained in a letter to her husband:

> Tucker—the soldier who has taken care of Captain Walsh's and our cows so long, shot one of ours, three days ago, because she would not come home just as he wanted her to. She had to be killed, the butcher made beef of her. The soldier says he will pay for her.[42]

[41] Organizational Returns, Tenth Cavalry, June–September, 1871; Major G. W. Schofield to Grierson, August 12, 1871, Grierson Papers; Lieutenant Samuel Woodward to Grierson, August 30, 1871, Grierson Papers. Lieutenant Price, a graduate of West Point, was assigned to the Tenth Cavalry in June, 1870, and resigned April 27, 1872. Heitman, *op. cit.*, I, 807.

[42] Mrs. Grierson to Grierson, August 31, 1871, Grierson Papers. The Grierson Papers contain numerous letters written by Mrs. Grierson in behalf of enlisted men guilty of minor infractions.

It is doubtful that Tucker got as much as a lecture for his misdeed, as Mrs. Grierson was ever quick to intervene in behalf of a buffalo soldier in trouble.

With the return of the mules and the march of two strong columns into the western reaches of the reservation, Grierson and Tatum hoped for better behavior on the part of the Kiowas, but strong patrols were kept moving along Red River to turn back bands attempting to slip into Texas. Most of the Kiowas were quieted, temporarily at least, but close friends and relatives of Satank and Satanta were thirsting for revenge—and they got it. On September 22 they killed and scalped two of Tatum's herders, Patrick O'Neal and John Johnson, within sight of the post. Three days later Grierson received word that a small band, presumed to be Kiowas, had ambushed three troopers of B Company as they scouted along Red River and mortally wounded bugler Larkin Foster. A strong detachment had pursued the slayers, but the trail had been lost.[43]

As usual, raids and depredations eased off with the coming of winter, but by early spring the Comanches were again marauding in Texas and they were soon joined by such restless Kiowa raiders as White Horse and Big Bow. The buffalo soldiers maintained their ceaseless patrols along the Red, but to little avail. On the reserve both tribes behaved reasonably well, but efforts by the Five Civilized Tribes, at their annual conference held at Okmulgee in midsummer, to persuade their Plains neighbors to adopt the "white man's road" were scorned, and a visit to Washington by several of their prominent chiefs under the auspices of the Indian Bureau had little effect. In fact, the visit proved a serious mistake, for the Commissioner of Indian Affairs, in a blush of enthusiasm, promised the release of Satanta and Big Tree on March 1, 1873.[44]

Raiding in Texas was a "legitimate" and "honorable" occupation for Tatum's Indians, but this was not the sole source of in-

[43] Grierson to the AAG, Department of the Missouri, September 25, 1871, SLR, AGO; Organizational Returns, Tenth Cavalry, September, 1871.

[44] *Annual Report of the Commissioner of Indian Affairs for the Year 1872*, 99; Tatum, *op. cit.*, 125; *Army and Navy Journal*, Vol. X (October 26, 1872), 165.

spiration for depredations. Whisky peddlers and unlicensed traders sneaked across the Kansas border, established "ranches," and supplied both liquid encouragement and weapons for Indian raiders. *Comancheros* from New Mexico hovered on the western borders of the reservations trading arms and ammunition for stolen cattle and horses. Many undesirables, the off-scourings of the frontier, were attracted to the Territory by railroad construction and were ready to steal or murder anything on foot, including Indians and their herds. Ever a problem, these vultures of the frontier so increased their activities that Grierson and his troopers had great difficulty in coping with them.

In an effort to deal more effectively with such people, Grierson moved his headquarters to Fort Gibson in June, 1872, along with four companies of the regiment. With two companies under Davidson at Camp Supply and six companies at Fort Sill, commanded by Major G. W. Schofield, it was believed the "intruder" problem could be more effectively dealt with. A concerted effort resulted in the arrest and expulsion of hundreds of these vermin, but punishment was often so trivial as simply to encourage the same characters to reappear time and again. A not untypical case was the experience of Lieutenant Pratt and Company D at Camp Supply.[45]

In January, 1873, John D. Miles, who had succeeded after Brinton Darlington's death as agent to the Southern Cheyennes and Arapahoes, complained to Davidson that there were five "ranches" selling whisky to his Indians on the northern border of the reservation. He wished these places broken up and their owners arrested. Davidson ordered Pratt to take a detachment and carry out the agent's request. With temperatures well below zero, Pratt and twenty troopers, bundled in their heaviest winter gear, two wagons, and an Indian guide left to find the "ranches."

A severe and cutting north wind made the march a miserable one, but it also confined the peddlers to their cabins and Pratt was able to round up fifteen intruders, a large quantity of foul whisky,

[45] Bigelow, "Sketch"; Organizational Returns, Tenth Cavalry, June, 1872; Post Returns, Fort Sill, June, 1872.

late-model rifles, revolvers and ammunition, and considerable stores of sugar, coffee, and bacon, as well as buffalo robes and cattle which the Indians had traded. In extreme cold, Pratt and and his men convoyed peddlers, supplies, and cattle back to Camp Supply. Thirteen buffalo soldiers were hospitalized at once for severely frostbitten hands and feet. They must shortly have had cause to wonder about the necessity for their suffering, for the peddlers were sent for trial to Topeka, Kansas, where each was fined ten dollars and sentenced to a month in jail.[46]

When spring arrived a change of command occurred in the Tenth. Grierson was ordered to St. Louis as Superintendent of the Mounted Recruiting Service and Lieutenant Colonel Davidson took command of the regiment. An able though erratic officer, Davidson was jealous of Grierson's popularity with the officers and men, and, unlike his tolerant predecessor, he was a strict disciplinarian. Almost immediately, he forced the resignations of Grierson's old staff but was overruled by the Adjutant General on the grounds that Grierson's assignment was a temporary one and the good of the service would not be promoted by a staff overhaul of a transitory nature. Davidson gained nothing from his maneuver but the enmity of many of his officers.[47]

Enlisted men as well were soon aware that there was a new regime. New regulations forbade the men to gamble in the barracks, and they were forced to resort to pushing up the ceiling boards and gambling in the attic. Anyone who walked on the grass while crossing the parade ground was subject to immediate arrest, but, ironically, the first culprit was Davidson's son. According to one officer at the post, Mrs. Davidson gave her husband "hell" when guards arrived with their offspring in tow.[48]

46 Post Returns, Camp Supply, January, 1873; Organizational Returns, Tenth Cavalry, January, 1873; Pratt, *op. cit.*, 49–53.
47 Colonel J. B. Fry, AAG, Military Division of the Missouri, to General Augur, December 31, 1872, SLR, Department of Texas, 1873, AGO, NA; Davidson to the AG, April, 1873, Tenth Cavalry, LS.
48 Henry O. Flipper, *Negro Frontiersman*, 3–4. Davidson was a graduate of West Point and served in the Mexican War. He had extensive service in the West prior to the Civil War, at which time he was a captain in the First Cavalry. By February, 1862, he was a brigadier general of volunteers and became Chief of Cavalry, Military Division of the West, in 1864. At the end of the War he was a brevet major general

Temporarily, Davidson could afford some time in improving deportment at Fort Gibson, for he assumed command of the regiment in a period of comparative quiet. In the fall of 1872, Mackenzie and his Fourth Cavalry had struck the Kwahadis of the Staked Plains a heavy blow and, for the first time, these Indians had come in to the reservation. Mackenzie captured more than a hundred of their women and children and held them as hostages to secure Comanche good behavior. During the early months of 1873, therefore, the Texas frontier enjoyed a period of almost unprecedented peace.[49]

The "honeymoon" did not convince Agent Tatum that the peace would last. When Satanta and Big Tree were released and the Comanche captives restored to their people, the war parties were sure to be on the prowl again. Utterly disillusioned, he resigned in March, 1873, and was succeeded by James Haworth, who was in thorough accord with the peace policy and had none of Tatum's confidence in the military. One of this first acts as agent was to dismiss the detachment of soldiers guarding the agency.[50]

Military authorities shared Tatum's gloom and Davidson was ordered to move his headquarters from Gibson back to Fort Sill and temporarily to concentrate most of the regiment there. Davidson was pleased with the move, not only from the standpoint of strategy, but in the interest of "regimental efficiency." He had not served with many of the companies and proposed to look them over with a rigorous eye. There is reason to doubt that so great a concentration at one post achieved the efficiency Davidson had in view, for a quarrel among the officers over quarters provided gossip for the garrison for months to come.

Lieutenant William Foulk accused Captain T. A. Baldwin, Captain William Kennedy, and Major Schofield of persecuting

with numerous citations for gallant and meritorious service. He accepted a lieutenant colonelcy in the Tenth Cavalry, in December, 1866, and remained in that rank until he left the regiment in 1879. He died of injuries when a horse fell on him in 1881. Heitman, *op. cit.*, I, 355–56.

49 Carter, *op. cit.*, 377–78; *Army and Navy Journal*, Vol. X (November 16, 1872), 213; *Annual Report for the Department of Texas, 1873*, RG 94, NA.

50 *Annual Report of the Commissioner of Indian Affairs for the Year 1873*, 219; Tatum, *op. cit.*, 132.

him and of making uncomplimentary remarks about his family. Baldwin went to Foulk's quarters to soothe over the dispute, whereupon Mrs. Foulk flailed at him with a horsewhip and the two Foulk boys, "holy terrors" on the post, threw books at him. Most of the officers supported Baldwin and a number signed a resolution not to associate with Lieutenant Foulk. Davidson solved the problem by managing a promotion for Foulk, giving him command of D Company, and transferring the new commander, his company, and his family to Fort Griffin, Texas. The arrival of the two Foulk children at the latter post probably signaled a new wave of on-post terrorism, for they seem to have dedicated their young lives to the cause of promoting adult misery.[51]

The shift of the Tenth to Fort Sill, and later the transfer of several companies to Texas, was dictated by the need not only to strengthen frontier defenses in that state and along Red River, but also to interlink the companies of the Ninth Cavalry with those of the Tenth in the interest of more "homogeneous" garrisons as regarded color. The dictates of frontier defense thus joined hands with the mandates of racial prejudice.

Shortly after Davidson's arrival at Fort Sill, Major John Hatch, on orders from General C. C. Augur, commanding the Department of Texas, arrived on a tour of inspection. He found morale and spirit high among the troopers, although many new recruits were in need of training. But Hatch was astounded when he viewed the horses and equipment. Many of the mounts were castoffs from the more favored Seventh Cavalry, others had been in the artillery service, and some were so old they had been ridden in the War of the Rebellion. F Company had only forty-eight serviceable horses and all but three were over fifteen years of age. The troopers had taken excellent care of these ancients, but Hatch was convinced a campaign might founder, if dependent on these hoary steeds.

Most of the equipment was very old, though again, well cared for. F Company had saddles more than three years old, while

71

Captain Nolan's A was using thirty saddles that had long since been condemned, and the men were worried about harming their horses' backs. The artillery was so old that Hatch did not believe a single piece would stand more than a shot. Ammunition too was in short supply, which was just   as well for the artillery, but Captain Kennedy's G Company had only twenty-five rounds of carbine cartridges per man and few of the other companies were much better off. Horses, new equipment, and adequate ammunition were essential at once.

Hatch's report was but an echo of complaints by officers and men of the Tenth for years. Even their regimental standard had been made by the men and was faded and worn, but higher headquarters had never seen fit to supply the regulation silk-embroidered standard. Yet the regiment had a good, if not spectacular, record, discipline was excellent, and desertions had steadily declined to the point that the rate was among the lowest of any unit in the army. Courts-martial for drunkenness, a curse in the frontier army, were lower than for comparable white units. Given the many handicaps, Grierson's "orphans" had done rather well—they would do even better.[52]

In April and May seven companies were transferred to Texas posts. E, I, and L marched to Fort Richardson, C and D to Fort Griffin, and A and F to Fort Concho. For these troopers and their officers, the days of "occupation" were over and they were free to fight hostile Indians wherever they might be found. But if they expected a warm welcome from the Texans, they were swiftly disillusioned. The citizens of a former slave state, in the throes of Radical Reconstruction, were hardly likely to welcome anyone in a blue uniform and much less so if that uniform encased a black frame.[53]

Jacksboro, adjacent to Fort Richardson, was typical of the wild little frontier towns that grew up in the vicinity of army posts.

[52] Major John Hatch to the AAG, Department of Texas, April 2, 1873, SLR, Department of Texas; Chauncey McKeever, AAG, Department of Texas, to Davidson, May 17, 1873, *ibid.;* Captain Nolan to Chief Ordnance Officer, Department of Texas, May 28, 1873, *ibid.;* Davidson to Chief Quartermaster, San Antonio, Texas, June 13, 1873, Tenth Cavalry, LS.

[53] Organizational Returns, Tenth Cavalry, April–May, 1873.

It boasted a population of about two hundred, many of them drifters, gamblers, prostitutes, and thieves. Twenty-seven saloons ministered to the needs of a thirsty population, among the more popular being the "Gem," "Emerald," "Island Home," and "Jimmy Nolan's Dance House." Mackenzie's Fourth Cavalry had its troubles while at Richardson. Troop B had burned down a house of prostitution because one of their buddies had been killed there, and threatened to burn the whole town. Fighting and friction between citizens and the buffalo soldiers was frequent, and as one observer put it "Jimmy Nolan's . . . was resonant with sound and frequently the scene of an inquest."[54]

But it was not always fighting and friction; in fact, more often it was co-operation. Detachments of six to ten troopers were on constant escort for contractors' trains and stages, and were kept busy assisting civilians in running down rustlers, and maintaining law and order. A representative item in reports to Departmental Headquarters ran as follows:

> April 22, 1873. Corporal John Wright, Company "L," 10th Cavalry, with two (2) privates, fully armed and equipped, mounted, furnished with rations . . . left Post for Weatherford, Texas for the purpose of assisting Deputy Sheriff in taking to that place one Reddy Draper, an escaped criminal, the Sheriff having reported himself unable to perform the duty without military protection.[55]

For the troopers at Griffin and Concho, life differed little from that of their comrades at Richardson. Griffin had its "Flats" and Concho its Saint Angela, and either could just as easily have been spelled "Trouble." As the post surgeon at Fort Griffin put it, when payday came he knew "killings would occur."[56]

Trouble of a different kind and in plenty was brewing in Indian Territory. The Kiowas remained in their camps during the spring and summer, angry at the failure of the government to return

54 Hatch to the AAG, Department of Texas, April 4, 1873, SLR, Department of Texas; H. McConnell, *Five Years a Cavalryman* (Jacksboro, Texas, J. N. Rogers and Co., 1889), 160–61.
55 Colonel H. Clay Wood to the AAG, Department of Texas, May 5, 1873, SLR, Department of Texas.
56 Medical History, Fort Griffin, Texas, Vol. 103.

Satanta and Big Tree in March as promised, but held in check by pledges that the chiefs would be released in the fall. Small Comanche war parties, however, slipped into Texas despite efforts of some of their chiefs to restrain them, and when the government returned the captive Comanche women and children in June, the lid was off. From Fort Griffin, Lieutenant Colonel George Buell, Eleventh Infantry, commanding the post, reported, "the Indians . . . have been quite troublesome this month and . . . I have run my cavalry about down."[57] Captain Charles Viele of C and Captain Foulk of D and their buffalo soldiers could certainly agree with the post commander, for in June alone they had scouted nearly a thousand miles.[58]

At Fort Sill Agent Haworth stoutly insisted that his Indians were not raiding, but Davidson distrusted the agent and had no faith in the peace policy. In July he sent out three troops, B, H, and M, the whole under Captain Carpenter, to scout along the Red and in the Pease River country of Texas. While encamped on the Pease, hostiles fired into the camp and Carpenter found many trails leading from the reservation into Texas. This was enough for Davidson. He prepared to take all five companies at Sill, march along the southern line of the reservation and "hit anything that came out."[59]

On August 19 Davidson left Fort Sill with G, H, K, and M. Captain John Vandeviele's B remained at the post because of the poor condition of his horses. The column marched west along the Red to Gilbert's Creek, where E and I under Captain Baldwin, operating out of Richardson, joined the command. The westward march continued without incident until August 28, when Groesbeck Creek was crossed. Here a fresh grave was found with a crude headstone on which was engraved "Hank Medley, killed by Indians August 25, 1873." A detachment soon located Medley's companions, members of a surveying party. The party chief, a Mr.

[57] Buell to the AAG, Department of Texas, June 15, 1873, SLR, Department of Texas.

[58] Organizational Returns, Tenth Cavalry, June, 1873. The troopers at Richardson and Concho were on almost constant scout during the entire summer.

[59] Davidson to the AAG, Department of Texas, July 25, 1873, SLR, Department of Texas; Organizational Returns, Tenth Cavalry, July, 1873.

Maddox, reported that Medley had gone hunting and was killed by eight Indians before his companions could come to his rescue.

Davidson pushed on until he reached the hundredth degree of longitude and then turned north across the Salt Fork, Elm Fork, and North Fork of the Red before turning eastward to Fort Sill which was reached on September 14. The scout had covered some four hundred miles, and Davidson had reached some firm conclusions:

> . . . that these Indians confine themselves to no particular belt of operations, but shoot straight from wherever their camps happen to be into Texas, that the reservation is a "city of refuge" for these marauders, that hunting for any enemy who has the eye of a hawk, and the stealth of a wolf over the arid plains and salty sandy beds of streams, I have traversed, is like hunting needles in hayricks, and that an effective method of meeting this condition of affairs, while the Government is feeding and clothing reservation Indians, is to dismount them, and make them answer a daily roll-call.[60]

To the north Agent Miles was watching the growing restlessness of his Southern Cheyennes with increasing apprehension. This proud and turbulent people had given no real trouble since 1871, but Kiowa and Comanche couriers were constantly in their camps urging the warpath and occasionally induced some of the young men to raid with them. And, despite all Miles' efforts, whisky dealers were demoralizing the Cheyennes. In one day in 1873 the agent saw twelve hundred Cheyennes dead-drunk. Late in March a party of warriors attacked a group of United States surveyors near Camp Supply, killing E. N. Deming, the crew chief, and three of his assistants. The bulk of the Cheyennes remained peaceful, however, but many of the young men were raiding in the summer and fall and Miles was unable to stop the steady flow of liquor to them.[61]

[60] Davidson to the AAG, Department of Texas, September 16, 1873, SLR, Department of Texas; Lieutenant S. L. Woodward to Grierson, August 18, 1873, Grierson Papers; *Army and Navy Journal,* Vol. XI (October 4, 1873), 117, and (December 20, 1873), 292.

[61] *Annual Report of the Commissioner of Indian Affairs for the Year 1873,* 220–23; T. H. Barrett, U.S. Surveyor, to Miles, March 8, 1873, Cheyenne-Arapaho Files, Indian Archives Division, Oklahoma State Historical Society, Oklahoma City, Oklahoma.

At Fort Sill Agent Haworth was also fearful. Satanta and Big Tree were still in a Texas prison and the Kiowas were on the point of becoming unmanageable. Release of the chiefs, promised by the Indian Bureau as no later than March 1, 1873, had struck a snag. Governor Davis of Texas had refused to turn them loose. Finally, however, yielding to pressure from President Grant, Davis agreed to return the chiefs to their people, but with some conditions attached. Satanta and Big Tree were brought to Fort Sill under military escort early in September and confined in the guard-house. Governor Davis arrived on October 3 with several members of his staff and was greeted by E. P. Smith, Commissioner of Indian Affairs, and the Superintendent for the Plains Tribes, Enoch Hoag.

Davis wished a formal council with the Kiowas to inform them of the terms under which he would release the chiefs, and arrangements were made at once for a meeting at the post on October 6. In view of the impatience of the Kiowas and a fear of violent reaction to any delay in the release of the chiefs, Davidson took every possible precaution to quell trouble if it arose. Every buffalo soldier at Fort Sill was on the alert, fully armed and equipped, with his mount saddled and ready for instant action.

At the appointed time, the Kiowas assembled and listened with growing anger to Davis' demands. In effect they would have to become farmers, permit spies in their midst, surrender their arms, and conduct themselves as white men before their chiefs were returned to them. Even then, their chiefs would be subject to immediate seizure and imprisonment if any raids occurred. The council broke up when Indian pleadings failed to move Governor Davis.

Commissioner Smith, Superintendent Hoag, and Agent Haworth all converged on the governor to persuade him to soften his terms, call for another council, and release the captive chiefs. Adamant at first, Davis finally yielded, and a second council was called for October 8. Meanwhile, in the Kiowa camps a decision had been reached to regain their chiefs by force if necessary. Tension ran high and the buffalo soldiers and their officers maintained a round-the-clock vigil.

When the council met, Davis surprised everyone by agreeing to let Satanta and Big Tree go and asked only that five Comanches, known to have been raiding in Texas recently, be surrendered to civil authorities for punishment. On this note the council ended, and the danger of a blood bath on the post was averted.[62]

On the same day Smith, Hoag, and Haworth met with the Kiowas and Comanches at the agency to remind them of the necessity for turning over the raiders that Governor Davis had demanded. After much angry discussion, a young Comanche chief, Cheevers, agreed to lead a few warriors and a detachment of troops in search of the raiders, and Smith gave him thirty days to get results.

Cheevers, with nineteen warriors, came to Fort Sill, and on October 12, with Captain P. L. Lee and fifty picked troopers, set out to find the offending Comanches. The expedition was a wild-goose chase, for Cheevers led Lee over a wide area of northwest Texas, but with no results. Not an Indian had been seen when the little column plodded wearily back to Fort Sill.[63]

At first the Indian Bureau took a firm line with the Indians. The five Comanches must be turned over, else rations and annuities would be withheld. The threat backfired. Many small bands immediately left the reservation to raid in Texas, but a few days later the Bureau changed its mind and issues were made. The vacillation had been a costly one when coupled with the long delay in releasing Satanta and Big Tree. Davidson and his regiment had nothing to do in influencing these floundering switches in policy,

---

62 *Annual Report of the Commissioner of Indian Affairs for the Year 1873*, 219; C. E. Campbell, "Down Among the Red Men," *Collections of the Kansas State Historical Society*, XVII (Topeka, 1929), 638–39; Thomas C. Battey, *The Life and Adventures of a Quaker Among the Indians* (Boston, Lee and Shepard, 1875), 199–200; Hoag to Haworth, August 12, 1873, Kiowa Files; Davis to Davidson, August 14, 1873, Kiowa Files.

63 Battey, *op. cit.*, 211–12; Campbell, *loc. cit.*, 639; Organizational Returns, Tenth Cavalry, October, 1873; Davidson to Lee, October 9, 1873, SLR, Department of Texas.

but the results were to keep the buffalo soldiers in the saddle almost constantly for many long months.[64]

Weary troopers at Fort Richardson and Fort Griffin could have told the Indian Bureau that far more than five Indians had been giving them sleepless days and nights for weeks. Colonel Buell, commanding at Griffin, reported that he was virtually helpless to stop widespread raiding. His only cavalry consisted of Captain Viele's C and Captain Foulk's D companies and every man in both companies was pursuing hostiles. There were no additional troopers to respond to the calls for aid that poured into his post. E, L, and I were operating out of Richardson without respite and badly in need of remounts.[65] Colonel W. H. Wood, commanding at Richardson, wrote department headquarters that these three companies were "about worn out" and that he could mount a total of only 116 men largely because of "unserviceable horses."[66]

Davidson at Fort Sill was certain large-scale field operations were imminent, yet his regiment was in dire need of more than three hundred horses, along with much new equipment. Seventy-seven mounts had been received in August, but of these only twenty-one were "suitable . . . for soldiers who are expected to pursue and overtake Indians." It was not until near the end of the year that the buffalo soldiers received some "fair" horses along with new .45-caliber Springfield carbines and Colt revolvers.[67]

Throughout the fall and early winter Indian raiders took scalps, cattle, and horses along the Texas frontier. Colonel Wood at Richardson complained that he had never known Indians to be so "numerous, desperate or persistent."[68] Nor were depredating redmen the only source of trouble. White thieves were also active, and often they raided Indian pony herds, insuring retaliatory action in

[64] Woodward to Grierson, December 5, 1873, Grierson Papers; Battey, *op. cit.*, 229.

[65] Buell to the AAG, Department of Texas, August 8, 1873, SLR, Department of Texas.

[66] Wood to the AAG, Department of Texas, September 3, 1873, *ibid.*

[67] Major Schofield to Davidson, August 17, 1873, *ibid.*; E. D. Townsend, AG, to General Sherman, December 24, 1873, *ibid.*; Davidson to Schofield, October 9, 1873, Tenth Cavalry, LS.

[68] Wood to the AAG, Department of Texas, October 10, 1873, SLR, Department of Texas.

Texas. It was a severe challenge to a badly scattered regiment, riding the poorest horseflesh in the army, and many raiders, both Indian and white, often escaped, but not always. Between September and December, detachments of the Tenth recovered nearly twelve hundred head of stolen animals, killed four white horse-thieves and captured seventeen others, had a dozen brushes with Indian war parties, and inflicted an undetermined number of casualties.[69]

During the winter of 1873–74, two events occurred which had far-reaching consequences, contributing to a major Indian war and ending completely the role of the Tenth as an "army of occupation." On December 9, Lieutenant C. L. Hudson, Fourth Cavalry, and a detachment of forty-one men intercepted a party of Indian raiders on the West Fork of the Nueces River. In the fight that followed, nine Indians were killed. The war party consisted of an elite group of young Kiowa and Comanche warriors from the reservation, and among the dead were Tau-ankia, son of Lone Wolf, and Gui-tain, son of Lone Wolf's brother, Red Otter.[70]

When news of this fight reached the Kiowa camps in January, the whole tribe went into mourning, and Lieutenant Woodward wrote Grierson from Fort Sill that Lone Wolf burned nearly everything he had, killed many of his ponies, and "slashed himself all up."[71]

Disaster also struck the Comanches. Winter raiding had been so extensive that Davidson stationed most of his troopers in stockaded camps on a line between Sill and Griffin. In this way he could move more swiftly to hit raiding parties or, failing to intercept them, could relay information far more quickly to Buell at

[69] Wood to the AAG, Department of Texas, November 1, 1873, *ibid.;* Organizational Returns, Tenth Cavalry, October–December, 1873; Wood to the AAG, Department of Texas, November 30, 1873, SLR, Department of Texas; Lieutenant T. C. Lebo to Wood, October 21, 1873, SLR, Department of Texas; *Record of Engagements,* 37.

[70] Lieutenant Hudson to the PA, Fort Clark, Texas, December 15, 1873, Office of Indian Affairs, LR, Kiowa, *Army and Navy Journal,* Vol. XI (January 3, 1874), 324; *Weekly Democratic Statesman,* Austin, Texas, December 25, 1873; Nye, *op. cit.,* 182–83.

[71] Woodward to Grierson, February 24, 1874, Grierson Papers.

Griffin regarding the probable direction in which the Indians were heading. And the new system soon brought dramatic results.

Late in January Buell received information that a party of Comanches had stolen some stock and were headed in the direction of the Double Mountains, about one hundred miles west of his post. With Captain P. L. Lee, Lieutenant R. H. Pratt, and fifty-five buffalo soldiers of D and G companies, and guided by eighteen Tonkawa Indian scouts, Buell left Griffin in search of the raiders. On February 5 he found his quarry in the valley of the Double Mountain Fork of the Brazos and in a running fight killed eleven warriors and recovered sixty-five animals.[72]

The twin blows of Hudson and Buell brought a burning desire for revenge to the camps of the Kiowas and Comanches. Many of the warriors could think of nothing but war, and their couriers found ready ears in the lodges of the restless Southern Cheyennes. The spring winds of 1874 brought with them all the elements of a major war.

[72] Davidson to the AAG, Department of Texas, March 20, 1874, SLR, Department of Texas; Post Returns, Fort Griffin, February, 1874; Organizational Returns, Tenth Cavalry, February, 1874; Medical History, Fort Griffin, Vol. 103.

Lieutenant Richard H. Pratt, Tenth Cavalry. (Courtesy National Archives)

Above: *Tenth Cavalry troops building officers' quarters at Fort Sill in 1870. Probably a Soule photograph.* (Courtesy U.S. Army Artillery and Missile Center Museum, Fort Sill)

Below: *Encampment of Tenth Cavalry battalion.* (Courtesy National Archives)

Shown in front of Evans and Fisher trading store, Fort Sill, are Tenth Cavalry soldiers, Indians, civilians, laden horses, and lounging Indian dogs. In the center, with a peace treaty medal on his chest, is Tosh-a-way, chief of the Penateka Comanches. Probably a Soule photograph. (Courtesy U.S. Army Artillery and Missile Center Museum, Fort Sill)

Captain Louis H. Carpenter, Tenth Cavalry. (Courtesy National Archives)

Captain Theodore A. Baldwin, Tenth Cavalry. (Courtesy National Archives)

Lieutenant Colonel Wesley Merritt, Ninth Cavalry. (Courtesy National Archives)

IV

THE NINTH IN TEXAS

WHILE THE BUFFALO SOLDIERS of the Tenth Cavalry labored and fought to assist in paving the way for peaceful settlement of the Central Plains, Hatch and the Ninth were no less involved in promoting the advance of civilization in West Texas and along the meandering Río Grande. For eight long years they sweated, bled, and died to make life and property secure on one of the most turbulent and strife-ridden frontiers in the history of American westward advance.

The movement west of the Ninth to Forts Davis and Stockton in the summer of 1867 was accompanied by initial orders to protect the mail and stage route between San Antonio and El Paso, search out and defeat marauding Indians infesting the region, and maintain law and order on the troubled Río Grande. It was no mean assignment for a single regiment, particularly one whose early history provided scant encouragement that it would ever develop into an efficient and reliable military unit.

Mere patrolling of the vast region in their charge was a well-nigh impossible task. It was characterized by hundreds of miles of brush jungle along the Río Grande, by vast areas of plain, desert, and mountain where water was often scarce or entirely absent, where terrain was incredibly rough and broken, where temperatures ranged from above one hundred degrees in summer to well below freezing in winter, and where violent and sudden changes were the norm. But the Ninth faced more formidable challenges than those posed by weather and terrain.

This remote and sparsely settled portion of West Texas had long been a favored haunt for a number of predatory Indian tribes.

For many years the Mescalero Apaches had swept down from nests in the Guadalupe Mountains to prey upon cattle herds, stages, wagon trains, and unwary travelers. Literally swarms of Kiowa and Comanche warriors came down from the north, spreading devastation and terror from the Red River to the Río Grande and for hundreds of miles into Mexico. It was no accident that Fort Stockton was located at Comanche Springs, astride the "Great Comanche War Trail," the well-trod highway for warrior elite, running from the shallow waters of the Arkansas to the haciendas of Durango.[1]

Indian raiding was not one-way traffic. Vengeful Mexican Kickapoos, refugees from the United States, combined their considerable talents for rapine and murder with those of the Lipans to carry on unrelenting warfare north of the Río Grande. It is probable that no other tribes equaled, much less surpassed, these Indians "for calculated viciousness, vindictiveness and destruction of life and property" when raiding against their Texan enemies.[2] Alone they could have well absorbed the energies of a full regiment of cavalry.

Marauding Indians, Mexican or American, were only one problem, however. The Republic of Mexico, born of revolution and torn by half a century of sporadic civil war, spawned almost countless bandits and revolutionaries—often the difference between the two was merely a matter of semantics—and many of these by reason of birth or convenience made their homes on the North Mexican frontier. Here the weak and languid arm of the federal government posed no real threat to their activities. They had many sympathizers among the Mexican population on the American side of the river, which they crossed and recrossed, killing, thieving, or organizing as need and whim dictated.[3]

[1] Fort Stockton was established on March 23, 1859, to protect the San Antonio–El Paso stage route. Named for Commodore Robert Stockton, it was abandoned by federal forces in April, 1861, and occupied by Confederate troops for a brief time and burned by them. Hatch and four companies of the Ninth reoccupied the post on July 7, 1867, and began the work of reconstruction. It was finally abandoned on June 30, 1886. Frazer, *op. cit.*, 162; Organizational Returns, Ninth Cavalry, July, 1867.

[2] A. M. Gibson, *The Kickapoos*, 210.

[3] Henry Bamford Parkes, *A History of Mexico* (Boston, Houghton Mifflin Co.,

The activities of these groups brought affairs on the Río Grande to a state of near anarchy for more than twenty years, but the woes of the Texas frontier, and thereby the problems of the Ninth, did not end here. White riffraff abounded, ever ready with gun, knife, rope, and branding iron to ply any trade which afforded an easy and illegal dollar. And lurking in the background was the shadowy and elusive *comanchero* with his trade goods, whisky, guns, and ammunition to reward those who stole cattle and horses for him. There was a steady and lucrative market for these animals in New Mexico Territory and A. B. Norton, Superintendent of Indian Affairs for New Mexico, in his annual report for 1867 related that the Territory was "filled with Texas cattle."[4]

Such challenges were enough to occupy fully every soldier in Texas, but of three regiments of cavalry in the state only one, the Ninth, was assigned exclusively to the frontier and not more than half of four regiments of infantry were available for such service. For too long, ranking officers such as Sherman and Sheridan refused to believe conditions were as bad as painted by thousands of frontier petitioners and, besides, Texas was undergoing the throes of Reconstruction and many troops were needed in the interior of the state.[5]

In the face of near-overwhelming responsibilities, the untried Ninth was forced to contend with a problem that compounded the difficulties of their tasks. Citizens on the frontier might rage and storm, demand and plead for greater protection, but they gave scant comfort and support when that protection arrived in the form of a Negro soldier. Raiding Indians, Mexican bandits and revolutionaries, pistol-happy border scum, and stealthy *comancheros* might wipe out cattle herds and hundreds of lives, but they did not suffice to wipe out the poison of racial prejudice.

1928), 242–50; Brevet Major General J. J. Reynolds to the AG, U.S. Army, October 21, 1869, *Annual Report for the Department of Texas, 1869.*

[4] *Annual Report of the Commissioner of Indian Affairs for the Year 1867,* 194–95.

[5] *Annual Report of the Secretary of War for the Year 1866,* 15. Sheridan's view was that there certainly had been depredations on the frontier, "but they are not very alarming." The other cavalry regiments assigned to Texas were the Fourth and Sixth.

There was too much to be done, however, for Hatch and his troopers to waste time complaining. Forts Stockton and Davis required complete rebuilding, and details were put to work at once cutting logs, making adobe bricks, constructing sinks, and erecting quarters and corrals. There were few comforts to compensate for the heavy work. The food was poor in quality and lacking in variety. The meals seldom deviated from coffee, bread, beans, and beef, with molasses, corn bread, and sweet potatoes added to spice up the evening meal. Rest for weary bodies was found on bedsacks filled with straw, tossed across slats on bunk irons.[6]

The work progressed slowly, for more than half the troopers were constantly in the field and so active were Indian raiders that from the first heavy herd guards and lookouts on high ground were necessary to prevent these matchless thieves from running off the horse herds. Scouting detachments were in the saddle from dawn to dusk probing along the Pecos, Concho, and Devils rivers, while others patrolled the San Antonio–El Paso road, escorted trains and stages, and guarded the mail stations to the east and west.[7]

Green troopers and officers unfamiliar with the country had little success in intercepting marauding Indians. Further, for a time at least, small parties seemed to prefer a quick hit-and-run for cattle and horses or the killing of a lonely shepherd. News of such small-scale activity was slow to reach the isolated posts and pursuit was all but useless. As summer faded into fall, however, the Indians grew bolder. Late in October a revenge-bent party of Kickapoos drew first blood from the buffalo soldiers. They ambushed and killed Corporal Emanuel Wright and Private E. T.

[6] Hutcheson, *loc. cit.*, 282; Post Returns, Fort Stockton, July–August, 1867; Organizational Returns, Ninth Cavalry, August–September, 1867. Fort Davis, located near Limpia Creek, Presidio County, was established in October, 1854, to protect the San Antonio–El Paso road. Named for Jefferson Davis, then secretary of war, the post was evacuated by federal troops in April, 1861. Indians and Mexicans used the buildings from time to time but also destroyed them. Merritt and six companies of the Ninth reoccupied the fort in July, 1867, and rebuilt it completely. Though isolated, the general climate and healthfulness made it a desirable post at which to serve. Frazer, *op. cit.*, 148; Joseph H. and James R. Toulouse, *Pioneer Posts of Texas*, 151–54.

[7] Organizational Returns, Ninth Cavalry, August–September, 1867. Companies A, B, E, and K were at Stockton, C, D, F, G, H, and I were at Davis, while L and M remained at Brownsville.

Jones of D Company as they escorted the mail from Camp Hudson to Fort Stockton. On December 5 more than one hundred Mescaleros attacked the stage, eastbound from El Paso, killed Private Nathan Johnson, a member of the escort, and in a running fight wounded four horses. The Apaches did not give up the chase until the stage came within sight of Eagle Springs Station where they were driven off by Captain Henry Carroll and Company F who were encamped nearby.[8]

Near the end of the year a force of Kickapoos, Lipans, Mexicans, and some white renegades, estimated at nine hundred strong, attacked the bivouac of Captain William Frohock and K Company at old Fort Lancaster, some seventy-five miles as the crow flies east of Fort Stockton. It afforded the buffalo soldiers their first opportunity to face their foes "toe to toe" and they responded with grim enthusiasm. A vicious three-hour fight left K Company in possession of the field after killing twenty of their attackers and wounding a large number. Three herd guards, Privates Andrew Trimble, William Sharpe, and Eli Boyer, who had been taken by surprise, roped, and dragged away, were missing and presumed dead.[9]

The fight at Fort Lancaster proved the virtues of hard work, discipline, and a sense of purpose, and should have removed any doubts concerning the combat effectiveness of the Ninth's black troopers. Certainly there were none in the minds of those who fought them on that cool, clear, December day nor in the minds of Hatch and his officers, but others still remained to be convinced—in other regiments and in the higher echelons of command.

While raiding Indians showed a decided reluctance after Fort

---

[8] *Ibid.,* October, 1867; General George Thomas, AG, to the Secretary of War, February 20, 1868, SLR, AGO.

[9] Organizational Returns, Ninth Cavalry, December, 1867; Post Returns, Fort Stockton, December, 1867; San Antonio *Weekly Express,* January 9, 1868; J. Lee Humfreville, *Twenty Years Among Our Hostile Indians* (New York, Hunter and Co., Publishers, 1889), 178. The remains of Trimble, Sharpe, and Boyer were found three months later near the scene of the fight. Fort Lancaster was established in August, 1855, on Live Oak Creek near its junction with the Pecos. Named for Captain Stephen Lancaster, First Infantry, it was abandoned in 1861 and was never reactivated, although troops often camped there after the Civil War. Frazer, *op. cit.,* 183.

Lancaster to indulge in pitched battles with troopers who showed such relish for fighting at close-quarters, there was no letup in their hit, steal, and run tactics. To counter these thrusts more effectively, Hatch moved L and M companies upriver from Brownsville to Forts Duncan and Clark. Fort Quitman, on the river northwest of Fort Davis, was reactivated and garrisoned by a strong detachment under aggressive Major Albert P. Morrow. With all companies of the regiment in position to co-ordinate their operations, Hatch planned a vigorous offense when spring arrived, but in February, 1868, he was appointed assistant commissioner of the Freedman's Bureau for Louisiana and placed on detached service. Lieutenant Colonel Merritt replaced Hatch as commander of the Ninth.[10]

Merritt was eager to carry out the plans of his predecessor, but the spring and summer of 1868 found the region literally swarming with small war parties that stretched the strength and endurance of his command to the limit. A year of campaigning had changed the face of the Ninth. It was a tough, hard-hitting unit, but intercepting the flitting red phantoms was almost as difficult as getting a firm grasp on a group of ghosts and, when hard pressed, the raiders almost invariably turned and fled across the Río Grande into Mexico and thumbed their noses at the frustrated troopers who were forced to pull up at the water's edge.

Kickapoo war parties threatened to devastate whole counties. In one swoop into Atascosa County they killed three men and drove off four hundred head of horses. Within three months they had killed five more citizens and stolen another three hundred head of animals in the same county. A ranchers' posse caught up with them only to be badly whipped and routed. Duval, Schlei-

---

10 Organizational Returns, Ninth Cavalry, January–April, 1868; Hatch to the AG, October 31, 1868, SLR, AGO. Morrow rose through the ranks during the Civil War from a sergeant in the Seventeenth Pennsylvania Infantry to lieutenant colonel, Sixth Pennsylvania Cavalry, with citations for conspicuous gallantry in action. In July, 1866, he accepted appointment as captain in the Seventh Cavalry but transferred to the Ninth with the rank of major in March, 1867. He served with the regiment for the next fifteen years and was one of its ablest officers. He retired in 1892 as colonel of the Third Cavalry. Heitman, *op. cit.*, I, 729.

cher, and Uvalde counties were equally hard hit. Mescalero and Comanche raids were almost as devastating.[11]

It was too much for one regiment. The Ninth was spread too thin, their enemies were far too numerous, the region simply too vast, and an international boundary too convenient for effective defense. Not all of the raiders escaped unscathed, however. On September 26 two hundred Apaches struck a train near Fort Stockton, ran off all the stock, and wasted no time in heading for sanctuary across the Río Grande. With orders from Merritt to spare neither men nor horses, Lieutenant Patrick Cusack, sixty-one men of A Company, and ten civilian volunteers took up the pursuit.

The trail was found without difficulty and followed into the wild and broken country southeast of Stockton. The search ended in the rugged Santiago Mountains where Cusack overhauled his quarry and, though badly outnumbered, attacked at once. In a running fight of five miles the buffalo soldiers soundly whipped the Apaches, killing twenty-five, wounding as many more, and recovering two hundred animals and two captive Mexican children. Cusack's only casualties were two men wounded.[12]

The raids eased somewhat as winter came on but were renewed early in 1869 and continued throughout the year. Between January and April, savage Kickapoo raids in Bexar, Frio, Uvalde, Zavala, Medina, and Atascosa counties cost the lives of sixteen persons, the loss of hundreds of horses, and thousands of dollars in other property. With the advent of summer, Kiowa and Comanche warriors raced down from their reservation in Indian Territory leaving havoc in their wake. Burnett, Comanche, Johnson, Parker, and Tarrant counties were especially hard hit.[13]

---

11 Wilbarger, *op. cit.*, 633; Gibson, *op. cit.*, 212–13; *H.R. Exec. Doc. No. 13*, 42 Cong., 3 sess., Vol. 5, 1–3.

12 Organizational Returns, Ninth Cavalry, September, 1868; *Army and Navy Journal*, Vol. VI, No. 8 (October 10, 1868), 114.

13 "Report of Felonies Committed by Indians in the Fifth Military District," *Annual Report for the Department of Texas, 1869; Annual Report of the Secretary of War for the Year 1869*, 144–45. Three hundred and eighty-four murders were committed in Texas in this single year, although not all of these resulted from Indian attacks.

The men of the Ninth literally rode their mounts into the ground over thousands of dusty miles in blistering heat, pursuing war parties that seemed everywhere and yet nowhere, and the usual result was a bleak sentence or two such as appeared in the *Post Returns* for Fort Concho in July, 1869:

> Indians ran off mail mules and government horses from mail station at head of the Concho July 29. Pursuit by Captain Gamble, Company "B" Ninth Cavalry with detachment failed to overtake the Indians.[14]

General Joseph J. Reynolds, commanding the Fifth Military District, reported that the troops were on continuous scout and "all that is possible for their number to do has been done to protect the people and property of the frontier counties."[15] This was cold comfort to the overworked buffalo soldiers who longed to come to grips with their elusive red antagonists, and in September their dogged persistence finally brought concrete results.

Emboldened by their successes, a strong war party of Kiowas and Comanches committed depredations in the vicinity of Fort McKavett on the San Saba River and headed north for the reservation. Captain Carroll and Captain Edward Heyl, with ninety-five men of B, E, F, and M companies, took up the pursuit. The trail was lost, supplies ran low, and the command was forced to halt at Fort Concho to refit. But Henry Carroll could find Indians as well as any officer on the frontier, and he had no intention of giving up the search. Once supplied, he returned to the pursuit with renewed determination.

Pushing north from Concho, Carroll regained the trail which led to the headwaters of the Salt Fork of the Brazos and a camp of nearly two hundred lodges. The eager troopers barely had time to clench their teeth on a generous chunk of chewing tobacco before Carroll gave the order to charge. The blare of bugles and the thunder of hoofs were enough for the Indians who sought safety

14 Post Returns, Fort Concho, Texas, July, 1869.
15 *Annual Report of the Secretary of War for the Year 1870*, 41. Reynolds pointed out in his report that the troops were also busy with construction work—lumbering, quarrying stone, making adobes, burning brick and lime, and driving wagons.

in wild flight. For eight miles shouting, cursing, and exultant buffalo soldiers chased the panic-stricken Comanches and pulled up
only when their mounts had given out. They had struck their foe
a heavy blow. More than a score of Indians had been killed or
wounded, and their entire camp and all its equipage had been
captured and destroyed. It was a weary but elated column that
reached Fort McKavett forty-two days and six hundred miles
after departure from that post.[16]

Hatch, meanwhile, had returned from detached service and
established his headquarters at Fort Davis. Distressed over lack
of success in curbing Indian raids, but encouraged by Carroll's
strike, he determined on an all-out campaign to drive the Kiowas,
Comanches, and Mescaleros from the region under his care. Detachments from six companies of the Ninth were concentrated at
Fort Concho under Captain John Bacon, G Company. On October
10, Bacon led his command out of Concho and marched to the
site of old Fort Phantom Hill on the Brazos where a detachment
of the Fourth Cavalry and twenty Tonkawa Indian scouts joined
him. Then, with 198 men at his back, he moved upriver near the
headwaters and went into camp.

Bacon intended sending out scouting parties on the morning
of October 28, but five hundred Kiowa and Comanche warriors
spared him the trouble by attacking at sunrise from all sides. For
the second time in two years, hostile Indians were bold enough
to assault a camp of buffalo soldiers, and for the second time they
found themselves in a hornets' nest. In a bitter and at times an

16 Post Returns, Fort McKavett, September–October, 1869; Organizational Returns, Ninth Cavalry, September–October, 1869; *Army and Navy Journal*, Vol. VII,
No. 15 (November 27, 1869), 224. Carroll was a New Yorker who enlisted in the
army in 1859 and rose through the ranks. Commissioned a second lieutenant in the
Third Cavalry in May, 1864, he was promoted to first lieutenant in April, 1866. He
joined the Ninth Cavalry as a captain in January, 1867, and remained with the regiment for eighteen years. He retired from the service as a colonel, Seventh Cavalry,
in May, 1899, after forty years in the regular army. Heitman, *op. cit.*, I, 286. Fort
McKavett, located near the source of the San Saba River, was the third Texas post
to be completely rebuilt by the men of the Ninth. Established in 1852 and named for
Captain Henry McKavett, Eighth Infantry, killed during the Mexican War, it was
abandoned in March, 1859. It was occupied by Confederates during the Civil War,
but was not reoccupied by federal troops until March, 1869, to curb Indian raids. Companies F and M, Ninth Cavalry, began the work of reconstruction. Frazer, *op. cit.*,
154–55; Organizational Returns, Ninth Cavalry, March, 1869.

eyeball to eyeball struggle, the Indians were whipped and forced to flee. But neither Bacon nor his troopers were satisfied and they set out to find the Indian encampment. Their efforts were rewarded near midafternoon on October 29, and a fierce charge scattered the demoralized redmen in all directions. Bacon placed their loss at forty killed and seven women and fifty-one horses captured. His own casualties were eight wounded, none fatally.[17]

December and January brought bitter cold weather, but Hatch pressed his campaign relentlessly. On January 20, 1870, Captain Francis Dodge of D Company with two hundred men from A, C, D, H, I, and K companies marched northwest from Fort Davis to carry the war into Mescalero country. While slogging through rain and sleet, the column came upon a Mescalero rancheria "in the most inaccessible region of the Guadalupe Mountains." As the troopers approached, the Apaches fled and took refuge on a nearby peak. Dodge had the men dismount and the ascent began at once.

Precarious footing and heavy Indian gunfire made the climb a slow and cautious one, but the troopers continued to press on and gained the summit just as night fell. The Apaches fled and the exhausted buffalo soldiers slept on the peak. Next morning ten Apache dead were counted and others were believed to have been carried away during the night. Dodge rounded up twenty-five ponies, destroyed a large number of robes, bows and arrows, and other supplies, and after a search in the immediate vicinity, retraced his steps to Davis.[18]

17 Hatch to the AAG, Department of Texas, November 7, 1869, SLR Relating to the Ninth and Tenth Cavalry, AGO; Post Returns, Fort Concho, November, 1869; Post Returns, Fort McKavett, November 1869; *Army and Navy Journal*, Vol. VII, No. 20 (December 4, 1869). Fort Concho was a home for the buffalo soldiers of both Hatch and Grierson. Established late in 1867, it was located at the junction of the North and South Concho rivers on the site of present San Angelo. Because of its strategic location, it became one of the most important of the Texas frontier posts. Frazer, *op. cit.*, 147. See also J. Evetts Haley, *Fort Concho and the Texas Frontier*.

18 Hatch to Brevet Colonel H. Clay Wood, AAG, Department of Texas, February 2, 1870, SLR, AGO. Dodge, a native of Massachusetts, rose through the ranks and was a captain in the Second Cavalry when the Civil War ended. He accepted appointment as a first lieutenant in the Ninth Cavalry in July, 1866, and was promoted to captain in July, 1867, and to major in January, 1880, at which time he transferred to the Department of the Paymaster General. On March 22, 1898, nearly twenty years

It was a bad winter for the Apaches, for as Dodge fell upon them in the Guadalupes, the enterprising Bacon struck another Mescalero camp some seventy-five miles southwest of Fort McKavett. He captured the camp and chased the occupants for fifteen miles, before turning back to destroy the lodges, all camp equipment, and six hundred beautifully dressed hides. In addition his troopers drove eighty horses and mules back to McKavett.[19]

Hatch was not content to rest on his laurels. Once the weather moderated, he proposed to launch a campaign in the Guadalupe Mountains designed to clean out the Mescalero nests and stop raids on the Texas frontier from that quarter. This assignment he gave to Major Morrow, stationed at Fort Quitman. Morrow left that post on April 3 with ninety-one men of H and I companies and, in summerlike heat and dust, marched upriver to El Paso where Mexican guides were employed. Here the command turned almost due east and set out for Pine Spring in the Guadalupes, the site agreed upon for a supply camp and a rendezvous with reinforcements from Forts Stockton and Davis.

If Morrow hoped to catch the Mescaleros off guard, he was doomed to disappointment. On April 9, while encamped in the Cornudas Mountains, the grass was fired accidentally by Private John Johnson of I Company. Racing flames spawned huge columns of smoke "without doubt alarming all the Indians in the country."[20] Alarmed the Apaches were, for as the column moved on to Pine Spring, it was accompanied by an "escort" of smoke signals on all sides.

The rendezvous was reached on April 11 and work began at once to construct a base camp. Some of the wagons had not come up, however, and Corporal Ross of I was ordered to take the back trail and urge the laggards on. And he made the first strike of the campaign. Scarcely a mile from Pine Spring three Mescaleros tried to interrupt his errand. Ross immediately dropped his bridle,

after the fight, he was awarded the Congressional Medal of Honor for his gallantry in the Milk River Battle against the Utes in September, 1879. Heitman, *op. cit.*, I, 376.

19 Post Returns, Fort McKavett, January, 1870; *Army and Navy Journal*, Vol. VII, No. 27 (February 19, 1870), 422.

20 Morrow to the AAAG, SubDistrict of the Presidio, June 1, 1870, SLR, AGO.

spurred his mount to a full run, and drove at his foes with carbine flaming. He killed one warrior and sent the remaining two scurrying for safety. Ross then located the tardy wagons and brought them into camp.

On April 12, Lieutenants Gustavus Valois and M. B. Hughes reached Pine Spring with sixty men, and Morrow was under way at dawn next morning marching northeast to the scene of Dodge's fight in January and then plunged into the heart of the Guadalupe Range. Cañon after cañon was scoured and in nearly all of them abandoned rancherias were found. Morrow reported:

> The guides knew nothing of the country we were now in but . . . again took up the trail and after marching four or five hours found myself back in the camp of the night before. In this march we passed about two hundred recently occupied lodges. . . . Our guides, although the best in the country were completely lost and baffled by the multiplicity of trails running in every direction crossing and retracing. They finally succeeded in finding a trail leading down what appeared an impassable ravine, the horses and pack mules had to be lifted down over the rocks. One or two fell into crevices and could not be extricated. Toward evening we came across a rancheria of 75 lodges which the Indians abandoned at our approach leaving a large amount of mezcal bread, about a hundred gallons of an intoxicating beverage brewed from the maguey and other commissary supplies, a great number of hides, robes, dressed and green skins, baskets, ojos, and all sorts of utensils and furniture pertaining to an Indian village.[21]

This camp was in sight of the Sacramento Mountains of New Mexico and Morrow bivouacked at Cuervo Springs on the evening of April 21. The men were in woeful condition. Their boots had fallen to pieces and most were barefoot, their clothing was in tatters, and half the command was dismounted, so great had been the loss of horses. For two days the troopers mended their rags, made moccasins for bruised and bloody feet, and gained as much energy as they could from hardtack and bacon.[22] Morrow moved

21 *Ibid.*
22 *Ibid.*; Journal of the March of Indian Expedition as Kept by Brevet Colonel George A. Purington, Captain, 9th Cavalry, from April 3, 1870 to May 26 '70 Inclusive, *ibid.*

out again on April 23, marched to the Peñasco River, and then turned eastward to his supply camp at Pine Spring.

After a brief rest, Morrow struck directly southwestward, skirted the eastern base of appropriately named Sierra Diablo, and headed for Rattlesnake Spring. Here the advance surprised a small party of Mescaleros who fled without offering any resistance and left the troopers in possession of thirty lodges and twenty-two horses. When extensive scouting turned up nothing more of significance, Morrow moved on in to Fort Quitman after fifty-three days in the field. Few Indians had been killed, but scores of lodges had been destroyed, along with great quantities of stores. No Mescalero would ever again feel entirely secure in the old haunts in the Guadalupes, their raids on the Texas frontier diminished, and the Ninth could claim a victory.

In his official report Morrow had nothing but praise for the performance of his troops. They had

> . . . marched about 1,000 miles, over two hundred of which was through country never explored by troops, drove the Indians from every rancheria . . . destroyed immense amounts of . . . food, robes, skins, utensils and materiel and captured forty horses and mules. I cannot speak too highly of the conduct of the officers and men under my command, always cheerful and ready, braving the severest hardships with short rations and no water without a murmur. The negro troops are peculiarly adapted to hunting Indians knowing no fear and capable of great endurance.[23]

Morrow's appraisal of the buffalo soldiers received no little reinforcement from the heroics of tiny Sergeant Emanuel Stance of Captain Carroll's F Company, stationed at Fort McKavett. On the morning of May 20, Stance and ten troopers left the post for a scout toward Kickapoo Spring some twenty miles to the north. Scarcely half the distance had been covered when a party of Indians was seen driving a herd of horses. Stance formed his men in line and charged at a dead run with Spencers blazing, routed the astonished Indians, and captured nine horses. He then proceeded on to Kickapoo Spring and encamped for the night.

[23] Morrow to the AAAG, SubDistrict of the Presidio, June 1, 1870, *ibid.*

Tenth Cavalry buffalo soldier.
Courtesy National Archives

The next morning Stance decided to return to his post with the captured animals but had traveled only a short distance when a party of warriors was spied preparing to attack a small train. Once more Stance charged, forced the Indians to flee, and captured five more horses. But the redmen were not quite ready to call it a day. They soon reappeared at Stance's rear and opened fire at long range, but the diminutive sergeant would have none of this. He wheeled about and "turned my little command loose on them . . . and after a few volleys they left me to continue my march in peace."[24] This was Stance's fifth successful encounter with Indians in two years and Carroll was unstinting in his praise. The result was a Congressional Medal of Honor for the redoubtable Sergeant Stance.[25]

While considerable success had been achieved against the Mescaleros, the Kiowas, Comanches, Kickapoos, and Lipans remained a sore problem. At Fort Davis, a fuming Hatch believed his regiment could make short work of the latter two tribes if he could only pursue their raiding parties to their villages in Mexico. In October he submitted a plan to General Reynolds for a winter campaign with this objective in view. The Ninth would take the field with every effective trooper that could be mustered, advance toward the Río Grande on a broad front driving every Indian they could flush before them, and, crossing the river, co-operate with Mexican troops in gaining an overwhelming and decisive victory.

Hatch's proposal was sound and won the swift approval of his superiors but just as swiftly struck a diplomatic snag. Mexican officials professed their willingness to co-operate but notified Thomas Nelson, United States minister to Mexico, that foreign troops could operate on Mexican soil only with the express consent of the Mexican Congress and that body would not convene until April, 1871. This situation ruined Hatch's plans for a winter campaign in 1870, but any future co-operation such as he envisioned was shunted aside as well when a suspicious and lethargic

[24] Sergeant Emanuel Stance, F Company, 9th Cavalry, to the PA, Fort McKavett, Texas, May 26, 1870, *ibid.*

[25] Stance to the AG, Washington, D.C., July 24, 1870, *ibid.* This was Stance's letter of appreciation for his reward.

Mexican Congress on April 29, 1871, refused entry of American troops to Mexican soil even if in "hot" pursuit of raiders.[26]

A high price had already been paid for lack of co-operation along the river frontier, and as Hatch was pleading for combined action a grisly affair just south of the border should have lent great force to his proposal. An American, Charles Keerl, his wife, and a party of seven were attacked by Apaches, and all but one were killed and the bodies mutilated. Keerl's head and that of his wife were severed and her head was placed upon his shoulders. Belated efforts by Mexican forces under Colonel Joaquin Terrazas, commanding in Chihuahua, failed to run down and punish the guilty tribesmen. It was only one of many such affairs that had occurred in the past and lay in the future.[27]

Hatch, meanwhile, was relieved of any immediate concern for affairs in West Texas. In December, 1870, he was ordered to St. Louis as Superintendent of the Mounted Recruiting Service, and command of his regiment once more fell to Lieutenant Colonel Merritt. It was many months before Hatch again returned to the Texas frontier.[28]

While a lack of decisive victories over elusive Indian foemen was frustrating to Hatch, Merritt, and their men, one salient fact did not escape them. They had scouted, pursued, and mapped in areas never before penetrated by troops, and the information thus gained would certainly shorten the time required to pacify the warring redmen. And, in the summer of 1871, a routine affair sent troopers of the Ninth into one of the last portions of West Texas still regarded as "safe" by Indian hostiles.

On the evening of June 16, bold Indian raiders ran off forty-three animals from the herd of Company A, Twenty-fourth Infantry, bivouacked at Barella Springs between Forts Davis and Stockton. Lieutenant Colonel William R. Shafter, Twenty-fourth

[26] Hatch to the AAG, Department of Texas, October 4, 1870; *ibid.;* Thomas Nelson to Hamilton Fish, Secretary of State, April 29, 1871, *ibid.*

[27] Galveston *News,* April 13, 1871.

[28] Organizational Returns, Ninth Cavalry, December, 1870; Post Returns, Fort Davis, January, 1871.

Infantry, commanding at Davis, set out for Barella with a detachment of buffalo soldiers and was joined there by Captain Michael Cooney and A Company of the Ninth. On June 21, Shafter, with six officers, seventy-five troopers, and two guides, set out on the Indian trail and followed it northeast to the Pecos.

From the Pecos the trail led north into the virtually unknown White Sands region where Shafter managed to find water after a two-day search. Trails led through the sand in every direction, and for ten searing days the dogged Shafter and his tough Negro troopers plowed back and forth along a maze of trails, suffering intensely from thirst and heat. Finally, with the command at the point of utter exhaustion, Shafter marched back to Fort Davis.

The immediate results of the march were meager. An abandoned village of some two hundred lodges was destroyed, there had been a bit of long-range skirmishing with furtive Comanches, one woman had been captured, along with a few horses and mules and a small quantity of powder and lead. Ample evidence had also been discovered that the "Sands" was a place of barter for the *comancheros*. The real significance of the dreary search, however, lay in the destruction of a myth—that soldiers could never operate in such country. The buffalo soldiers could, and never again would an Indian or a *comanchero* close his eyes with any guarantee of unbroken sleep in the once mysterious White Sands.[29]

Despite increased military activity and the penetration of old sanctuaries, Indian raiders continued to plague ranchers and their herds. In late August they stole three hundred head near Fort Mc-Kavett, and detachments of F and M of the Ninth set out in pursuit. On September 1, Lieutenant John L. Bullis, Twenty-fourth Infantry, and four troopers of M, while scouting some distance from the main column, came upon three Indians driving the stolen cattle. Bullis attacked immediately and soon found himself in possession of the herd—but not for long. The initial three raiders returned with reinforcements to the number of fifteen,

29 Shafter to H. Clay Wood, AAG, Department of Texas, July 15, 1871, SLR, AGO.

and for an hour and a half Bullis and his intrepid four skirmished, charged, retreated, turned, and fought again, eventually retiring with two hundred head of the cattle still in their possession.[30]

By the close of the year the Ninth had seen nearly five years of the hardest kind of service with no respite. Most of the men had not seen their homes since enlistment, and efforts of their officers to secure extended furloughs for them were denied—at a high cost in veterans when enlistments expired. Their stations were among the most lonely and isolated to be found anywhere in the country, and mere service at such posts would seem to have called for honorable mention. Discipline was severe, food usually poor, recreation difficult, and violent death always near at hand. Prejudice robbed them of recognition and often even of simple justice.

A buffalo soldier in the Ninth could expect little mercy at the hands of a court-martial, even for trivial offenses. A dishonorable discharge and one year at hard labor was virtually automatic for drunkenness while on duty. The same sentence was the fate of Privates George Perry and Richard Talbot, both of Company I. Perry purloined a jar of candy from a saloon, while Talbot stole one dollar from a civilian. Private William Tolliver of A Company took a cat nap on guard duty and paid for his leisure with a stint of six months in the post guardhouse. Private John Curtis of H spent two months at hard labor for telling his sergeant to "go to hell" when ordered to help feed the company horses. The court was lenient with Private Andy Clayton of H, who was charged with entering the quarters of laundress Mrs. Lydia Brown, drawing a knife, and threatening, "I cut you if you don't undress and let me sleep with you." The verdict was "not guilty." Generally, however, the punishment meted out was more harsh than that in white regiments.[31]

Poor meals, like poor horses, were constant companions of Negro troopers. The post surgeon at Fort Concho put it bluntly. The food was inferior to that provided at other posts. The bread

---

[30] Post Returns, Fort McKavett, September, 1871; *Army and Navy Journal*, Vol. IX, No. 16 (December 2, 1871), 243.

[31] Cases tried by a general court-martial at Fort Concho, Texas, June, 1874, LR Relating to Texas, AGO, RG 94, NA.

was sour, beef of poor quality, and the canned peas not fit to eat. There were none of the staples common at other posts—molasses, canned tomatoes, dried apples, dried peaches, sauerkraut, potatoes, or onions. The butter was made of suet, and there was only enough flour for the officers. Certainly there were no visions of a sumptuous repast in the minds of worn-out troopers coming in to Concho after days or weeks in the field.[32]

Off-post recreation, of a sort, was available in the sordid little towns that blossomed around the posts, but a Negro soldier had no cause to seek trouble—it was awaiting him. If a trooper was unfortunate enough to lose his life in a clash with a white citizen, his comrades could hardly expect that justice would be served. One such citizen, John Jackson, a settler near Fort McKavett, murdered a Negro infantryman, Private Boston Henry, in cold blood, long eluded the law, and in the process shot and killed Corporal Albert Marshall and Private Charles Murray of Captain Carroll's F Company stationed at Fort McKavett. When finally apprehended and brought to trial, a jury quickly set him free.[33]

Such conditions could have demoralized any regiment, yet morale in the Ninth remained high. Desertion, the curse of the frontier army, dwindled steadily to the point that the rate was the lowest of any unit on the frontier. Proud, tough, and confident, the Ninth was the equal of any similar combat unit in the country, and it was well that this was so for the most trying years were still in the future.[34]

Conditions on the Río Grande, turbulent and bloody for years, worsened in the eighteen seventies. Control by the Mexican government was loose at best, and its border states of Tamaulipas, Nuevo León, Coahuila, and Chihuahua were fertile breeding grounds for revolutionary activity, particularly as Porfirio Diaz and his followers undermined and then overthrew the government of Sebastián Lerdo de Tejada in 1876.[35] Border chieftains with large am-

[32] Medical History, Fort Concho, Vol. 404.
[33] Organizational Returns, Ninth Cavalry, February, 1870; Haley, *op. cit.*, 264ff.
[34] *H.R. Exec. Doc. No. 1*, Part 2, 45 Cong., 2 sess., 49.
[35] See Frank Averill Knapp, Jr., *The Life of Sebastian Lerdo de Tejada, 1823–1889*; Parkes, *op. cit.*, 283–84.

bitions were numerous and their activities were often indistinguish-able from outright banditry. Their lust for blood, pillage, and cattle theft was seldom if ever satiated, and these leaders showed a remarkable impartiality as between their own countrymen and those of the United States.

To make a bad situation worse, the river country was plagued with young desperadoes who had fought in the Civil War, become accustomed to violence, and "had carried the habit into civil life." Gambling, stealing, killing, and drinking were a way of life, and often these men combined in such numbers as to overawe civilian authorities. If they entertained any compunctions about killing one of their own kind, they had none about killing a Mexican. Their common brag concerning the number of their victims was qualified by indicating they were not counting Mexicans. This feeling was shared in reverse by many a Mexican "hardcase" who felt that killing a Texan deserved a medal.[36]

By 1872 the activities of bandits, desperadoes, and revolu-tionaries, when combined with those of marauding Indians, drove law-abiding citizens and state officials to the brink of despair. Losses in cattle and horses ran into the thousands, ranches were looted and their owners shot down, post offices and customhouses were systematically robbed, and murders so frequent as to be commonplace. Many officials charged with enforcing the law were either in league with the lawbreakers or too fearful of reprisals to make the effort. If culprits were apprehended, prosecutors were afraid to prosecute and juries unwilling to convict. Little wonder that Governor Richard Coke could write to President Grant that he feared the whole country between the Nueces River and the Río Grande would be depopulated.[37]

Faced with this ugly situation and well aware that the spring of 1872 would bring red swarms pouring south from the reserva-tions in Indian Territory, General C. C. Augur, who succeeded

36 Governor Richard Coke of Texas to President Grant, May 29, 1875, Records of the AGO, LR, Consolidated File No. 1653, Affairs on the Río Grande and Texas Frontier, NA (hereinafter cited as File No. 1653).

37 *Ibid.;* Report of the AG of the State of Texas for the Year 1875; *ibid.;* N. H. Davis to Inspector General R. B. Marcy, May 14, 1875, *ibid.*

General Reynolds as commanding general, Department of Texas, in November, 1871, made the best possible disposition of troops available to him. The whole of the Fourth Cavalry, under Colonel Ranald S. Mackenzie, was sent to West Texas, while Merritt was ordered to rotate the companies of the Ninth counterclockwise southeastward so as to bring the bulk of the regiment along the line of the Río Grande. Supporting the cavalry were the Twenty-fourth and Twenty-fifth infantry regiments. Thus disposed the troops formed a vast fourteen-hundred-mile arc stretching from just south of Red River to near the mouth of the Río Grande.[38]

On April 16, 1872, in obedience to these orders, Merritt and his staff, with the regimental band and Companies A and H, left Fort Stockton to take up headquarters at Fort Clark. On the afternoon of April 20, the command reached Howard's Well on the San Antonio–El Paso road to find the still smoldering remains of a contractor's train. Bodies of men, women, and children were strewn about, some of them burned to a cinder. All the animals of the train were missing.

Captain Cooney with A Company took up the pursuit immediately, with Lieutenant F. R. Vincent and H hard on their heels. The trail led into a valley up which both companies advanced in parallel ranks. Many of the men were raw recruits and the veterans gave instructions while on the march. Shortly, the Indians were found entrenched on steep rocky slopes, and the troopers began the ascent but were greeted with a withering volley that killed or wounded nine horses. Cooney's mount fell, pinning its rider, then rose and started dragging him. Only quick action by Trumpeter William Nelson and Private Isaac Harrison saved their commander's life.

Cooney withdrew, had the men dismount, and then advanced to fight on foot. Once more the attempt was made to climb the rugged slopes, and once again the Indians leveled a heavy fire. Lieutenant Vincent was shot through both legs and bled profusely but, wishing to set an example for his green troopers, he refused to

---

[38] *Annual Report of the Secretary of War for the Year 1872*, 54–55; Organizational Returns, Ninth Cavalry, January–April, 1872.

leave the field. Darkness fell and still the stubborn foe held their positions. With water exhausted and ammunition running low, Cooney was forced to order a retreat to Howard's Well, with four troopers carrying a dying Vincent in a blanket.

In camp was Mrs. Marcella Sera, captured during the attack on the train, who had made her escape during Cooney's fight. More than one hundred Indians had struck the train with devastating force and overwhelmed the defenders. Eight men had been tied to wagon wheels and burned to death. Mrs. Sera, the lone captive, had been forced to watch while her husband, small child, and mother suffered agonizing deaths. The woman told Merritt that four Indians had been killed in the attack and that Cooney had killed six more. She believed, mistakenly as it turned out, that the war party had come from Mexico.

Next morning Merritt buried eleven bodies and believed others had been burned to ashes. This grim task accomplished, he had little other choice than to move on to Fort Clark, as rations were barely sufficient to see the command into the post, ammunition was nearly exhausted, and he was encumbered by a large quantity of baggage.[39]

The repulse at Howard's Well set the tone for the year. Raids and depredations increased and no regiment ever tried harder, but interceptions were rare. Merritt was convinced that both bandits and Indians were aided by Mexican citizens. The pattern seldom varied. Raiders struck, and his troopers pursued with the trail taking the most direct route to the Río Grande, and here pur-

[39] Merritt to the AAAG, Department of Texas, April 29, 1872, SDLR, 1872–76, AGO, RG 94, NA; Captain Cooney to PA, Fort Clark, Texas, May 9, 1872, *ibid.* The raiders were Kiowas and Comanches under the implacable leaders White Horse and Big Bow. Affidavit of Marcella Sera to Lieutenant Patrick Cusack, June 20, 1872, *ibid.* Michael Cooney was one of the ablest company commanders in the Ninth. A native of Ireland and a professional soldier, he enlisted in the regular army in 1856 and was a private in the Sixth Cavalry at the outbreak of the Civil War. He rose to a captaincy in the Fifth Cavalry by the end of the war and was commissioned a first lieutenant in the Ninth Cavalry in July, 1866. He remained with the regiment until December of 1888 when he transferred to the Fourth Cavalry with the rank of major. Heitman, *op. cit.,* I, 325. Lieutenant Vincent, a Missourian, rose through the ranks to a captaincy in the Missouri State Cavalry during the Civil War. He was appointed second lieutenant in the Ninth in June, 1867, and promoted to first lieutenant in July, 1869. Heitman, *op. cit.,* I, 967.

suit had to stop. According to Merritt, the Mexicans never seemed to bother the thieves.[40]

On occasion there was a bit of good fortune. In August Captain Dodge and a detachment of D Company were returning to Fort Stockton after escorting a herd of cattle to the Seven Rivers country of New Mexico. Near the post they discovered a fresh trail and after a short pursuit closed quickly upon an Indian camp. The warriors took to their heels, leaving all their property behind. With great gusto the troopers destroyed twenty tipis and all their contents with the exception of one item for each man—Indian bonnets which they wore gaily as they trotted into Fort Stockton.[41]

The experience of Captain Cooney, an able and aggressive officer, was, however, typical:

FORT CLARK, TEXAS, November 28, 1872

To: *Post Adjutant*

SIR:

I have the honor to submit the following report of a scout made by Troop "A," 9th Cavalry under my command and in compliance with letter of instructions from Post Headquarters dated November 17, 1872.

I marched from Fort Clark, Texas at 3 o'clock P. M. November 17 with my command consisting of 1st Lieut. Patrick Cusack and thirty enlisted men of Troop "A", 9th Cavalry, also a guide, with rations for seven days which was made to last ten days. I marched that night to Cope Ranch on West Fork of Nueces River to Kickapoo Springs with the intentions of crossing the country between the West Fork of the Nueces and Devils River. I found the country almost impracticable for travel being alternate mountain and valley with neither high land or valley favorable to travel. No permanent water between the two rivers. Some water was found in niches from recent rains. On the 21st we came in sight of Devils River but found great difficulty in getting down to it. However, after several hours search a place of descent was found and an Indian camp which appeared to have been abandoned about twenty four or thirty hours

40 Merritt to the AAAG, Department of Texas, November 29, 1872, SDLR, 1872–76, AGO.

41 San Antonio *Weekly Express*, August 22, 1878; Organizational Returns, Ninth Cavalry, August, 1872.

previous was found. I crossed over to the west bank and marched down the river in search of trail or their camp. After marching some distance a party of (4) Indians were seen on the east side of the river and coming toward the camp referred to as abandoned. They were driving eight animals. I detached Lieut. Cusack with a party toward them but they left the animals and rode off at speed. It was now dark and after search an ascend to the left bank could not be found. I drew in the detachment and encamped intending to cross as early as possible next morning. On the morning of the 22nd I sent Lieut. Cusack across as early as possible but the eight animals were in the same place and no trace of the Indians could be found. One of the animals had died during the night and of the seven remaining two died next night. We recrossed again to the west bank after resting the animals. The trail being found, meantime, it was taken at as fast pace as possible under the circumstances and followed to the El Paso road about two miles south of California Springs where it crossed. I found Lieut. Valois with his command on the trail at this point he having just arrived after marching out of Clark. We arranged that he should follow the trail immediately and I would encamp and follow in the morning. Lieut. Valois followed the trail as far as possible that night and was on it again at daylight. I was also on the march at daylight and pursued his trail. Lieut. Valois followed the trail to the Rio Grande River and could see signs of the Indians having crossed the day previous and encamped on the Mexican side that night. I met Lieut. Valois about ten miles this side of the Rio Grande and after him reporting these facts to me I gave up the pursuit and turned homeward. I arrived at Fort Clark on the 27th of November after a march of about 250 miles in eleven days over country almost impracticable between this post and El Paso road. My animals suffered greatly from the roughness of the country and want of grass. The men also suffered and were forced to lead and pull the horses over at least half the distance travelled but they did not complain and would feel compensated for all if they could only get a brush with the Indians.

Very Respectfully,
Your Obedient Servant
MICHAEL COONEY
Captain, 9th Cavalry.[42]

42 Cooney to the PA, Fort Clark, Texas, November 28, 1872, SDLR, 1872–76, AGO.

Ill feeling and lack of co-operation hurt law-abiding citizens on both sides of the river. In December a band of American renegades attacked the small village of Resurrección in Mexico. As soon as the news reached Fort Clark, Lieutenant Cusack and a strong detachment marched to the west bank of the Río Grande opposite the village and managed by signals to induce the alcalde to come down to the riverbank. Cusack tried to obtain information about the raid by shouting across the river, but the alcalde's reply was so sarcastic that Cusack felt himself accused of having inspired the attack.[43]

Revolutionaries were an increasing headache to the Ninth and kept patrols constantly on the lookout. Captain C. D. Beyer with Company C, working out to Fort McIntosh, should have received a decoration from the Mexican government, for he seemed to have a "nose for revolutionaries" and consistently located, arrested, and disarmed rebel leaders and their followers. In December he gathered up seven officers and thirty-seven privates in one swoop and learned that their commanding officer was in Mexico with an equal number of men. Beyer haunted the area for a week and had the pleasure of picking up a colonel and forty enlisted men.[44]

General Augur probably spoke for every officer and man of the Ninth when he noted in his annual report for 1872:

> The labor and privations of troops in this Department are both severe. The cavalry particularly are constantly at work, and it is a kind of work too that disheartens, as there is very little to show for it. Yet their zeal is untiring, and if they do not always achieve success they always deserve it. I have never seen troops more constantly employed.[45]

"Constantly employed" was an apt description of the buffalo soldiers and there were no indications of any change, for conditions along the Río Grande did not improve and Augur shifted five companies of the Ninth still farther downriver.

---

[43] Cusack to the PA, Fort Clark, Texas, December 2, 1872, *ibid.*
[44] *Annual Report of the Secretary of War for the Year 1872*, 58.
[45] *Ibid.*, 59–60.

Colonel Hatch returned to his regiment in March, 1873, and established headquarters at Ringgold Barracks. B, C, G, H, and L companies were quartered at Ringgold with detachments thrown out for miles along the river guarding crossings. Of necessity the other companies of the regiment were scattered at Forts Concho, Stockton, Davis, and McKavett to fend off Kiowa and Comanche war parties and to keep the El Paso road open.[46]

Less than half a regiment supported by a few companies of infantry was woefully inadequate to cope with the Río Grande troubles, and while conditions on the northwestern frontier of Texas were far from satisfactory, Augur, after conferences with General Sheridan, transferred the Fourth Cavalry to Fort Clark. In April, Colonel Mackenzie was apparently given carte blanche to cross the Río Grande if, in his opinion, circumstances warranted such action. On May 16, Mackenzie received word that a fresh trail had been discovered near the river, and he set out at once from Fort Clark with six companies of his regiment, a detachment of the Twenty-fourth Infantry, and a few scouts.

The trail led to the Río Grande which was crossed and the pursuit continued into Mexico. Early on the morning of May 18 Mackenzie surprised and destroyed three Indian villages, killing nineteen warriors, capturing forty women and children and the Lipan chief, Castillitos, along with sixty-five ponies. Mackenzie was back at Fort Clark before surprised Mexican officials could move to intercept him, and strong protests by their government failed to move President Grant who supported his vigorous commander.[47]

Augur reported optimistically that Mackenzie's raid had done much to quiet the Río Grande frontier, but this was hardly the case. A single raid, nineteen dead Indians, and a few captives

46 Organizational Returns, Ninth Cavalry, March, 1873.

47 Carter, *op. cit.*, 416ff; Mackenzie to the AAG, Department of Texas, SDLR, 1872–76, AGO. Ringgold Barracks, headquarters for the Ninth for more than two years, was situated a short distance below Río Grande City. Established in 1848, the post was named for Captain Samuel Ringgold, Third U. S. Artillery, who was killed at the Battle of Palo Alto during the Mexican War. It was evacuated by federal troops in March, 1861, and reoccupied in June, 1865. The name was changed to Fort Ringgold in December, 1878. Frazer, *op. cit.*, 158–59.

scarcely brought a new order of things. If so, the buffalo soldiers
—who had longed to make just such a raid—failed to feel or per-
ceive it. There were many times more than nineteen Indians, bandits, and white renegades infesting the border—more than enough
to keep the troopers in the saddle from morning until night—and
they were still not permitted to cross that frustrating ribbon of
water to overhaul their tormentors.[48]

For two more long, grim, and frustrating years Hatch and
nearly half his regiment sought to bring peace and order to a tortured frontier, and they did succeed in cutting down on cattle
losses and breaking up bands of outlaws, but conditions remained
so bad as to defy description. The country for thirty miles back
from the river was a brush jungle and the population was almost
entirely Mexican, with these people living on either side of the
Río Grande as convenience or necessity suited them. Small parties
organized, stole, killed, plundered, and swiftly dispersed. Such
lawlessness was almost impossible to prevent, and spies were
everywhere reporting on the location and movement of troops.
And, in this witches' brew, the marauding Indian was never far
away.[49]

Detachments of the Ninth could not be everywhere, but to
their everlasting credit they tried. Patrols moved from ranch to
ranch, from river crossing to river crossing in constant motion.
Others were stationed at or near the small border towns where the
"deputy collectors could not stay a day without troops at those
places."[50] When raiders were caught, there was no guarantee of
punishment, for local juries showed a decided preference for a
verdict of "not guilty."

The Ninth's effectiveness was in no small measure hampered
by harassment from local officials who disliked anything in a blue
uniform, particularly if Negroes wore that uniform. Among minor

[48] C. C. Augur to the AAG, Military Division of the Missouri, September 30,
1873, SDLR, 1872–76, AGO. Some historians have gone overboard on the importance
of the Mackenzie raid, even to indicating it brought a new era along the border. See
Haley, *op. cit.*, 210–13.
[49] Major James Wade, 9th Cavalry, to the AAG, Department of Texas, File
No. 1653.
[50] *Ibid.*

nuisances at Fort Ringgold were professional gamblers who infested the post on paydays to relieve the men of their earnings. Hatch was determined to stop the practice and in December, 1874, had post guards bring one member of the gambling fraternity, a Mr. James Johnson, to his office. Hatch delivered a tongue-lashing and ordered this somewhat dubious pillar of the community off the post.

Promptly, a Starr County grand jury indicted Hatch for "false imprisonment" and he was forced to retain a lawyer to quash the indictment. The attorney general's office refused to countenance payment of the legal fees and Hatch found himself faced with a suit by his erstwhile legal counsel for five hundred dollars.[51]

Far more serious was an affair the following month. On the evening of January 26, 1875, Sergeant Edward Troutman and four privates of G Company, on patrol out of Ringgold, encamped near the Solis ranch house some sixteen miles from their post. As the troopers prepared their supper, bullets whistled near their heads. Believing the shots had come from the ranch house, Troutman approached and questioned a number of men lounging about. He received evasive answers, noticed the men were all heavily armed, and returned to his camp.

After discussing the situation with his fellow troopers, Troutman ordered them to mount and move off. They had traveled only a short distance when they were fired upon from ambush. A vicious short-range fight ensued in which Privates Jerry Owsley and Moses Turner were killed, Privates Charley Blackstone and John Fredericks managed to escape into the brush, and Troutman fought his way out of the ambush and made his way back to Ringgold. Troutman believed his patrol had killed at least one man and wounded several others.

Early next morning, an angry Hatch, with sixty troopers from B and G companies and Deputy Sheriff T. Davis, marched to the scene of the attack and found the horribly mutilated bodies of Owsley and Turner. In a shack nearby, the uniforms and other equipment of the slain men were found. Hatch then moved on to

[51] The AG to the Secretary of War, January 7, 1875, SDLR, 1872–76, AGO.

the ranch house and "arrested every suspicious character I could find." Two of those arrested were suffering from bullet wounds. A grand jury at Río Grande City indicted nine Mexicans for the murders, but only one was tried and quickly acquitted. The remaining eight were permitted to go free.[52]

The affair did not end here, however, for troopers Troutman, Blackstone, and Fredericks, in Río Grande City to testify for the prosecution, found themselves in arrest and under indictment for murder of one of their attackers. Shortly thereafter Hatch and Lieutenant J. H. French were also indicted—for burglary. They had illegally entered the shack from which they had taken the effects of the murdered Owsley and Turner! Starr County, Texas, took excellent care of its own.

Hatch, French, and the three troopers were eventually cleared of the charges against them, but were forced to employ legal counsel and obtain a change of venue to do so. According to their attorney, Stephen Powers, malice in the area toward Hatch and his men was very great and their indictments stemmed from "gratification of purely local prejudice."[53] If the army high command drew a "water line" for the Ninth, it was also true that the people of the border drew a "color line."

Under such conditions matters could only grow worse, and a report of Captain Francis Moore of Company L was typical of many:

EDINBURG, TEXAS, March 1st, 1875

To the Post Adjutant
Ringgold Barracks
Sir:

    On the evening of the 27th instant about 7 P. M. the Sheriff of this county applied to me for a detachment of men to proceed to

---

[52] Hatch to the AAG, Department of Texas, January 26, 1875; *ibid.*; Major James Wade to the AAG, Department of Texas, May 12, 1875, File No. 1653.

[53] Attorney Stephen Powers to Major J. G. Boyle, U.S. District Attorney, November 27, 1875, File No. 1653. A tragic aftermath of this affair occurred at Fort Stockton on April 26, 1876. Private Charley Blackstone shot and killed Private John Fredericks, apparently in a quarrel over attorneys' fees borrowed to secure their release from the murder indictments of the year before. Organizational Returns, Ninth Cavalry, May, 1876.

the ranch of Fulton, about 9 miles below here, a Mexican having just come in and reported that he had seen men firing and running in and around his house and store. I immediately saddled up and with 14 men accompanied the Sheriff arriving at Fulton about 8:45 we found a group of frightened Mexicans, who reported that six men (Mexicans) had attacked the store about dark killing Mr. Fulton and his assistant, a Mexican. The body of the clerk was lying just at the door shot through the head, and Fulton's body about 200 yards distant, also shot through the head. He had evidently run from the store when he had had a struggle with the robbers from one of which he had seized a pistol and wounded one. They robbed his person and with their wounded comrade crossed the river near the ranch. It is not known how much money was taken, a small sum was found in the drawers of a counter, which was probably forgotten in their haste.

It is the general impression that one or more of Fulton's employees were accessories, as there were 7 or 8 men in and around the premises at the time of the attack who tell very contradictory stories, although all of them deny any knowledge of the perpetrators. I placed a detachment of one noncommissioned officer and six privates at the disposition of the Sheriff to assist in taking care of the murdered man's goods. I also offered him as many men as he might require to assist him in making arrests.

> Very Respectfully,
> Your obedient servt.
> FRANCIS MOORE
> *Capt. 9th Cavalry*
> *Commdg.*[54]

On April 2, Mexican bandits crossed the Río Grande in great force, surrounded and began looting the border town of Roma. It required Captain Beyer and his entire Company C to drive them off and free the town. Two weeks later, another band struck Carrizo, Texas, murdered the postmaster, D. D. Lovell, robbed his store of seven thousand dollars, and plundered the office of the deputy collector. Once again a detachment of the harried Ninth

[54] Moore to the PA, Ringgold Barracks, Texas, March 2, 1875, File No. 1653.

[55] J. L. Hayes, Customs Collector, to the Secretary of Treasury, May 13, 1875; *ibid.;* Organizational Returns, Ninth Cavalry, April, 1875.

went in pursuit and was closing fast with the bandits when it was forced to halt on the banks of the Río Grande.[55]

Shortly after this affair, however, the Ninth gained some measure of revenge and satisfaction, even if indirectly. A body of Mexican bandits carried out a successful cattle raid and was driving a large herd to the river when overtaken by Captain L. H. Mc-Nelly and a company of Texas Rangers on Palo Alto prairie near Brownsville. McNelly and his men killed twelve of the raiders and recovered more than two hundred head of cattle. A strong relief force of bandits crossed the river to attack McNelly but found itself facing two companies of grim buffalo soldiers and retired quietly to the south side of the Río Grande.[56]

At this point, General Augur was replaced by General E. O. C. Ord, the latter under instructions not to disperse his troops in small detachments, but to keep them at posts in at least company strength. Sherman believed that Ord should call upon sheriffs and local citizens to form posses and send word immediately to military posts as quickly as they discovered that raiders were in the vicinity. Sherman had a lot to learn about co-operation from citizens along the river.[57]

Governor Coke had a far more realistic view of how to cope with the situation. He pleaded with President Grant to permit troops to cross into Mexico in pursuit of raiders and punish them wherever caught. Ord agreed with Coke, but received unequivocal instructions that no troops were to cross the river without express permission from Washington.[58]

Meanwhile, disgusted with lack of local co-operation on the lower river, Secretary of War William Belknap telegraphed Governor Coke that if harassment of federal forces by civil authorities did not stop, he would remove all troops "from that locality." And, to lend weight to the threat, Hatch was ordered to transfer his headquarters to Fort Clark and "draw in" outlying companies from

[56] Statement of J. P. O'Shaughnessy, June 16, 1875, File No. 1653.

[57] Sherman to Ord, May 1, 1875, *ibid.;* Ord to the AAG, Military Division of the Missouri, September 10, 1875, *ibid.*

[58] Coke to Grant, May 29, 1875, *ibid.;* Ord to the AAG, Military Division of the Missouri, November 5, 1875, *ibid.*

Fort Ringgold.[59] These moves proved a preliminary to transfer of the Ninth from Texas. Sheridan wrote his superiors that the time had come to give officers and men of the regiment some relief. For eight years they had garrisoned the worst posts on the frontier and carried out their duties under the most trying conditions. As a result, Hatch received orders in September, 1875, transferring the regiment to the District of New Mexico. The Eighth Cavalry took its place along the river and soon had the privilege denied the men of the Ninth—permission to cross the Río Grande in "hot pursuit" of marauders.[60]

[59] Belknap to Coke, May 18, 1875, *ibid.;* Sheridan to Townsend, May 22, 1875, *ibid.*

[60] Sheridan to Belknap, June 5, 1875, *ibid.;* Organizational Returns, Ninth Cavalry, September, 1875.

V

THE RED RIVER WAR

T HE QUAKER POLICY of President Grant had failed by 1874, if not before. Fundamentally the chance of success, if indeed there had been any, foundered on the hard rock of Indian resistance to a radical change in their way of life. But the war came when it did as a result of many factors which merged to inflame Indian resentment and produce among them the urge to war that for most was irresistible.

Despite the continuing efforts of Indian agents and constant vigilance by the military, bootleggers managed to smuggle large quantities of whisky into the Indian camps, and it was flowing like water in the spring of 1874. Unlicensed traders, utterly indifferent of consequences, sold late-model arms and ammunition to the Indians in exchange for buffalo robes, cattle, and horses. Arms and whisky in an Indian camp formed a deadly mixture, providing both a stimulus and a means for depredations.[1]

White horse-thieves drove the Indians to the point of frenzy. Agent Haworth wrote Superintendent Enoch Hoag that he did not believe the number of stock stolen by his charges in Texas greatly exceeded that stolen by Texans from his Indians. Agent Miles believed that white thieves were the major source of unrest among the Cheyennes, and that a raid on an Indian pony herd invariably led to a counterraid by outraged tribesmen.[2]

Indian tempers were further inflamed by the activities of

[1] George W. Fox, Indian trader, to Davidson, April 2, 1874, Kiowa Files, Depredations; J. S. Evans to Haworth, April 27, 1874, LR, Office of Indian Affairs, Kiowa; Battey, *op. cit.*, 261.

[2] Haworth to Hoag, February 23, 1874, LR, Office of Indian Affairs, Kiowa; *Annual Report of the Commissioner of Indian Affairs for the Year 1874*, 236.

113

buffalo hunters. Prior to the construction of the transcontinental railroads, white hunters had sought these stupid and lumbering beasts primarily as a source of food, but the development of adequate transportation, combined with the growth of a market for the hides in New England, led to an incredible slaughter. The once vast herds, cornerstone of the Indian way of life, were fast disappearing by 1874. Unless the buffalo hunters were driven from the country, the tribes would have to suffer starvation or accept agency rations and take the white man's road. The Indian hated the buffalo hunter and with cause.

The heavy losses sustained by war parties in Texas during the winter of 1873–74 aroused an overwhelming desire for revenge on white men south of the Red, and when age-old raiding proclivities were added, it formed a potent witches' brew.

The activities of bootleggers, arms traders, white horse-thieves and buffalo hunters, the thirst for revenge, and the demands of a warrior culture all coalesced in the spring of 1874 to bring on an upsurge of raiding and then open warfare.

As their ponies grew stronger on the rich plains grass, Comanche and Kiowa raiders left the reservation to depredate in Texas. And they served notice on the buffalo soldiers by firing into their stockaded camps along Red River. The practice became a habit, and a wrathful Davidson wrote department headquarters requesting permission to pursue the snipers into the reservation. The request was approved, subject to the injunction that great care be taken to insure that no innocent Indians suffered. One more string that had fettered the effectiveness of the Tenth had thus been removed.[3]

Snipers were a minor nuisance when compared with the problem of coping with war parties which were marauding over hundreds of miles along the Texas frontier. Davidson kept his troopers on constant scout and pursuit as did Buell at Fort Griffin, but initial results were meager. Captain J. B. Vanderviele's B Company scouted more than five hundred miles in a single month in

---

[3] Davidson to the AAG, Department of Texas, April 15, 1874, SLR, Department of Texas.

a vain attempt to corner small bands of hostiles. Captain A. S. B. Keyes, who replaced Captain Foulk as commander of D Company, scoured the Double Mountain country, but the Indians managed to evade him. Extensive scouts by F and G from Griffin proved fruitless. It was almost worthy of a celebration when L Company struck a small party on the Big Wichita River and recovered a number of stolen horses.[4]

Colonel Merritt, at Fort Concho with Companies A, D, E, F, and K of the Ninth, reported that every trooper able to mount a horse was in the field. He needed more cavalry desperately, but with the critical state of affairs along the Río Grande, he could not call on Hatch for additional support. Merritt's problems were complicated by stepped-up activity on the part of white cattle rustlers, who were quick to take advantage of the opportunity afforded them when wide-scale Indian raids pinned down the available cavalry. Lieutenant Cusack, with a detachment of A Company, and a citizens' posse from Brownwood had broken up one gang of thieves, and detachments under Sergeants Allsup and Morgan had recovered some stolen stock, but more men were needed to curb the rustlers effectively.[5]

Early in May bitter Lone Wolf with a large party of warriors eluded the river patrols and set out to recover the body of Tau-ankia, slain in the fight with Lieutenant Hudson the previous winter. The remains were found and the Indians were returning north when they were spotted by a detachment of Fourth Cavalry, under Major H. C. Bankhead, and pursued in the direction of Fort Concho. Here the Indians obtained fresh horses by stealing twenty-three animals from the herd of Company D, Ninth Cavalry, encamped near the post. Thus mounted, Lone Wolf escaped to the reservation, but pursuit by detachments under Lieutenants Cusack

4 Organizational Returns, Tenth Cavalry, May, 1874. Keyes, a native of Massachusetts, rose through the ranks during the Civil War and was promoted to second lieutenant July 5, 1864. He remained in service after the war and held the rank of first lieutenant in the Twelfth Infantry until his transfer to the Tenth Cavalry in April, 1870. Promoted to captain in December, 1873, he remained with the regiment until October, 1892, when he transferred to the Third Cavalry. Heitman, *op. cit.*, I, 595.

5 Lieutenant Cusack to the PA, Fort Concho, Texas, February 28, 1874, SDLR, 1872–76, AGO; Merritt to the AAG, Department of Texas, December 3, 1873, SLR, Department of Texas.

and Hughes of the Ninth and Major Bankhead of the Fourth had been so hot that he was forced to abandon the body of his son. All the mission accomplished was to increase the chief's burning desire for revenge.[6]

Meanwhile, on the Cheyenne reservation white horse-thieves provided the match which exploded that Indian powder keg. They stole forty-three prize ponies from the herd of Chief Little Robe. The chief's son set out with a small party of warriors to recover the stock, failed to find the thieves, and then ran off horses and cattle near Sun City, Kansas, to replace their losses. They were pursued and overtaken by a detachment of the Sixth Cavalry, and in the skirmish that followed Little Robe's son was wounded severely. There was no doubt thereafter as to Cheyenne intentions. A large body of warriors came to their agency, reassured the white employees there that they would not be harmed, and then, "They shook hands with us and rode off and began killing people."[7]

Late in May the Comanches held a Sun Dance on the North Fork of Red River. Many Kiowas and an impressive delegation of Cheyennes and Arapahoes were also present. They were harangued by a Comanche medicine man, Isatai, who urged a war of revenge on the whites and his words found ready ears. Most of the Comanches and Cheyennes, and some of the Kiowas, smoked the war pipes, while those who desired to remain at peace moved hastily toward their agencies.

From the Sun Dance the war parties swarmed forth to strike the Texas and Kansas frontiers. The Cheyennes killed three men near Medicine Lodge, Kansas, attacked several parties of buffalo hunters along the Canadian, and placed the Camp Supply–Fort Dodge road under virtual siege. Kiowa and Comanche raiders had every trooper in Indian Territory and West Texas in the saddle and riding hard to fend off attacks.[8]

6 Lieutenant Orleman, Tenth Cavalry, to the PA, Fort Richardson, May 1, 1874, Kiowa Files, Military Relations; *Army and Navy Journal,* Vol. XI (June 20, 1874), 708; Captain C. A. Wickoff, Eleventh Infantry, Fort Concho, to Commanding Officer, Fort Sill, May 22, 1874, Kiowa Files, Military Relations.

7 Quoted in James Mooney, "Calendar History of the Kiowa Indians," *Seventeenth Annual Report of the Bureau of American Ethnology, 1895–1896,* 199; Berthrong, *op. cit.,* 383; *Annual Report of the Commissioner of Indian Affairs for the Year 1874,* 233.

On June 27 several hundred Comanche, Kiowa, and Cheyenne warriors sought to wipe out a party of buffalo hunters at Adobe Walls on the Main Canadian in the Texas Panhandle. They were driven off by accurate rifle fire, losing nine warriors while killing only three of the hunters. The Cheyennes had better luck nearer their agency where they killed five men in the first three days of July and caused a frightened Agent Miles to appeal to Davidson for troops. Davidson ordered Lieutenant M. M. Maxon and Company M to the Cheyenne agency, but Maxon and his troopers were diverted by a courier from Fort Sill to the Wichita Agency at Anadarko, where Acting Agent J. Connell feared an attack. Miles, without troops for defense, gathered up his employees and made fast tracks for Fort Dodge, where he telegraphed both Commissioner Smith and military authorities apprising them of the outbreak.[9]

The Comanches, and some Kiowas, beaten by the buffalo hunters at Adobe Walls, relieved their frustrations with devastating raids into Texas. The most spectacular success was achieved by Lone Wolf on the afternoon of July 12. With a medicine man, Maman-ti, and about fifty warriors, he ambushed and badly shot up a party of Texas rangers in Lost Valley northwest of Fort Richardson. One of the rangers managed a daring getaway and reached the post. Captain Baldwin with I Company galloped to the rescue and reached the scene early on the morning of July 13, but the Indians had drawn off, leaving two rangers dead, two wounded, and twelve horses killed.[10]

8 Haworth to Hoag, May 9, 1874, LR, Office of Indian Affairs, Kiowa; Battey, *op. cit.*, 302–303; *Annual Report of the Commissioner of Indian Affairs for the Year 1874*, 220; Haworth to Hoag, June 3, 1874, LR, Office of Indian Affairs, Kiowa; Post Returns, Camp Supply, June, 1874; Organizational Returns, Tenth Cavalry, June, 1874; Buell to the AAG, Department of Texas, June 11, 1874, SLR, Department of Texas; *Annual Report of the Secretary of War for the Year 1874*, 30.

9 Davidson to Lieutenant M. M. Maxon, July 6, 1874, SLR, Department of Texas; Leckie, *op. cit.*, 190–93; Mooney, "Calendar History," 203; B. K. Weatherell to Enoch Hoag, July 4, 1874, Kiowa Files, Depredations; *Annual Report of the Commissioner of Indian Affairs for the Year 1874*, 233–34.

10 Walter P. Webb, *The Texas Rangers: A Century of Frontier Defense*, 312–13; Post Returns, Fort Richardson, July, 1874; Interpreter Phil McCusker to Lieutenant M. M. Maxon, July 30, 1874, LR, AGO, 1874, File No. 3300–1874, NA (hereinafter cited as File No. 3300–1874).

Colonel Buell at Griffin sent every trooper at his post after the raiders. Captain P. L. Lee with G, Captain William Kennedy with F, and Lieutenant Pratt with D combined in a five-day search for the hostiles, but the birds had flown and their trail was lost.[11]

Prowling Comanches attacked a wood camp less than a dozen miles from Fort Sill on July 13. A detachment of the overworked Tenth arrived in time to deprive the hostiles of fifty-two head of freshly stolen stock and to bury one man who had been killed and scalped. When two more men were killed next day at Elm Spring Station, Davidson, over the protests of Agent Haworth, took decisive action. He telegraphed department headquarters for more cavalry and issued the following general order:

HEADQUARTERS POST OF FORT SILL, I. T.
July 17, 1874

GENERAL ORDERS
NO. 46.

The hostile bands of Comanches, Cheyennes, and Kiowas having committed depredations and murder upon government employees within the Reservation, and within a few niles of the Post, some marked line must be drawn between the hostile and friendly portions of those tribes. In order then that troops and others may be able to distinguish those who are friendly—all such Indians must form their camps on the east side of Cache Creek at points selected by the Agent.

No Indian hereafter will be permitted to approach this post nearer than the Agency, and must come in to the Agency from the east side of Cache creek.

When friendly Indians desire to visit the Post Commander they must come from the direction of the Agency, and with a messenger from the Agent stating the Chief and the number of his party.

J. W. DAVIDSON
Lieut. Col. 10th Cavalry
Bvt. Maj. General USA[12]

---

[11] Medical History, Fort Griffin, Vol. 103; Post Returns, Fort Griffin, July, 1874; Organizational Returns, Tenth Cavalry, July, 1874.

[12] General Order No. 46, Fort Sill, July 17, 1874, Kiowa Files, Military Relations. For a summary of Indian depredations near Fort Sill, see Davidson to the AAG,

Despite the gravity of the situation, an incident occurred on the evening this order was issued to provide considerable amusement for the garrison. Horace Jones, the post interpreter, paid a visit to the trader's store and spent several hours drinking with some old cronies. His weaving return to the post was interrupted by one of Davidson's sentries, a raw recruit fresh from the depot in St. Louis, who challenged Jones and refused to let him pass. When the interpreter demanded indignantly to know why, the trooper replied, "I am sorry, but the new post order says you cannot enter the post unless accompanied by an Indian." And a suddenly sobered Mr. Jones was forced to make a trip to the guardhouse and provide what was undoubtedly a profane explanation of his visit before being allowed to proceed to his quarters.[13]

The scope of hostile action had been so great as to assume the proportions of a general war and forced the War and Interior departments to agree on a common policy to cope with the situation. On July 21, General Sherman telegraphed Sheridan that a decision had been reached. Reservation lines were to be disregarded and hostile Indians pursued and punished wherever they could be found, but great care was to be taken to insure that the innocent were separated from the guilty. The former were to be enrolled and concentrated at their agencies to avoid their being harmed. Sheridan forwarded these instructions to Generals Pope and Augur, and Commissioner Smith so informed the Indian agents.[14]

Davidson received orders on July 26 to proceed immediately with enrollment of the "friendlies" at Fort Sill, and the process was completed on August 8. Few Comanches came in and most of that tribe was regarded as hostile. An overwhelming majority of the Kiowas were enrolled, although the reliability of many was

Department of Texas, July 20, 1874, LR, AGO, 1874, File No. 3144–1874, NA (hereinafter cited as File No. 3144–1874).

13 Nye, *op. cit.*, 202.

14 Sherman to Sheridan, July 21, 1874, LR, AGO, 1874, File No. 2815–1874, NA (hereinafter cited as File No. 2815–1874). Woodward to Grierson, August 8, 1874, Grierson Papers; *Annual Report of the Secretary of War for the Year 1874*, 41; Acting Commissioner of Indian Affairs, H. R. Clum, to Haworth, August 15, 1874, Kiowa Files, Depredations; Enoch Hoag to Agent Richards, Wichita Agency, July 21, 1874, Kiowa Files, Depredations.

subject to question. Virtually all the Kiowa-Apaches remained at peace. The Arapahoes submitted quietly to registration at the Cheyenne agency, but of some two thousand Cheyennes, fewer than three hundred remained on the reservation. Acting Agent Connell at Anadarko had little difficulty enrolling the Wichitas and affiliated tribes but was concerned over Comanche and Kiowa hostiles who lurked in the vicinity.[15]

A few days after enrollment closed, a number of Comanche chiefs sent word to Davidson that they wished to come in. Only one, Assanonica and his people, received permission, as all the others, including Big Red Food, a Nokoni, had taken part in the attack on the buffalo hunters at Adobe Walls. These "outs" proceeded forthwith to join the other "out" Comanches near Anadarko. This development made Davidson uneasy, for if these Indians mixed with the friendlies at that agency, he was faced with a delicate situation which could bring great harm to many peaceful Indians.

Shortly, conditions at Anadarko became explosive. Some enrolled Kiowas killed six men in two days near Fort Sill. Many of them, fearing retaliation by the army, left the agency and joined the hostiles under Lone Wolf who were demanding rations from Connell, stealing food from his Indians, and ignoring his pleas for them to leave.[16]

Connell consulted with Captain Gaines Lawson, Eleventh Infantry, commanding the single company at the post, and both agreed that reinforcements were necessary and the quicker the better. Lawson, therefore, sent an urgent appeal to Davidson. The latter received Lawson's message at six o'clock on the afternoon of August 21 and began preparations at once. By ten o'clock that evening, C, E, H, and L under Captains Viele, Robinson, Car-

15 Davidson to the AAG, Department of Texas, August 10, 1874, File No. 3300–1874; *Annual Report of the Commissioner of Indian Affairs for the Year 1874*, 238; Haworth to E. P. Smith, August 17, 1874, LR, Office of Indian Affairs, Kiowa.

16 Davidson to the AAG, Department of Texas, August 10, 1874, File No. 3300–1874; Haworth to Smith, August 25, 1874, LR, AGO, 1874, File No. 3490–1874, NA (hereinafter cited as File No. 3490–1874). *Annual Report of the Secretary of War for the Year 1874*, 41. Prominent among those who enrolled and then left for the Wichita agency were Satanta and Big Tree.

penter, and Little were armed, mounted, and ready to march. Davidson led them out of the post and headed swiftly for Anadarko.

Near noon next day, Davidson crossed the Washita and entered the agency grounds. The river curled to the south at this point, forming a large arc which was closed on the north by a range of wooded bluffs. Within this rough rectangle the agency buildings were scattered badly. The agent's house, shops, school, and stables were all under the bluff and a mile from the river. On the bluff to the northwest was the agency sawmill, while Shirley's store was to the northeast. The commissary and corral were near the river.

August 22 was Saturday and issue day at the agency. Most of the Wichitas, Caddoes, Pawnees, Delawares, and Penateka Comanches were in or near the commissary, while the camp of Big Red Food was not more than two hundred yards away and close to the Penateka camp. Connell sent at once for Big Red Food, and when the chief arrived Davidson told him that he and his warriors had been given every opportunity to enroll, that they had not done so, and that enrollment had been completed. Now they must surrender, turn over their weapons, and move back to Fort Sill as prisoners of war.

At first the chief was reluctant, but after some urging by Tosh-a-way, a friendly Penateka, he agreed to Davidson's demands and, under escort by Lieutenant Woodward and forty troopers, he went to his camp to gather up the weapons. Here an argument developed over the surrender of bows and arrows which the chief wished to retain for hunting purposes. Woodward hesitated, then sent a trooper to Davidson for an answer. In the interim some of Lone Wolf's Kiowas, who were close by, began taunting Big Red Food and his Nokonis, asking them if they were women and if they intended allowing a few buffalo soldiers to disarm them.

The chief was no coward and the jibes were too much for him. Suddenly he gave a loud whoop, leaped from his pony, and escaped into the brush with a volley from the troopers whistling around his ears. Hostile Kiowas and the Nokonis returned the fire and the battle was joined. Lawson's infantry, acting under Davidson's orders, moved at once toward the agency sawmill to cut off any Indians trying to escape up the Washita, while the latter faced his companies toward Big Red Food's camp and advanced.

But Davidson found himself in an awkward position. Friendly Indians were flying in all directions and, having no desire to harm these people, he was hesitant to open fire. Yet, as his troopers moved forward, Kiowa warriors, who had taken positions behind the commissary and corral, fired into them from the rear, wounding Sergeant Lewis Mack of H and Private Adam Cork of E. A number of horses were also hit, and Davidson swerved his command abruptly into the thick timber along the river and dismounted to fight on foot.[17]

Captain Little with L moved out and drove the Kiowas from the commissary and corral, but most of these Indians circled Little's right flank, crossed the river, and headed for the farm and home of a Delaware named Black Beaver. Carpenter with H Company pursued these Indians, charged, and routed them, but not before they had killed four men who were in the fields cutting hay and two more near Black Beaver's home. Davidson now regrouped his command and moved swiftly to protect the agency which was threatened by a swarm of warriors who had gained the bluffs and gutted Shirley's store. The troopers reached the agency in time to prevent an attack, and Viele with C Company cleared the bluffs as dusk fell and brought an end to the day's fighting.

During the night Davidson posted detachments at Shirley's, the commissary, and the agency cornfield, while others destroyed the camp of Big Red Food and dug trenches on the south side of the river.

The Indians had not been idle. By early morning nearly three hundred of them had gathered to recapture the bluff and were beginning the ascent. Captain Carpenter took E, H, and L and drove these warriors off just as they reached the top. Frustrated in their efforts to gain the bluffs, the Indians fired the dry grass in an effort

[17] Davidson to the AAG, Department of Texas, August 27, 1874, File No. 3490–1874; Augur to Sheridan, September 13, 1874, *ibid*.

to burn the agency. The troopers started counterfires and with much hard work managed to save the agency buildings.

The "fire fight" ended the battle of Anadarko. Davidson had four troopers and six horses wounded. He believed that fourteen Indians had been "shot off their horses" and at least four ponies had been killed.[18]

The affair at Anadarko served to clear the air on a number of matters, and at least two of these were of no little shock to the Indians. The presence of a Quaker agent was no longer any guarantee of immunity, and an agency was no sanctuary in time of bad behavior; a few buffalo soldiers freed from restrictions were nothing to be trifled with—they could fight, and they fought very well. They had not wavered when fired on from the rear, Little's men had advanced on the corrals in steady, even file, Carpenter's H had charged with zest, and Viele's C had ascended and cleared the bluff in a manner that would have pleased a Sherman.

The fight also served to separate clearly the hostile and friendly bands. When news of the fighting reached Fort Sill, nearly all the Indians stampeded, but within less than a month most of them returned. The hostile Kiowas and Comanches moved toward the western reaches of Indian Territory or on to the Staked Plains to join the Kwahadis. The warring Cheyennes were nearby on the edge of the Plains and more than two hundred miles southwest of their agency. It was the task of the army to find, defeat, and drive these Indians back to their reservations. Once this project had been accomplished, they were to be disarmed, dismounted, and their leaders punished.[19]

Sheridan, Augur, and Pope had completed their plans for the

18 Davidson to the AAG, Department of Texas, August 27, 1874, *ibid;* Augur to Sheridan, September 13, 1874, *ibid.;* J. Connell to Miles, August 25, 1874, Cheyenne–Arapaho Files, Military Relations, Indian Archives, Oklahoma State Historical Society, Oklahoma City, Oklahoma. Connell believed Satanta to be among the Kiowas firing on the troops from the commissary and corral. An excellent account of this fight from the Indian point of view is in Nye, *op. cit.,* 206–10.

19 *Annual Report of the Secretary of War for the Year 1874,* 42; Davidson to the AAG, Department of Texas, August 27, 1874, File No. 3490–1874; Sherman to Sheridan, July 20, 1874, File No. 2815–1874; *Annual Report of the Commissioner of Indian Affairs for the Year 1874,* 234.

campaign in July. Lines separating the Departments of Texas and Missouri were to be disregarded and the reservations invaded if necessary. Five strong columns were to converge on the Indians from the north, south, east, and west in a continuing operation, until a devastating defeat had been inflicted. One column, under Colonel Nelson A. Miles, would march south from Fort Dodge toward the headwaters of Red River, while another, commanded by Major William R. Price, would move eastward from Fort Bascom, New Mexico, and effect a junction with Miles. A third command under Colonel Mackenzie would sweep the Staked Plains northwest of Fort Concho and establish contact with Miles. The buffalo soldiers formed the backbone of the remaining two columns. One of these, largely of Ninth Cavalry under Lieutenant Colonel Buell, was concentrated at Fort Griffin, with the other organized at Fort Sill by Colonel Davidson. Buell and Davidson were to operate between Miles and Mackenzie and drive the hostiles westward into their paths.[20]

All five commands were scheduled to take the field in August, but the trouble at Anadarko, and a delay in receiving supplies, detained Buell and Davidson, and it was not until early September that they were ready to march. Meanwhile, the columns of Miles, Price, and Mackenzie had proceeded as planned.

Miles set out on August 14 and in torrid weather pushed far southward to the Salt Fork of Red River where, on August 30, he overtook and drove a large body of Cheyennes out on to the Staked Plains. His command was too used up and supplies too low to follow them, so he retraced his steps to the Canadian and established a supply camp on that stream and others on the Washita and Sweetwater. From these camps he kept a number of small columns in constant motion and prevented any Indians from escaping to the north.

Price accomplished very little. He left Fort Bascom on August

20 Pope to Sheridan, July 27, 1874, SLR, Department of Texas; Miles to the AAG, Department of the Missouri, March 4, 1875, File No. 3490–1874; *Annual Report of the Secretary of War for the Year 1874*, 40; Post Returns, Fort Sill, August–September, 1874; Post Returns, Fort Griffin, August–September, 1874; Woodward to Grierson, August 12, 1874, Grierson Papers.

28 and reached Miles on September 7 as the latter was falling back to the Canadian. He then moved northward to find his train, which he had earlier sent toward the Antelope Hills, and on September 12 he stumbled into a literal hive of Kiowas and Comanches near the Dry Fork of the Washita and was fought to a standstill. From this fight Price marched on to the Canadian where he merged his force with that of Miles.[21]

The operations of Miles and Price assisted Mackenzie in scoring a spectacular success. The latter left Fort Concho on August 23 and set out to scour the Staked Plains northwest of that post. On September 25, his scouts located a large Indian camp in Palo Duro Cañon on the Prairie Dog Town Fork of Red River. Mackenzie found a trail leading into the cañon, effected a complete surprise, and routed a large force of Kiowas, Comanches, and Cheyennes, many of whom had taken refuge there from Miles's columns. Mackenzie inflicted few casualties, but he captured and destroyed huge quantities of supplies as well as a pony herd of more than one thousand animals. Until the end of the year this command remained in the field scouting the breaks of Red River and along the headwaters of the Brazos.[22]

Buell left Fort Griffin on September 1 and marched for Fort Sill where he arrived a week later. Here he completed the organization of his command and loaded supplies on thirty wagons, drawn by six-mule teams. He moved out of Sill on September 24 and five days later established a supply camp on the North Fork of Red River a few miles above the mouth of Otter Creek. At the supply camp final plans were made, and the command divided into two battalions. Major Morrow commanded the first, consist-

21 Miles's command consisted of Companies A, D, F, G, H, I, L, and M, Sixth Cavalry, and Companies C, D, E, and I, Fifth Infantry—some 750 men. On September 9, one of his supply trains was hit and badly mauled by the same hostiles who fought Price. The latter had four companies of the Eighth Cavalry, two howitzers, and a few Navaho scouts. For details see Miles to the AAG, Department of the Missouri, March 5, 1874, File No. 3490–1874, and Price to the AAG, Department of the Missouri, September 23, 1874, File No. 2815–1874.

22 Mackenzie had eight companies of the Fourth Cavalry, four companies of the Tenth Infantry, one company of the Eleventh Infantry, and about thirty Tonkawa Indian scouts. His campaign is well described in Carter, *op. cit.*, 473–506. For official reports consult File No. 2815–1874.

ing of Companies A, E, F, and K, Ninth Cavalry, while Companies A and E, Tenth Cavalry, formed the second under Captain Nolan of the Tenth. Each battalion had a few Tonkawa scouts, and the train was guarded by two companies of the Eleventh Infantry.

On the morning of October 3 the columns got under way with twenty-five days' rations. Each trooper carried forty rounds of carbine and twenty rounds of pistol ammunition on his person. The only equipment allowed consisted of an overcoat, a poncho, a shelter tent, and one change of socks and underwear, carried on the horses. Almost immediately fresh pony tracks were found, and shortly thereafter a small party of warriors was sighted and pursued. The Indians made their escape but lost two horses in the process.

Five days of uneventful marching followed, but late on October 8 one of the Tonk scouts came in to report that he had "shaken hands with a Comanche some twenty miles toward the south." Buell pushed on with greater speed, and before the day was out, his advance overtook and killed a Kiowa warrior who was spying on the column. The trails led toward the Salt Fork of Red River, and on the afternoon of the ninth a small party of warriors was sighted well to the front. Captain Ambrose Hooker, with E of the Ninth, charged them at a gallop and killed one warrior before the others vanished in the breaks along the Salt Fork. When the rest of the command came up, a deserted Indian camp of fifteen lodges was found and destroyed.

Here Buell waited impatiently for his train to come up, as signs indicated a large body of Indians was within striking distance. When the train finally arrived the following day, the decision was made to cut loose from it in order to march as swiftly as possible. Early on October 11, the pursuit was taken up and pushed relentlessly through the rough breaks and cañons of the Salt Fork and then northwest to the edge of the Staked Plains where a deserted camp of seventy-five lodges was destroyed. The trail now led across the Plains toward the headwaters of McClellan Creek and grew rapidly in size as small parties joined from both flanks. The track was also easy to follow, for it had been littered with abandoned camp equipage and worn-out ponies as the fleeing Indians sought to shake off their dogged foe.

On the morning of October 12, Buell had expectations of bringing the Indians to bay or driving them into either Miles or Mackenzie. These hopes were shattered when midafternoon brought him to a huge but abandoned camp of 475 lodges which he put to the torch. The Indians were undoubtedly heading for the Canadian, but the command was nearly out of supplies and the horses were nearing exhaustion. Buell encamped and conferred with Morrow and Nolan. Both were loath to give up the chase without a decisive action. Their rugged troopers were full of spirit and eager to push on. The decision was made to continue the pursuit while couriers rode hard for Fort Sill to request that a train with forty days' rations be sent out at once.

The column moved on northward, but on the evening of October 13 the couriers returned with disturbing news. They had been intercepted and pursued by a party of twenty-five warriors and were fortunate to get back to the main body with their hair. Buell was thoroughly alarmed. Indians might well have overwhelmed his lightly guarded train which was far to the rear. There was no other choice than a forced night march along the back trail, and before daybreak the train was found. Much to the relief of all, it had not been attacked.

Private Williams of E Company, Tenth Cavalry, and one of the scouts were sent into Fort Sill with the request for rations, and the command plodded back to the camp of the night before. Hardly had the animals been turned out to graze when firing was heard to the rear, and Buell was informed that his scouts were engaging a party of *comancheros*. This report proved false, for in the poor evening light the Tonkawa scouts had actually opened fire on one of Miles's detachments and discovered their error only when a howitzer shell screeched over their heads.

From the officer commanding the detachment, Buell learned of Miles's position which was to the front and right on the Canadian and about two days' march. Buell had driven several hundred Indians into Miles, and both were now following the same parties.

127

Buell pressed on with horses so weak the men were forced to walk at least half the time and reached the Canadian on October 16. Here the Indians had scattered in all directions. Buell sent the Tonkawas to locate the main body and ordered Major Morrow to be ready with one hundred picked men to take up the chase if the hostiles were found.

A bewildering maze of trails defied the best efforts of the Tonkawas, but indications were that many of the Indians had curled around the column's left flank and fled back southward. Buell at this point was three hundred miles from his base and in desperate need of forage and rations. A courier was hastened down the Canadian seeking Miles, while the command followed as rapidly as the condition of the animals would allow. Considerable difficulty was encountered in locating Miles who proved to be on the Washita, and his camp was not reached until October 24.[23]

With his needs partially satisfied, Buell wasted no time in ceremony, but threw out his scouts and marched south to the Sweetwater where the broken-down animals were sent on to the supply camp on the Salt Fork. While here, Captain Viele, with C Company of Davidson's column, came in and Buell learned that a large body of Indians had surrendered to Davidson on Elk Creek about forty miles to the front and that scouting reports indicated still other Indians were moving toward the Wichita agency to surrender.

Buell saddled up at once and marched to Elk Creek where a large trail was struck leading east. Major Morrow, with A, D, and E of the Ninth, was detached to follow the trail and make certain it was made by the band that had surrendered to Davidson. The rest of the column continued on south until a supply train was met on November 4. A much needed rest was taken and the command reorganized. By November 16, however, Buell was on the move again with eighty picked buffalo soldiers while the remaining men were sent in to Fort Sill.

Buell's intention was to scout the headwaters of Red River, but

---

[23] Buell to Miles, October 18, 1874, File No. 2815–1874; Buell to the AAG, Department of Texas, November 8, 1874, *ibid.*

he soon encountered "as severe weather as I have ever experienced" and was forced to hole up on the banks of the Salt Fork. The storm subsided somewhat on November 22 and Buell sent a detachment under Lieutenant Valois to scout along the Red, while the main column continued along the Salt Fork. Next day a deserted village of twenty-two lodges was found, along with a quantity of horse meat. The harried Indians had been reduced to killing and eating their ponies. After destroying the village, pursuit was undertaken in the face of a heavy snowstorm which soon turned to driving rain and stinging sleet. Doggedly the column pushed on, turned northward, and headed for Miles's supply camp.

But Buell and his troopers were reaching the limits of their endurance, and as the weather grew steadily worse, they soon found themselves fighting to advance in the teeth of a howling blizzard. It was too much, the buffalo soldiers were not clothed for this kind of weather, many of them were almost bootless, and they were forced to turn back to the supply train which was found only after a considerable search on December 3. Shortly thereafter Valois came in with his men badly frostbitten and the animals completely used up. He had gone well up the main Red when the storm struck and turned him back.

Buell had demanded and gotten an almost superhuman effort from his Negro troopers, and he could ask no more. He broke up the expedition and moved in to Fort Griffin. In his official report, Buell, ever sparse with praise, gave the buffalo soldiers a well-earned accolade, "I cannot give them too much credit for manly endurance without complaint."[24]

Buell's expedition was a devastating blow to the Indians. He killed only two warriors, but he destroyed nearly six hundred lodges, tons of supplies, and camp equipment. The grim, relentless pursuit broke down scores of Indian ponies and the will to resist of hundreds of Kiowas, Comanches, and Cheyennes. The campaign contributed materially to the success of Mackenzie,

[24] Buell to the AAG, Department of Texas, February 24, 1875, SLR, Department of Texas; Organizational Returns, Ninth and Tenth Cavalry, September–December, 1874; *Army and Navy Journal,* Vol. XII (December 26, 1874), 308.

Miles, and Davidson, yet curiously it received little notice. This treatment may have been strange to Buell, but it was an old story to the cheerful and willing buffalo soldiers.

The fight at Anadarko, and the necessity for providing an adequate garrison at the Wichita agency, delayed Davidson for nearly three weeks. Not until September 10 was the Fort Sill column ready to move. It consisted of Companies B, C, H, K, L, and M, Tenth Cavalry, three companies of the Eleventh Infantry, a section of mountain howitzers, and forty-four Indian scouts under Lieutenant Pratt. Forty-six wagons carried a three weeks' supply of rations and forage.[25]

The long column marched northward to the Washita which was found "bankfull" from recent rains. Davidson's plan was to follow the twisting course of the Washita northwestward and flush any Indians who might be between his command and that of Miles. If this action proved unproductive, he intended to search along the North Fork of Red River and McClellan's Creek, and, if no Indians were found, to scout the eastern base of the Staked Plains in the hope of driving hostiles into Mackenzie's arms, or to catch any that Mackenzie might be driving eastward.

Davidson marched westward on September 12 with scouts and detachments thrown far out in order to sweep an area forty miles wide. No trails or Indians were seen until September 17 when Pratt's scouts captured a lone Kiowa with three head of stock. Two days later a detachment found one of Miles's camps on the Sweetwater, and Davidson moved his whole command to that point and bivouacked, while couriers were sent to Miles who was then on the Washita. Miles came in on September 22 and conferred with Davidson, while the men of the command "washed up and refitted."

From this camp Davidson turned south and crossed the North Fork of the Red, while Pratt and his scouts probed the heads of that stream and McClellan Creek. On September 25, Pratt found a large herd of buffalo and had his scouts kill a number of them to supply the command with fresh meat. As he was moving off

25 Woodward to Grierson, August 12, 1874, Grierson Papers; Post Returns, Fort Sill, September, 1874; Organizational Returns, Tenth Cavalry, September, 1874.

to rejoin Davidson, a lone Indian was sighted some distance to the rear and was quickly pursued, overtaken, and captured. The Indian proved to be a Cheyenne who had mistaken the pony tracks of Pratt's scouts for those of his own people and had ridden virtually into the column before he discovered his mistake.[26]

For a week Davidson's troopers toiled south along the edge of the Staked Plains and into the breaks of Mulberry Creek and Red River "through some of the most broken country I ever saw."[27] When no trace of Indians was found, Captain Caleb Carleton with about two hundred troopers was detached to locate Buell and Mackenzie. A forty-eight hour search proved fruitless and Carleton rejoined the main command. By this time the men were on half rations, forage was exhausted, the grass scarce, and Davidson decided to turn toward Fort Sill. On October 2, while marching eastward along Red River, a band of Kiowas was surprised and pursued, but the worn-out animals were too weak to close the gap and the Indians escaped. The march continued to Herd Creek, about seven miles south of Fort Sill, and the troopers went into camp to rest and refit. Davidson had little to show for his efforts but fifty-eight dead horses and mules.[28] A tragic footnote was added to the campaign on October 16 when First Lieutenant Silas Pepoon of B Company, in a fit of despondency, shot and killed himself.[29]

By October 21, Davidson was ready to resume operations and marched northwest to Fort Cobb where he turned due west and advanced on a broad front. Almost immediate results were obtained. In the Pond Creek area Captain Carpenter with H and L companies captured forty-five Kiowas and fifty horses without a fight. On October 24, Major Schofield with B, C, and M surprised a large camp of Comanches on Elk Creek and forced their surrender after a slight skirmish in which Private Alfred Pinkston of

26 Pratt, *op. cit.*, 68–69.

27 Davidson to the AAG, Department of Texas, October 10, 1874, SLR, Department of Texas.

28 *Ibid.*

29 Organizational Returns, Tenth Cavalry, October, 1874. Pepoon was one of the original cadre of officers assigned to the Tenth.

131

M killed a "Kiowa warrior in personal combat."[30] At one swoop Schofield had bagged a number of prominent chiefs, including Big Red Food of Anadarko fame, sixty-four warriors, two hundred and fifty women and children, and the entire pony herd of two thousand animals. These Indians, fleeing from the tenacious Buell, and near exhaustion, had run squarely into Davidson.[31]

From Elk Creek the command continued westward in excellent weather with the troopers in high spirits. Wild game was found in abundance and veritable banquets of wild turkey, antelope, and deer replaced the normal bacon, beans, and hardtack. The honeymoon was brief, however, for difficult days were just ahead.

To his front Miles had a number of columns searching for Cheyenne hostiles. On November 6, Lieutenant Henry Farnsworth with twenty-eight men of H Company, Eighth Cavalry, while scouting toward McClellan Creek, ran afoul of one hundred Cheyenne warriors and succeeded in breaking loose only after one of his men had been killed and three wounded. Davidson and Miles established contact through couriers and moved to find these hostiles. On the morning of November 8, as the Sill column was searching the breaks of the North Fork of McClellan Creek, heavy firing was heard to the front, and a hastily abandoned Cheyenne camp of seventy-five lodges was soon found and destroyed.[32]

In an effort to overtake these Indians who had clashed with Miles, Davidson ordered Captain Viele to take 120 picked men, Lieutenant Pratt, and fifty scouts, and pursue as swiftly as possible. At first the trail led out on the Staked Plains in a northwesterly direction but then turned sharply toward the southwest. By late afternoon Pratt's scouts sighted the Cheyenne rear guard and a

---

[30] Davidson's command was the same as in his first campaign with the exception of K Company whose animals were in such bad condition as to prevent the company from taking the field. F Company took the place of K. See Organizational Returns, Tenth Cavalry, October, 1874, and Post Returns, Fort Sill, October, 1874.

[31] Davidson to the AAG, Department of Texas, October 30, 1874, File No. 2815–1874; Organizational Returns, Tenth Cavalry, October, 1874.

[32] Davidson to General Augur, November 23, 1874, File No. 2815–1874; Farnsworth to Price, November 7, 1874, *ibid.; Army and Navy Journal*, Vol. XII (November 14, 1874), 212. The body of Private William Dencham of Farnsworth's command was found and buried by a detachment of buffalo soldiers on November 10. See Pratt, *op. cit.*, 75.

long chase began, but Viele was unable to close with his foe, although rifle fire was exchanged at long range.

Nightfall brought pursuit to a halt, but at daybreak the command was on the trail again and stayed with it until nearly evening when Viele felt compelled to abandon the pursuit. The horses were giving out after a march of ninety miles in two days, rations and forage were nearly gone, and a cold north wind was blowing. There was nothing to do but plod wearily back on their out trail.[33]

The weather turned bitter cold, and sleet and snow pelted Davidson's column as it pushed slowly northward in the teeth of the storm to the Sweetwater. More than two dozen troopers were disabled with frostbite, one hundred of the animals froze to death, and supplies were fearfully low. In such a condition little could be accomplished, and Davidson turned back to the North Fork of the Red and then eastward toward Fort Sill with men and animals suffering intensely from the cold. The post was reached on November 29, and before a warm fire Davidson could look back with considerable satisfaction on his operations. Nearly four hundred Indians and more than two thousand animals had been captured, several score of lodges with much camp equipment had been destroyed, and all without the loss of a man. The troopers had performed admirably under the most trying conditions.[34]

While hundreds of hostiles had been captured, and other hundreds had moved in and voluntarily surrendered either at Fort Sill or at the Cheyenne agency, many remained out, and early in December the buffalo soldiers of the Ninth and Tenth made a final effort to drive in these last holdouts. Major Schofield took the field on the morning of December 7, with K, M, and D companies of the Tenth, and Company C, Eleventh Infantry. Enough supplies were carried to maintain a scout of twenty-five days.

Schofield marched north to the Wichita agency and then turned westward up the Washita searching for trails. Nothing of

[33] Davidson to Captain Carlton, November 17, 1874, File No. 2815–1874; Organizational Returns, Tenth Cavalry, November, 1874; *Army and Navy Journal,* Vol. XII (December 12, 1874), 276; Pratt, *op. cit.,* 76–77.

[34] Davidson to Augur, November 23, 1874, File No. 2815–1874; Organizational Returns, Tenth Cavalry, November, 1874; Lieutenant Pratt to the AAAG, Fort Sill Column, November 29, 1874, File No. 3490–1874.

any significance was discovered until December 18 when a hastily abandoned Cheyenne camp of fifteen lodges was found. Captain Keyes with Company D and ten men of Company M were detached to pursue these Indians, while Schofield pushed on toward the Canadian.

Keyes overtook the Cheyennes on Kingfisher Creek fewer than twenty miles from their agency, captured fifty-two men, women and children, and about fifty animals. Schofield scouted for more than two hundred miles in a vast arc between the Canadian and the Washita and found nothing. He took time out to allow the troopers a turkey shoot on Christmas Day and then set out for Fort Sill where he arrived on December 31.[35]

Major Morrow, who had been at Fort Sill with A, D, and E of the Ninth since mid-November, left the post on December 4 and marched to Buell's supply camp on the North Fork of the Red where he obtained three weeks' rations. He then set out for the main Red River and searched far upstream in intense cold. The scout was unproductive, and he turned to the Pease River for one final look under constant hammering by rain and snow. When fifty-four of his sixty mules froze to death, he called it quits and marched in to Fort Concho.[36]

There was little here to comfort the half-frozen soldiers and Post Surgeon William Buchanan filed a complaint with the post adjutant. The men had "just returned from a fatiguing campaign," yet there was little for them to eat. The bread was heavy and sour, the meat poor in quality; canned peas furnished as "fresh" were of Swiss origin, very old, and poisoned by the tin and solder; there were no crackers, molasses, sugar, cheese, canned pears, or sauerkraut. To add insult to injury, the roofs of the barracks leaked and the doors and porches needed repair. According to Buchanan, all these conditions were to be "regretted."[37]

For all practical purposes the Red River War was over at the opening of 1875, although Davidson and Miles continued to

[35] Schofield to the PA, Fort Sill, December 31, 1874, File No. 3490–1874.
[36] Morrow to the AAG, Department of Texas, January 23, 1874, *ibid.*
[37] William Buchanan to the PA, Fort Concho, Texas, February 28, 1875, SLR, Department of Texas.

harass the Cheyennes and round up small parties of beaten and destitute Kiowas and Comanches. And on March 6 the main body of the Cheyennes reached their agency and surrendered. Thereafter only the Kwahadis of the Staked Plains remained out, and in June they too came in peacefully and surrendered at Fort Sill. Sheridan summed up the war in a letter to Sherman, "This campaign was not only very comprehensive, but the most successful of any Indian campaign in this country since its settlement by whites."[38] Sheridan should have been pleased. There was little to criticize in the operations of Mackenzie and Miles, while the columns of Buell and Davidson had scouted more miles, captured more Indians, and destroyed more lodges and property than any other regiments in the war.

Meanwhile, the process of dismounting, disarming, and imprisoning ringleaders of the outbreak had gone on apace. And all went smoothly until April, when serious trouble occurred at the Cheyenne agency. This affair was sheer tragedy for the Cheyennes and at the same time provoked a bitter controversy among officers of the Tenth that cast a shadow over the outstanding effort of the regiment during the war. All but two companies of buffalo soldiers had been transferred to Texas in March—Captain Keyes and Captain S. T. Norvell, with Companies D and M, remained at the Cheyenne agency to assist the garrison there under Lieutenant Colonel Thomas H. Neill in watching over large numbers of Cheyenne prisoners of war.[39]

On the afternoon of April 6 a small detachment of Fifth Infantry under Captain Andrew Bennett brought a few prisoners to the agency blacksmith to have leg irons fitted. Nearby a group

---

[38] *Annual Report of the Secretary of War for the Year 1875*, 58; *Annual Report of the Commissioner of Indian Affairs for the Year 1875*, 269; Pope to Sherman, February 23, 1875, File No. 3490–1874; Davidson to the AAG, Department of Texas, February 3, 1875, SLR, Department of Texas.

[39] Organizational Returns, Tenth Cavalry, February, 1875. Satanta and Big Tree, with most of their followers, surrendered early in the war at the Cheyenne agency. Satanta was sent back to the penitentiary at Huntsville, Texas, where he took his own life in October, 1878. Other prominent Kiowas and Comanches imprisoned were Lone Wolf, Woman's Heart, Bird Chief, White Horse, Red Otter, and Maman-ti of the former tribe, and Pe-che-wan, Buck Antelope, Dry Wood, and Little Prairie Hill of the latter. Lieutenant Pratt to Davidson, March 12, 1875, SLR, Department of Texas.

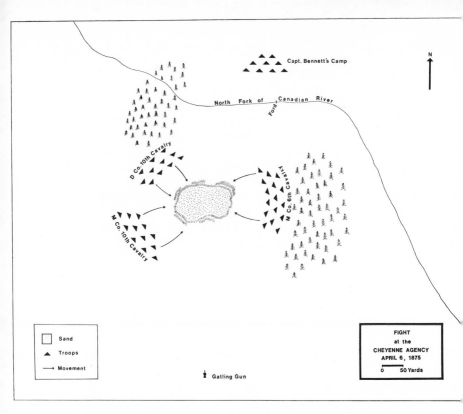

Sand

▲ Troops

→ Movement

Gatling Gun

North Fork of Canadian River

Ford

Capt. Bennett's Camp

D Co. 10th Cavalry

M Co. 10th Cavalry

M Co. 6th Cavalry

N

FIGHT
at the
CHEYENNE AGENCY
APRIL 6, 1875

0   50 Yards

of Indian women taunted the warriors as they were shackled. It was more than young Black Horse could bear. He kicked over the blacksmith and dashed madly for the Cheyenne camp. The guards called out to him to halt, but when he continued to run, they fired and killed him instantly. Some of the shots struck lodges in the Cheyenne camp and brought a volley of arrows which wounded two of Keyes's troopers who had just reached the scene. The fire from the camp was returned and the Cheyennes stampeded.

Between 100 and 150 warriors with a few women and children fled to an elevated sand hill on the south side of the North Fork of the Canadian, dug up arms and ammunition, apparently buried there prior to surrender, and entrenched themselves. Neill immediately ordered Captain William A. Rafferty, Sixth Cavalry, with M Company to dislodge the Indians, and shortly thereafter he sent Keyes and Norvell to assist him.

According to Neill's official report, Rafferty arrived on the east side of the sand hill in advance of Norvell and Keyes. He ordered his men to dismount, hold their fire, and advance. The Indians waited until he had approached within a short distance and then fired a volley into M Company, driving it back. When Keyes and Norvell arrived, they moved to the southwest side of the hill and opened fire.

It was near midafternoon when Neill arrived and surveyed the battleground. Long-range rifle fire was getting nowhere so he ordered a mounted charge. A courier from Norvell and Keyes brought word that the terrain on their front made a mounted charge impracticable, and Neill had a Gatling gun brought up to spray the Indian position at four hundred yards. He then ordered a charge on foot, but only Rafferty's men advanced and the attack failed. The Gatling gun again swept the sand hill and again a charge was ordered, but accurate Indian fire held off the troops until nightfall.

Neill called off the troopers and prepared for an early morning assault with every soldier at the agency, but the Indians fled during the night and a pursuit of nearly four hundred miles by a detachment from D and M of the Tenth failed to overtake them. The chase was taken up by Lieutenant Austin Henely, Sixth Cavalry, with sixty troopers from Fort Wallace. On April 23, Henely surprised the Cheyennes who had encamped on the North Fork of Sappa Creek in Kansas. Some of the Indians managed to escape, but nineteen warriors fought until all were killed along with eight women and children who remained with them.[40]

Back at the Cheyenne agency, Neill's report on the fight at the sand hill raised a storm of controversy. The report contained high praise for Rafferty and the troopers of the Sixth, and gave

[40] Neill to Lieutenant Colonel R. Williams, AAG, Department of the Missouri, April 7, 1874, SDLR, 1872–76, AGO; Lieutenant Henely to Major Hambright, Commanding at Fort Wallace, April 25, 1875, File No. 3490–1874. In addition to the twenty-seven Cheyennes killed by Henely, seven more were killed in the fight at the sand hill.

credit to Lieutenant Edward P. Turner of Keyes's company for leading a charge, but had not a word of commendation for the buffalo soldiers. Twice, according to Neill, he had ordered a charge, and twice the men of Norvell and Keyes had failed to support Rafferty. And he was supported by Lieutenant Turner who verbally charged that Keyes was a coward and the troopers of D and M a bunch of "god-damned Moacks who wouldn't fight; there was no charge in them."[41]

Captain Norvell was quick to counter both Neill and Turner. D and M had marched to the Cheyenne agency in February after a hard campaign with no more than thirty men to each company. While there they did not receive adequate shelter or clothing and at times were without rations. The men had not complained, however, and had performed their duties with customary cheerfulness. When the fight broke out and the Cheyennes fled, he and Keyes had marched swiftly toward the sand hill and, moving to Rafferty's left, had taken a position south of the hill and at a rough right angle from Rafferty.

Once in position, the companies dismounted and started to advance on foot when a courier arrived from Neill ordering them to fall back and mount, and they did. But then Norvell and Keyes had decided that a mounted charge was not practicable, due to the nature of the terrain, and Neill had been so informed. Orders were then received to advance on foot and the men pushed forward, but the Indian fire was accurate, a number of men were hit, there was no cover, and the advance halted.

It was at this time that the Gatling gun opened fire, and the balls came so close to D and M that Norvell felt momentarily he was being fired upon from the rear. Orders for another charge were received and the troopers of all three companies shouted and moved forward, but two men in his company (Norvell's) were shot down instantly and the other troopers had great difficulty in making headway in the deep sand on their front. Captain Keyes, and not Lieutenant Turner, with a few men, had succeeded in

41 Neill to Williams, April 7, 1874, SDLR, 1872–76, AGO; Norvell to the AAG, Department of the Missouri, May 15, 1875, *ibid.*

getting within sixty yards of the Indian position before being pinned down. Short-range firing had continued until dark when Neill ordered a general withdrawal.[42]

In concluding his report, Norvell demanded recognition for the buffalo soldiers. No such recognition was ever forthcoming, and higher headquarters apparently accepted Neill's version of the fight. Years later, Corporal Perry Hayman of Norvell's company wrote his version of the struggle at the sand hill. "As the first set of fours crossed the river, the Indians opened up on us and Corporal George Berry was wounded. We charged them. . . . While rolling around on the ground (when ordered to take cover) my rifle got some sand in the breech. I had to take a stick to clean it out, and in doing so I got in full view of the Indians. It was here that I got shot in the right side. I laid down behind a stump, and again those Indians fired a number of shots, but none of them hit me. Some came so close to me that they threw sand in my face. . . . I stayed there until dark, and then I managed to crawl away from my hiding place."[43] When pursuit was undertaken on the morning following the fight, Hayman related, "I crawled out of my tent and wanted to saddle my horse, but the captain made me go to the hospital."[44]

In the light of Hayman's story and in view of casualties incurred, Norvell's demand for recognition deserved a better fate. Rafferty's company had five men wounded, but only one severely. Keyes's D had eight men hit, five seriously, while Norvell's M had three wounded, one of them mortally. Of sixteen men wounded, eleven were among the buffalo soldiers, and they suffered the only fatal wound as well. For troopers who had refused to fight and "had no charge in them," they had certainly managed to get in the way of a disproportionate amount of lead.[45]

42 Norvell to the AAG, Department of the Missouri, May 15, 1875, *ibid.*
43 Quoted in an unpublished article by Don Rickey, Jr., "The Negro Regulars: A Combat Record, 1866–1891."
44 *Ibid.*
45 Casualties in D Company of the Tenth were: Sergeant Richard Lewis and Privates John Green, Robert Logan, David Saddler, Jacob Slimp, Ephraim Smith, Benjamin Smith, and Sammy Vincent. Norvell's M had Private Clark Young killed, Corporal Perry Hayman and Private George Berry wounded. Organizational Returns,

On this controversial note, the role of the buffalo soldiers in the Red River War came to an end. D and M were transferred to Texas to join the rest of their regiment in completing what their comrades in the Ninth had started—the task of making the vast reaches of West Texas safe for an advancing civilization.

Tenth Cavalry, April, 1875. Neill's report indicates nineteen men were wounded with five of these in Rafferty's company, but the Returns cited above do not bear out these figures. Norvell and Keyes preferred charges against Lieutenant Turner, and Colonel Grierson, who returned to the regiment in April, felt the case merited a general court-martial in justice to the Tenth, but the judge advocate general refused to hold an inquiry. Grierson to the AAG, Department of Texas, June 3, 1875, SLR, Department of Texas; Captain C. D. Emory to the AAG, Department of Texas, June 12, 1875, SLR, Department of Texas. Captain Stevens Thomson Norvell rose through the ranks in the Civil War and was commissioned a first lieutenant, Fifth Michigan Infantry, in February, 1863. He was assigned to the Tenth Cavalry as a captain in December, 1870, and was promoted to major in March, 1890. He ended a long career in 1898 as a lieutenant colonel in the Ninth Cavalry. Heitman, *op. cit.*, I, 753. Turner was a center of controversy until he resigned from the army in June, 1878, after eight years of service, *ibid.*, 974.

VI

THE TENTH IN WEST TEXAS

C OLONEL GRIERSON, after more than two years as superintendent of the Mounted Recruiting Service, resumed command of the Tenth Cavalry with headquarters at Fort Concho on
April 30, 1875. He found the regiment badly scattered. Six companies comprised the garrison at Concho, two others were at
Fort Griffin with Davidson in command of the post, two more
were at Fort McKavett, and one each at Forts Davis and Stockton.
In addition, the regiment was woefully undermanned, and, as
usual, poorly mounted. Some measure of relief was in order after
the rigors of the Red River War for rest, refitting, and recruitment,
but conditions on the Texas frontier did not permit any such
luxury.[1]

Small parties of "out" Comanches were active in the vicinity
of Forts Concho and Griffin, the Kickapoos and Lipans continued to harass settlers and ranchers along the Río Grande, while
depredations by outlaw bands of Mescalero and Warm Springs
Apaches were on the increase. White and Mexican bandits were
having a field day relieving owners of their herds, and Mexican
revolutionaries remained a source of real concern. Needs notwithstanding, the Tenth plunged into this maelstrom of violence
and lawlessness, while Grierson pleaded with General Ord for at
least two hundred more troopers and the animals to mount his
regiment properly.[2]

Bold white horse-thieves got quick attention from the Tenth.

1 Organizational Returns, Tenth Cavalry, April, 1875.
2 Grierson to the AAG, Department of Texas, May 5, 1875, SLR, Department
of Texas. Grierson had a total of 650 men and even fewer horses. Many of these
animals were old, broken down, or otheriwse unserviceable.

Five men, clumsily disguised as Indians, attempted to run off part of the herd of Captain Baldwin's Company I encamped near Fort Concho, but alert guards engaged them in a gun fight, put four of the thieves to flight, and captured one with a smoking pistol in his hand. The prisoner was turned over to civil authorities at Saint Angela, but a tolerant jury saw fit to release him.

Near Fort Griffin another gang had more success. It succeeded in stealing a number of ponies belonging to friendly Lipan Indians living adjacent to the post. Lieutenant George Evans, E Company, with four troopers investigated the theft, and with a Lipan serving as guide, soon found the trail. It led southeast to the pasture of a man named Cooksie, and here one of the stolen animals was found. Cooksie proved most helpful. He had no idea how the pony got into his pasture, but the thieves were undoubtedly a party of men who had recently passed his place and gone to the village of Picketville.

Inquiries at Picketville revealed no such party of men, and Evans returned to Cooksie's by a circuitous route and found another stolen pony tethered in some thick brush. Shortly thereafter Cooksie was encountered riding a horse that the Lipan identified immediately as one of those they were looking for. Cooksie wasted no time in conversation but spurred at a dead run into some heavy brush with the troopers at his heels. He managed to make his escape, however, and apparently kept right on running. Evans learned later that Cooksie and some companions had decided to leave the country.[3]

Renegade Comanches were also busy gathering up horses at outlying ranches and, when pursued, fled into the trackless wastes of the Staked Plains. Few such raiders could be overtaken, although on occasion they paid for their audacity. On May 6, 1875, an alert patrol under Sergeant John Marshall of Company A intercepted a party of eight Indians near Catfish Creek, killed one, and scattered the others in a running fight of seven miles. The following day on the North Concho, Lieutenant Thad Jones,

[3] Captain Baldwin to the PA, Fort Concho, Texas, May 28, 1875, *ibid.;* Lieutenant Evans to the PA, Fort Griffin, Texas, June 18, 1875, SDLR, 1872–76, AGO.

with a detachment of H Company, overtook a small party and recovered thirty-three head of stock.[4]

These raids were on a small scale, but the swift hit and rapid run tactics kept post commanders busy trying to fend off the attacks that often gained the troopers nothing more than exhausted mounts and bad tempers. The activities of a few Comanches were demanding far too much time and energy, and in May General Ord decided to settle this business once and for all. Since Grierson was unfamiliar with the country, Colonel Shafter was ordered from Fort Duncan to Concho to organize an expedition for the purpose of sweeping the Staked Plains of hostile bands. Shafter was also given an additional task. The westward flow of settlement was slapping at the edges of the Plains, and Shafter's orders required that he "show in detail, the resources of the country passed over, looking to its adaptability for cultivation and stock-raising" and to pay special attention to the location of bodies of water.[5]

Buffalo soldiers formed the backbone of Shafter's force. When preparations were complete, the command consisted of six companies of the Tenth, two companies of the Twenty-fourth Infantry, and one company of the Twenty-fifth Infantry. Lieutenants John L. Bullis and C. R. Ward led a body of Seminole and Tonkawa scouts. Sixty-five wagons drawn by six-mule teams and a pack train of seven hundred mules carried supplies for a four-month campaign, and a beef herd was driven with the command to provide a ready supply of fresh meat.[6]

The long column left Fort Concho in the steaming heat of July 14, 1875, and headed northwest for the Fresh Fork of the Brazos, some 180 miles away, to establish a supply camp. A week later at Rendlebrock Springs, about midway between the North Concho and the Colorado rivers, Shafter detached Captain Nolan

[4] Sergeant Marshall to the PA, Fort Concho, May 12, 1875, SLR, Department of Texas; Lieutenant Jones to the PA, Fort Concho, Texas, May 7, 1875, *ibid.*

[5] The AAG, Department of Texas, to Shafter, June 30, 1875, SLR Relating to Texas, 1875–76, AGO, NA (hereinafter cited as RT, AGO).

[6] Shafter to the AAG, September 29, 1875, *ibid.;* Post Returns, Fort Concho, July, 1875; Organizational Returns, Tenth Cavalry, July, 1875. Companies of the Tenth were A, C, F, I, G, and L under Captains Nolan, Viele, Kennedy, Baldwin, Lee, and Little.

143

with A and C companies of the Tenth, with twenty days' rations, to scout toward the west and rejoin the main command at the supply camp.

Nolan pushed west to Mustang Springs, which he reached on July 27, and next morning picked up the trail of a lone pony leading northwest. The trail grew larger as others fed into it, and by early afternoon the scouts sighted a large body of Indians to their front. Nolan made "all possible haste," but all he got for his pains was a deserted camp. Another mile and a half brought a second and larger village which the Indians had also abandoned, along with most of their supplies. Nolan halted and destroyed both camps, which contained seventy-four lodges, cooking utensils, robes, saddles, and a six months' supply of food. It was late afternoon by the time the work of destruction had been completed, and Nolan decided to encamp and resume pursuit early the next morning.

Dawn brought a hard rain which held the column up until well past noon when pursuit was again undertaken, but after a slogging march of eight miles, Nolan gave up hopes of overtaking the fleeing Indians. From a muddy bivouac he sent a report by courier to Shafter, and on the following morning he set out northeast for the supply camp on the Fresh Fork of the Brazos, which was reached August 6. Shafter was pleased with Nolan's destruction of the camps but much upset over what he regarded as a lack of vigorous pursuit. Ten days later, with the approval of General Ord, Shafter relieved Nolan of his command and ordered him to Fort Concho to await a court-martial.[7]

On August 5, Shafter left his supply camp with G, I, F, and L companies of the Tenth and a detachment of the Seminole and Tonkawa scouts. Rations were carried on pack mules, and a single wagon was used for medical supplies and to carry the sick. The intention was to run down the Indians Nolan had encountered, but it marked the beginning of one of the most demanding marches ever made by the buffalo soldiers—or any soldiers, for that matter.

[7] Nolan to Shafter, August 1, 1875, RT, AGO; Shafter to the AAG, Department of Texas, August 5, 1875; *ibid.;* the AAG, Department of Texas, to Shafter, August 16, 1875, *ibid.*

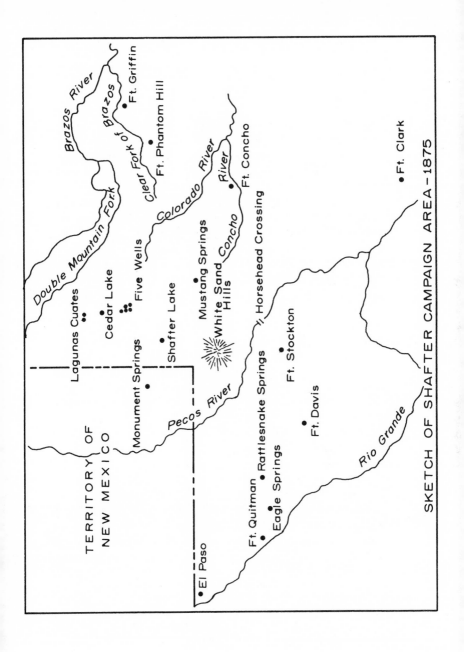

SKETCH OF SHAFTER CAMPAIGN AREA – 1875

Above: *Brigade drill of Tenth Cavalry soldiers.* (Courtesy National Archives)

Below: *Tenth Cavalry buffalo soldiers bringing Indian prisoners to court at Tucson, Arizona.* (Courtesy National Archives)

Ninth Cavalry drill on parade ground of Fort Davis, Texas, about 1875.
(Courtesy National Archives)

Ninth Cavalry, Fort Davis, Texas. (Courtesy National Park Service)

Aerial view of crumbling remains of once-thriving Fort Davis. (Courtesy U.S. Signal Corps, National Archives)

The route was almost due west for some one hundred miles to a lake called Casas Amarillas. Shafter had hopes of striking the Indians at this prominent watering place. No Indians were found, however, and Shafter

> . . . took a southwest course, hoping to find water sufficient in holes on the prairies, which I did for two days; but at the expiration of the 3rd day's march, finding no water I had either to strike for the Pecos or turn back. I determined to make for the Pecos, and did so the next night, marching in the two days and one night seventy seven miles, with water but once (a heavy shower of rain). From there I went down the Pecos as far as HorseHead Crossing, and after resting my stock a few days and getting rations from Stockton, I left the Pecos on the 5th of September at Pecos Falls, forty miles above HorseHead Crossing, on my return across the plains to Supply Camp which I expected to reach in ten days.[8]

Ten days turned into twenty, for as Shafter turned northeast and skirted the White Sand Hills, he failed to find water and had to turn westward into New Mexico by forced marches to reach Dug Spring on September 13. Here a large Indian trail was found leading north, and Shafter determined to follow it, although "we had but six days rations, and the heat, dust, sand and want of water had told greatly on the stock."[9]

Shortly after midnight, however, a party of warriors numbering about thirty came in on Shafter's back trail and fired into G Company. The guards returned the fire immediately and the hostiles scattered with no harm done on either side. At daybreak Shafter was in pursuit with forty-five picked troopers and followed the trail for twenty miles to an abandoned camp and a very large spring. The rest of the command was brought up and spent the better part of a day burning lodges and other camp equipage, while a detail went to a nearby hill and erected a stone marker seven and one-half feet high which could be seen for miles in every direction. It served as a beacon to guide the thirsty traveler to "Monument Spring."

[8] Shafter to the AAG, Department of Texas, September 29, 1875, *ibid*.
[9] *Ibid*.

145

Meanwhile, the Indians had scattered in all directions and Shafter decided to give up the chase. Rations were very low, the animals badly worn, and his base was two hundred miles away. These considerations turned the column northeast toward the supply camp which was reached on September 25 after an absence of fifty-two days and a march of more than 860 miles through country of which "nothing was known before by troops." Twenty-nine horses were the only casualties. In Shafter's absence, Captain Viele with A and C companies of the Tenth had crossed the Staked Plains to Portales, New Mexico, and, after returning to the supply camp for rations, had pushed north to Palo Duro Cañon to scout that old hostile "winter resort," but he had found no sign of Indians.[10]

Shafter remained in camp until October 12 resting his stock and reoutfitting his tattered troopers; then he moved southwestward to the Double Mountain Fork of the Brazos. Here he detached Captain Baldwin with F and I to scout through the Mucha Que country and on south to Sulphur Springs and Big Spring. Baldwin reached Big Spring after a march of 340 miles accompanied by much suffering, which included one stretch of thirty-eight hours without water. After giving his durable troopers a brief rest, he fanned out patrols to the south and west.

Shafter also moved south to Double Lakes where he left one company of infantry and then on southwest to Laguna Sabinas (Cedar Lake), a large lake but too salty for drinking purposes. Good water was found, however, by digging near the edge. Bullis, with his scouts, had preceded Shafter and found a large Indian encampment, but the Indians had escaped. He had captured twenty-five ponies, fifty sacks of mesquite beans, about four thousand pounds of buffalo meat, many buffalo hides, lodge poles, and cooking utensils, all of which he had destroyed.[11]

From Laguna Sabinas the trail was followed some thirty miles

[10] *Ibid.*; Organizational Returns, Tenth Cavalry, September, 1875. Shafter's scout convinced him that the Plains were clear of Comanches and that the Indians both he and Nolan had encountered were Apaches from New Mexico.

[11] Shafter to Colonel J. H. Taylor, AAG, Department of Texas, October 19, 1875, RT, AGO. Bullis came upon the Indian camp on the night of October 17.

south to "five large wells." The Indians had passed on south, and Shafter detached Lieutenant Andrew Geddes, Twenty-fifth Infantry, with Companies G and L of the Tenth and the Seminole scouts "to follow the trail as long as possible." Shafter, meanwhile, turned westward and marched sixty-three miles to Monument Spring where he arrived on October 23.

Geddes took Shafter literally and pursued the fleeing Indians with dogged determination as they turned southeast, west, and then south again to throw him off. He refused to be shaken, however, and on November 2 he overtook his quarry within sight of the Río Grande and charged. He deserved a better fate—most of the warriors had left the camp and he managed to kill only one warrior, capture four women and a small boy, and destroy the camp. It was a trail-weary command that turned back to Fort Clark for a brief rest and then marched on to Fort Concho where the troopers arrived on November 27, having covered more than 650 miles of very rough country since leaving Shafter at Laguna Sabinas.[12]

Shafter, at Monument Spring, found a large Indian trail on October 24 and followed it to the White Sand Hills where he decided to turn back, for the trail pointed in the direction of Baldwin's area of operations. Returning north to Laguna Sabinas, Shafter sent Lieutenant Lebo with A Company to Casas Amarillas. No Indians were found, but a lake was discovered which, not inappropriately, was named Lebo's Lake. When Lebo returned, Shafter marched back south and joined Baldwin at Big Spring on November 8. Five days later the command moved northeast to Tobacco Creek, established a new supply camp, and on November 15 began another sweep across the Plains to Monument Spring which was reached after six days of heavy going. Turning back east, Shafter reached the "five wells" and here received orders from Ord to break up his expedition and return to Fort Duncan.

Shafter's expedition killed but a single Indian and captured

12 Major A. P. Morrow to the AAG, Department of Texas, November 10, 1875, *ibid.;* Organizational Returns, Tenth Cavalry, November, 1875; Shafter to the AAG, Department of Texas, January 4, 1876, RT, AGO.

only five others. However, it had swept the Plains clear of Indians, and, more importantly, it provided the first thorough exploration of the Staked Plains and forever dispelled the myths and fears surrounding this heretofore mysterious and uncharted region.

Shafter's report and accompanying maps would surely have warmed the heart of a Staked Plains Chamber of Commerce had such existed. From Rendlebrock Spring north to the Fresh Fork of the Brazos was slightly rolling country with excellent grass and considerable mesquite—wonderful cattle country. North of Casas Amarillas was "an excellent place for sheep or horses." For nearly sixty miles east of the White Sand Hills was high, rolling prairie with fine grass. Shafter was cautious concerning water but indicated there were several good springs near the edge of Double Lakes and at Laguna Sabinas water could be obtained from dug springs.[13]

The report was widely circulated and read, and spawned a swift movement of cattlemen, sheepmen, and homesteaders to claim and settle this last great home of the Southern Plains Indians. But if the report had praise for much of the country over which Shafter had campaigned, it was silent in this regard on the officers and men who accompanied him. Except for Captain Nolan it neither condemned nor praised—it all but ignored them. Few incoming settlers knew, and perhaps even fewer cared, that over the trails they trod a tattered, patient, and bone-weary buffalo soldier had gone before.[14]

While half the regiment fought killing heat, thirst, and dust over hundreds of miles with Shafter, the remaining companies of the Tenth had also been hard at work. A detachment of thirty troopers was detailed for construction work on the United States Military Telegraph Line to connect Fort Concho and Fort Griffin.

[13] Shafter to the AAG, Department of Texas, January 4, 1876, RT, AGO. Shafter's report, as indicated, had considerable influence on Southern Plains settlement, but the Adjutant General was apparently not impressed for he approved a deduction of $52.00 from Shafter's pay for authorizing Captain Baldwin and I of the Tenth to expend two thousand rounds of ammunition "in hunting to provide food and improve aim."

[14] Shafter to the AG, USA, January 6, 1876, Correspondence, AGO, Document File No. 1876, NA.

Others provided the essential escort to surveying parties of the Texas and Pacific Railroad, stages, trains, and cattle herds.

The greatest activity and concern, however, was directed toward the Río Grande where conditions all but defied improvement. In the spring of 1876 guerrilla bands of Porfiristas and Lerdistas fought for control of the north Mexican frontier, with the losing parties frequently crossing to the American side of the river for sanctuary, and they were not averse to robbery and murder to recoup losses of arms, animals, and supplies. With these diversions combined with continuing raids of Mexican Indians and bandits, there was more than enough activity to keep every available soldier in almost constant motion.[15]

Troops were too few to guard the many river crossings, and scattered patrols were ineffective. Pursuit of brigands and raiding Indians rarely produced results, for escape, as in past years, required the mere crossing of the river. A change of policy was essential if peace was to prevail along the border, and in the spring of 1876 it came. General Ord was instructed to use his discretion in allowing troops in his department to continue pursuit across the Río Grande. Revolutionary bands crossing to the American side were to be rounded up as quickly as possible, arrested, disarmed, and interned until such time as they were prepared to give parole that they would not attempt to organize on American soil or disturb the peace of their native country.[16]

Mexican Indians soon learned that a new day had dawned. Kickapoos and Lipans had reaped a considerable harvest of cattle and horses in the spring and early summer of 1876, and in May they taunted the buffalo soldiers by quick thrusts within virtual gunshot of Forts Davis and Stockton. Efforts to overtake these raiders proved futile, for they always had a head start in the in-

15 Parkes, *op. cit.*, 283; *Annual Report of the Secretary of War for the Year 1876*, 26; Captain L. H. Carpenter to the PA, Fort Davis, December 2, 1875, SDLR, 1872–76, AGO. Carpenter voiced an old complaint—Mexican authorities encouraged, tolerated, and provided ready markets for loot brought back by raiding Indians from Texas, and he urged a more aggressive policy.
16 The AG to Commanding General, Department of Texas, March 10, 1876, File No. 1653; *H.R. Resolution No. 96*, April 4, 1876, 44 Cong., 2 sess.; Sheridan to Townsend, April 18, 1876, File No. 1653; *Annual Report of the Secretary of War for the Year 1876*, 493.

evitable dash for the Río Grande and safety. It was enough for General Ord—the time had come to "use his discretion." In July he ordered Colonel Shafter at Fort Duncan to form a strong column and attack a large camp of these Indians known to be in the vicinity of Saragossa [Zaragoza], Mexico.[17]

Shafter quickly assembled a force consisting of Companies B, E, and K, Tenth Cavalry, Lieutenant Bullis and a party of Seminole scouts, and detachments of the Twenty-fourth and Twenty-fifth Infantry. The command marched upriver and some twenty-five miles above the mouth of the Pecos splashed across the Río Grande into Mexico. It was a long-awaited opportunity for the buffalo soldiers and one that perhaps would never have come had General Ord not been so hard-pressed for cavalry. In his annual report Ord wrote:

> I must remark, however, that the use of colored soldiers to cross the river after raiding Indians, is in my opinion, impolitic, not because they have shown any want of bravery, but because their employment is much more offensive to Mexican inhabitants than white soldiers.[18]

A buffalo soldier might have replied that the attitude of Mexican citizens along the river left much to be desired in any case.

Shafter's column pushed southwestward for five days when a halt was called. There were growing fears that a Mexican force might cross the back trail and cut off a return to the river. Shafter proposed that he encamp, while Bullis with the Seminoles and Lieutenant George Evans, Tenth Cavalry, and twenty picked troopers would march on to the Indian village.

Bullis and Evans needed no urging. In just twenty-five hours they covered 110 miles and located the village of twenty-three lodges some five miles from Saragossa. At dawn on July 30 the village was assaulted, and after the first volley a savage hand-to-hand fight—clubbed carbine against thrusting lance—swirled

[17] *R.H. Doc. No. 1*, Part 2, 45 Cong., 2 sess., 81; Medical history, Fort Davis, Texas, Vol. 9; Edward S. Wallace, "General John Lapham Bullis, Thunderbolt of the Texas Frontier," *Southwestern Historical Quarterly*, Vol. LV, No. 1 (July, 1951), 82.

[18] *H.R. Exec. Doc. No. 1*, Part 2, 45 Cong., 2 sess., 80–81.

among the lodges. In a matter of minutes it was over with the Indians in full flight, but they left fourteen dead warriors, four of their women, and ninety horses behind. Bullis, with only three wounded, quickly destroyed the village and retreated to Shafter's camp with a force of Mexican regulars close on his heels. The united command then marched back to the Río Grande and crossed. Here the only loss to the command occurred. Trooper Joseph Titus of Company B was drowned.[19]

The buffalo soldiers were quick to follow up the strike at Saragossa. Captain Lebo with B, E, and K crossed the river on August 4 and headed for the Santa Rosa Mountains. An eight-day march led to a small Kickapoo nest of ten lodges which was destroyed, and sixty horses and mules were captured. Following this success, Grierson put virtually his entire regiment into the field. B, E, K, and M scoured the Pecos and Devils rivers area, and then moved into the Guadalupe Mountains, scattering small bands in all directions. A, D, F, and L operating out of Concho scouted more than a thousand miles between July and the end of the year. With the Tenth on an all-out hunt, it was becoming difficult for an "honest" thief to make a living. Not until December did the companies come in for a much needed rest.[20]

In partial compensation for a year of constant field operations, Grierson gave a Christmas party for the entire garrison at Fort Concho. The regimental band, ever a source of pride and satisfaction, provided the music while officers and men feasted on sandwiches, turkey, buffalo tongue, olives, cheese, biscuits, sweet and sour pickles, candy, raisins, pears, apples, and four kinds of cake —all washed down with gallons of coffee. A rare treat indeed for a buffalo soldier.[21]

If the winter rest was sweet, it was also of necessity short. The

---

[19] Shafter to the AAG, Department of Texas, August 3, 1876, File No. 1653; Wallace, *loc. cit.*, 83; Kenneth Wiggins Porter, "The Seminole Negro-Indian Scouts, 1870–1881," *Southwestern Historical Quarterly*, LV (January, 1952), 370; Organizational Returns, Tenth Cavalry, August, 1876.

[20] Organizational Returns, Tenth Cavalry, July–November, 1876; Post Returns, Fort Concho, Fort Clark, Fort Davis, and Fort Stockton, August–November, 1876.

[21] Mrs. Grierson to Robert Grierson, December 31, 1876, Grierson Papers.

undermanned Tenth was the only cavalry regiment in the whole of West Texas. With an authorized strength of 1,202 men, Grierson could count not more than 900 as the new year opened. So few men could at best provide a porous defense for hundreds of miles of frontier. Porfirio Díaz had defeated Lerdo after a year of civil war, but followers of the latter remained active along the Río Grande, as did bandit chieftains who defied all efforts of the new government to bring them to heel. The Kickapoos and Lipans had been hard hit but still continued to conduct small-scale raids, and they were joined by disgruntled Mescaleros from their reservation at Fort Stanton, New Mexico. And reports reached Fort Concho that restive Comanches were once again prowling the Staked Plains.[22] Efforts of the buffalo soldiers to meet and defeat these old enemies resulted in a mixture of triumph and tragedy.

On January 10, Lieutenant Bullis and his Seminole scouts teamed up with Captain Keyes and ninety troopers of B and D at Fort Clark for another march into Mexico after the Kickapoos and Lipans. A "hastily abandoned" camp was found and destroyed in the Santa Rosa Mountains. The north bank of the river was re-gained without a loss.[23] In February and March detachments of the Tenth made frequent dashes into Mexico with little result other than finding abandoned camps. F Company, however, suffered a sore loss in the Santa Rosa Mountains when gallant Sergeant Sandy Winchester was accidentally shot and killed. Sandy had been a member of F since its organization and had participated in the regiment's first action against the Cheyennes in Kansas on August 2, 1867.[24]

The swift forays of the buffalo soldiers kept the Mexican Indians constantly on the move and reduced the number of raids, but the Mexican government, alarmed at their growing frequency, protested vigorously. The protests were ignored, and in May the

[22] *H.R. Exec. Doc. No. 1,* Part 2, 45 Cong., 2 sess., 33; Parkes, *op. cit.,* 284; Organizational Returns, Tenth Cavalry, January, 1877; Medical History, Fort Concho, Vol. 404.

[23] Wallace, *loc. cit.,* 83; Organizational Returns, Tenth Cavalry, January, 1877.

[24] Organizational Returns, Tenth Cavalry, January–March, 1877.

United States minister to Mexico, J. W. Foster, telegraphed the American Secretary of State, William Evarts, that the Díaz government was sending forces under capable officers to the frontier to assist in curbing lawlessness.[25]

The initial effort of the Mexican troops was directed toward curbing revolutionary activity. On June 10 they attacked a party of Lerdistas above the mouth of Devils River, and when the latter fled to the north side of the Río Grande, the government troops crossed and attacked them on American soil. Captain Joseph Kelley with E Company, on patrol near San Felipe, rode immediately to the site of the attack where he arrested and disarmed fifty Lerdistas, but Mexican federal troops had crossed to their side of the river before he arrived.[26]

Small parties of bedraggled Lerdistas continued to cross into Texas, and on August 5 Major Schofield, while scouting out of Fort Duncan with a detachment of the Tenth, surprised and captured forty-four of these revolutionaries, forty-three horses, and a large quantity of arms and ammunition. With the twin blows of Kelley and Schofield and increasing pressure from Díaz troops, enthusiasm for revolution suffered considerable erosion.[27]

The Kickapoos and Lipans still managed to evade the ceaseless patrols and to depredate in Texas. On June 21 a small party of Lipans crossed near San Felipe and rode northeastward into Edwards County. Near Camp Wood they surprised farmer John Leary who was taking a siesta beside his wagon. The Indians opened fire, wounding Leary in the wrist, but with the courage of a cornered lion he pulled his revolver and cocked it by pushing the hammer against the wagon bed. In this manner he succeeded in driving off his attackers, but they ran off a horse. The raiders continued northward, stealing stock in both Kerr and Kimble counties before turning back toward their camps in Mexico.[28]

25 J. W. Foster to William Evarts, May 28, 1877, File No. 1653.

26 General Sheridan to General Townsend, June 12, 1877, *ibid.;* Organizational Returns, Tenth Cavalry, June, 1877.

27 The AAG, Military Division of the Missouri, to General Townsend, August 8, 1877, File No. 1653.

28 Statement of John M. Leary, June 21, 1877, *ibid.;* Faltin and Schriener to Dr. Peterson, July 22, 1877, *ibid.;* Organizational Returns, Tenth Cavalry, June–July, 1877.

153

Detachments of buffalo soldiers working the Río Grande both up and down the river from Fort Duncan failed to intercept the Lipans. The success of this raid encouraged others, and when the Mexican government failed to respond to calls for more energetic action against these hostiles, General Ord authorized another large-scale expedition into Mexico. Lieutenant Bullis with his Seminoles and Captain Lebo with a battalion of buffalo soldiers gathered at Pinto Creek near Fort Duncan. The Río Grande was crossed on September 28, and the command set out for the head-waters of San Diego Creek where a Lipan village was discovered. The attack was launched at once, but the Indians wanted no part of a fight and fled helter-skelter. Torches were applied to lodges and equipment, and by September 30 Bullis and Lebo were back in the camp on the Pinto.[29]

Two weeks later Bullis and his scouts were on the move again searching along the Devils and Pecos rivers. Finding nothing, Bullis returned to the Río Grande and crossed on October 28. A trail was found almost at once and followed to a large cañon near the Santa Rosa Mountains. The Indians were just driving out a herd of horses as Bullis came up and opened fire. After a hot skirmish, Bullis was forced to retire, for the warriors were too numerous for his small body of scouts. He set out for Fort Clark where he joined forces with Captain S. B. M. Young, Eighth Cavalry, then ready to take the field with a detachment of his regiment, and Company C, Tenth Cavalry, under Lieutenant William Beck.

Young, Bullis, and Beck left Clark on November 10 with the intention of crossing the river and marching "across that point of Mexican territory extending north in what is known as the 'Big Bend.' " The column found the going extremely rough, and on one day covered only six miles, as men and horses were forced to step carefully and ropes were tied to the pack mules to prevent a fall off precipitous trails. Despite the precautions, eleven ani-

29 The AAG, District of the Nueces, to Captain Lebo, September 13, 1877, File No. 1653; Organizational Returns, Tenth Cavalry, September, 1877; Porter, "Seminole-Negro Scouts," 374.

mals did slip and were lost along with nearly all the medicine and supplies. There was no thought of turning back, however, and a warm trail leading toward Mount Carmel was found on November 28.

Cold so bitter it froze water in the canteens struck as they pushed on with the buffalo soldiers suffering intensely, as they "were without great coats." And grim persistence was rewarded, for the Indians were overtaken in a steep cañon near Mount Carmel. The warriors turned to make a stand, and a blazing fight raged for a few minutes before the Indians broke and fled with troopers and scouts in hot pursuit. Eventually the quarry was lost in the broken country, and Young recalled his scattered force to round up twenty-three animals and destroy a large quantity of robes, hides, dried meat, saddles, and ropes.

This task accomplished, the return to Fort Clark began. The men were soon half frozen, for their clothing was in tatters and there was no escape from the bone-chilling cold. The post was a welcome sight on December 3, and the command received one of Shafter's rare commendations:

> Officers and men were exposed to very severe weather and having only pack animals were necessarily restricted to the small allowance carried on the saddle. The country scouted in was exceedingly difficult, more so than any part of Texas, officers and men deserving great credit for the patience, fortitude and energy, they exhibited on this scout, they are to be complimented on its successful issue.[30]

Campaigning on the Río Grande frontier had ended for the year on a note of achievement. Meanwhile, far to the north, other troopers of the Tenth had been busy with renegade Comanches and Mescaleros and, in so doing, had produced one of the most stark dramas in the history of the Southern Plains.

In the spring of 1877 a strong band of Comanches under Black Horse left their reservation and fled west to the Staked Plains. They made life precarious for numerous parties of buffalo hunters, and

---

30 Captain S. B. M. Young to the AAAG, District of the Nueces, December 18, 1877, File No. 1653; Lieutenant Bullis to the PA, Fort Clark, Texas, December 22, 1877, *ibid.*

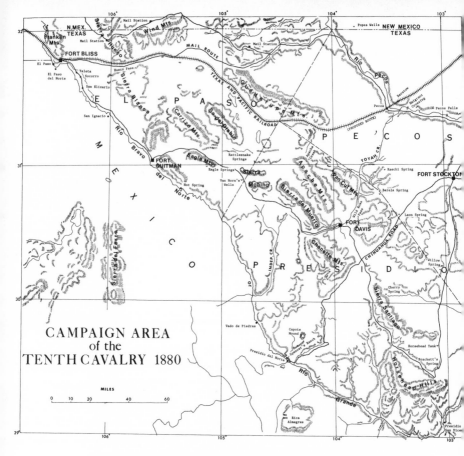

CAMPAIGN AREA
of the
TENTH CAVALRY 1880

MILES

0   10   20   40   60

on April 9 Captain Lee with C Company left Fort Griffin to search for them. On May 4 he located and attacked a Comanche camp at Lake Quemado, Texas, killed four warriors, and captured six women and sixty-nine horses. First Sergeant Charles Baker was shot in the breast and mortally wounded during this action. A detachment of I Company out of Fort Richardson also scouted more than a thousand miles for these Indians, but without result.

Small parties of Mescaleros were also on the prowl. In the spring and early summer, several stage stations along the San Antonio–El Paso road were attacked, and Sergeant Joseph Claggett with a detachment of H Company from Fort Davis pursued one band into the Guadalupe Mountains before losing the trail. Claggett was convinced that the Indians were from the Mescalero reservation. Lieutenant Charles Ayres, also of H Company, pursued a party of warriors in the same direction but lost them when eight of his horses died of exhaustion.[31]

The Tenth was committed too heavily along the Río Grande to permit of simultaneous sweeps against the Mescaleros and Comanches, but Grierson ordered Captain Nolan, who had escaped Shafter's displeasure with a reprimand, to take A Company and punish any marauders he could find on the Staked Plains. On July 10, Nolan, Lieutenant Charles Cooper, and sixty troopers with a four-wagon train left Fort Concho and marched up the North Concho River. The weather was dry and very hot and on the second day out one of the troopers suffered sunstroke, although he soon recovered. Nolan moved on to the headwaters and then northwest to Big Spring where he turned due north to the Colorado, and across that stream to Bull Creek in present Borden County, Texas. Here Nolan found a suitable site and established a supply camp. He also found reinforcements in the form of twenty-eight buffalo hunters who were out looking for Indians who had stolen stock from them.

With the hunters was a veteran guide, José Tafoya, who had been of great assistance to Colonel Mackenzie in his campaigns on the Staked Plains, and Nolan welcomed the opportunity to secure his services. Tafoya believed the Indians were at or near Laguna Sabinas due west of the supply camp, and Nolan and the hunters prepared to march for that point. Having no pack mules, Nolan took the eight lead mules from his six-mule teams to carry his rations and forage, and sent his wagons back to Fort Concho for additional supplies.

On the evening of July 19 Nolan set out westward with Lieutenant Cooper, forty troopers, and twenty-two buffalo hunters. Sergeant Allsup and nineteen men were left behind to care for

31 Organizational Returns, Tenth Cavalry, May–June, 1877; Medical History, Fort Griffin, Vol. 103; Post Returns, Fort Richardson, May, 1877.

the supply camp. On July 21, as the column made its way along Tobacco Creek, the first Indians were seen. They proved to be a party of Comanches under Chief Quanah Parker, but they had a pass from the Indian agent at Fort Sill which had been countersigned by Colonel Mackenzie, commanding at that post, indicating that the chief was on a mission to induce runaway Indians back to the reservation. Nolan was unhappy, but "he and party were liberally supplied with Government Horses, Equipments, Arms, Ammunition and Rations, I did not feel authorized in detaining him."[32] After the Indians left, Nolan marched on to Laguna Sabinas, which was reached on the evening of July 22. But it had been a dry year, and where Shafter had found plenty of water in 1875, Nolan was forced to dig holes and dip out water by the cupful.

The command rested for a day while Tafoya and a few of the hunters scouted south to the Five Wells for signs of Indians and also for water. They returned next day, after a waterless trip of thirty hours, to report that an Indian trail had been found running northeast toward Double Lakes. Nolan set out on the late afternoon of July 24, preferring to march at night to avoid the searing heat, and reached Double Lakes about noon the following day. No sign of Indians was found, and once again the men were forced to dig for precious water.

The guide, with some of the hunters, rode west to Dry Lake, a distance of about seventeen miles, while Nolan remained in camp. Next morning two of the hunters returned to report that Tafoya had seen a party of forty Indians just west of Dry Lake, and Nolan saddled up and marched for that point where he arrived about sundown and joined Tafoya. There was no water, but the guide assured Nolan a supply could be obtained about fifteen to twenty miles westward along the trail taken by the Indians. Nolan made a fateful decision. He decided to push on in the direction indicated by the guide and did so until nightfall when a dry camp was made—Tafoya had been unable to find water.

[32] Nolan to the AAG, Department of Texas, August 20, 1877, LR, Department of Texas, 1877, AGO, RG 94, NA (hereinafter cited as LR, AGO).

Next morning the trail was followed over gently undulating country dotted occasionally by bunches of stunted mesquite, scrub oak, and patches of grass over which the thirsty troopers dragged their blankets in hopes of obtaining a bit of moisture for their parched throats. Nolan was forced to call a halt after twenty-five miles. His animals were giving out and the Indians, apparently aware of the pursuit, had scattered. While the men rested, Tafoya searched for the main trail, which he managed to find, and the weary, thirsty column moved out again, plodding slowly westward into a barren sandy plain.[33]

After a few miles the heavy going, heat, and lack of water began to exact their toll. One trooper fell from his mount of sunstroke and others were beginning to straggle. Nolan, now genuinely concerned, asked Tafoya how much farther it was to water, and when told it was another six or seven miles, he gave the guide one of his private horses and urged him to lead on as rapidly as possible. The command would follow with as much speed as the condition of men and animals permitted.

Tafoya rode off in a westerly direction and then turned northeast with Nolan doing his utmost to keep up, but this proved impossible for two more troopers suffered sunstroke, and others were so dehydrated and exhausted that they kept falling from their saddles. Nolan halted briefly, detailed Sergeant William Umbles to stay with the two sick men, picked eight of his strongest men, gave them all the canteens they could carry, and sent them on to follow the guide. It was the last he would see of those eight men for many days.

Nolan limped on for a few more miles and then was forced to bivouac. Shortly thereafter Sergeant Umbles and the two sick men passed within easy hailing distance but failed to respond to repeated shouts and disappeared in the darkness. Eleven men were now missing, the guide had not returned, and Nolan's plight was becoming desperate.

At daylight on July 28 there was still no sign of Tafoya or

33 *Ibid.;* Curtis W. Nunn, "Eighty-six Hours Without Water on the Texas Plains," *Southwestern Historical Quarterly,* XLIII (January, 1940), 356.

the eight troopers, and the buffalo hunters were "scattered over the plains, their ponies gone." Nolan and Cooper conferred with the hunters, and the decision was made to follow in the direction taken by the guide the day before, but after some fifteen miles with no sign of water or Tafoya, Nolan decided to turn back and make for the Double Lakes some fifty-five miles to the southeast. The buffalo hunters disagreed; water must be nearby somewhere to the northeast and they bade Nolan farewell.[34]

Every mile was agony now for Nolan and his troopers. The heat was blistering, exhausted horses were staggering, and the men were constantly falling from them. Discipline became the victim of thirst and fear. Corporal Charles Gilmore deserted after being detailed to care for a trooper who had fainted, and the little column was straggling so badly that Nolan called a halt to await sundown. Mouths were so dry that neither bread nor mesquite beans could be swallowed and some of the men were becoming delirious. One of Lieutenant Cooper's horses, completely broken down, was killed and the warm blood drunk to slake partially an all-consuming thirst.

Not until 2:00 A.M. on July 29 was the column able to start moving again. Officers and men were so weak that three hours had been required to pack and saddle up. Morning brought out the broiling sun again to beat down upon half-crazed men. Corporal George Frémont and two other troopers struck off on their own, and forty men had shrunk to twenty-four. Thirst was so overpowering that the urine of both horses and men was sweetened and drunk with relish which brought momentary relief, then greater suffering. More horses died and their blood was drunk as tortured officers and men fell, lurched, and staggered another twenty-five miles before sheer exhaustion forced a halt near midafternoon beside some scrub mesquite that gave partial shelter from the blistering rays of the sun.

All were now despairing their lives, but big, rawboned Pri-

[34] Nolan to the AAG, Department of Texas, August 20, 1877, LR, AGO; Nunn, *loc. cit.*, 357. The hunters reached water at Casas Amarillas late that day.

vate Barney Howard summoned the energy to go from man to man giving encouragement and telling cheerful stories. He reminded Lieutenant Cooper of the pretty, dark-eyed wife that awaited him at Fort Concho, and that he must not disappoint her. Barney Howard deserved a medal, but there is no record that he ever received one.[35]

Near sundown Nolan ordered the men to abandon all their rations and surplus property and gird themselves for a last effort. Then the column set out, although this was no longer a disciplined march but an individual struggle to reach life-giving water. Fifteen more agonizing miles brought them at last in little groups to Double Lakes during the early morning of July 30. They had been on the Staked Plains for eighty-six hours without water.[36]

As soon as thirst was quenched, Nolan counted faces. One trooper, Private J. T. Gordon, was missing, and a brief search failed to locate him. The men were in no condition for a thorough scout, and Nolan rested his command until the morning of July 31 when he sent out a detail with two pack mules to return to the last camp, gather up the abandoned supplies, and look for stragglers. While awaiting their return, Nolan spied a long column on the horizon to the north and soon welcomed Captain Lee and G Company who were scouting out of Fort Griffin. Lee rendered immediate assistance and sent out a strong detachment along Nolan's back trail with plenty of food and water to find any men still lost and to retrieve discarded property. Meanwhile, the detail that Nolan had sent out earlier in the day returned with the abandoned rations, but the troopers had found no stragglers.

On August 1, while the command recuperated at Double Lakes, Corporal Frémont and another trooper came in. They reported that they had straggled and become lost, all their animals had died, and Private Isaac Derwin, who had also been with them, had perished. Nolan placed both men under arrest as deserters and sent a detail to bring in Derwin's body, but the men failed to locate

---

35 John R. Cook, *The Border and the Buffalo*, 284–85.
36 Nolan to the AAG, Department of Texas, August 20, 1877, LR, AGO.

the remains. Three days later Sergeant Allsup with fifteen men arrived from the supply camp on Bull Creek overjoyed to find their commander alive and safe.

Sergeant Umbles and the two men with him, as well as Corporal Gilmore, had reached the supply camp and told Allsup that Nolan and the rest of the command had become lost and died of thirst. Umbles, Gilmore, and another trooper had then ridden on to Fort Concho to bear the grim news to the garrison, while Allsup had marched at once to find Nolan. The latter immediately sent a courier to Concho to give the lie to Umbles' story and to request that both he and Gilmore be placed in arrest.

On August 5, Nolan broke camp at Double Lakes and, escorted by Captain Lee, marched for his supply camp, which was reached at noon the following day. Here he found the eight troopers whom he had sent on for water on July 27. Shortly thereafter a relief force from Concho headed by Lieutenant Robert G. Smither and Assistant Surgeon J. H. King arrived, having marched in response to the news Umbles had brought to the post. After rest and treatment, Nolan set out for Fort Concho where he arrived on August 14.[37]

Nolan's ill-fated expedition cost the lives of four troopers. Privates Isaac Derwin, John Gordon, John Bond, and John Isaacs died of thirst and exhaustion. Twenty-five horses and four mules were also lost. Sergeant Umbles, Corporals Gilmore and Frémont, the latter the post librarian, and Private Alexander Nolan were court-martialed, dishonorably discharged, and sentenced to a year of imprisonment for desertion, although Colonel Grierson had recommended leniency because of the extenuating circumstances involved.[38]

37 *Ibid.;* Medical History, Fort Griffin, Vol. 103.

38 Nolan to the AAG, Department of Texas, August 20, 1877; LR, AGO; Organizational Returns, Tenth Cavalry, August, 1877; Susan Miles, "Fort Concho in 1877," *West Texas Historical Association Yearbook* XXXV (October, 1959), 49. Nolan was a native of Ireland who joined the regular army in 1852 and was promoted to second lieutenant, Sixth Cavalry, in 1862. He was a first lieutenant at the close of the Civil War and was commissioned a captain in the Tenth Cavalry in July, 1866. He remained with the Tenth for sixteen years before transferring to the Third Cavalry in December, 1882, with the rank of major. He died less than a

Leniency may well have been in order, for desertion was the most common serious offense in the frontier army. For twenty-five years after the Civil War a third of all men recruited became deserters, and in 1873 the army made an effort to curb the practice by adopting a policy of amnesty for those who surrendered voluntarily. The four troopers of Nolan's Company A fell in this category, and Grierson's request was in accord with then current policy. In addition, the buffalo soldiers of both the Ninth and the Tenth had an outstanding record for faithful service with a desertion rate well below any other units in the army. For the year 1877, despite the most arduous service in one of the most demanding regions of the country, Grierson's Tenth had a total of 18 desertions as compared with 184 for Mackenzie's famous Fourth.[39]

The year had been a difficult one in any case at Fort Concho, and particularly for Captain Nolan, whose wife had died earlier in the year. Young Lieutenant Hans J. Gasman had returned from a scout to find his infant child, whom he had never seen, dead at the age of six days. One of the telegraph operators had gone insane from loneliness, and Surgeon King's maid had begun "eating dirt." Neither Grierson nor his troopers were popular in the nearby village of Saint Angela, the sole source of night life in the immediate area. Grierson described the place as a "resort for desperate characters and is mainly made up of gambling and drinking saloons and other disreputable places."[40]

Dreary and dangerous though Saint Angela's "resorts" were for a Negro trooper, there had been only minor clashes until the fall of 1877 when, oddly enough, the arrival of a few Texas Rangers brought serious trouble. Several rangers visited Nasworthy's saloon to drink and dance, and discovered that a number of troopers were doing likewise, whereupon they pulled their six-shooters and pistol-whipped the soldiers. When the incident

year later on October 25, 1883, after thirty-one years of service. Despite many ups and downs, he was an able and humane officer. Heitman, *op. cit.*, I, 750.

39 Rickey, *op. cit.*, 143, 154; *H.R. Exec. Doc. No. 1*, Part 2, 45 Cong., 2 sess., 49. The rate in 1877 for the Ninth Cavalry was only 6 as compared to 172 for the Seventh Cavalry.

40 Grierson to the AAG, Washington, D. C., January 12, 1880, LR, AGO; Miles, *loc. cit.*, 29.

was reported at the post, Grierson asked the ranger captain, John S. Sparks, for an apology and instead got the braggart answer that the little ranger company could whip the entire Fort Concho garrison. Fortunately for all concerned, Grierson's temper was equal to the occasion.

The affair did not end here, however, for the angry troopers armed themselves, went back to Nasworthy's, and shot up the place, killing an innocent bystander. Responsibility for this unfortunate turn of events pointed squarely at Captain Sparks, and he left the ranger service.[41]

A few months later more serious trouble occurred in Morris' saloon where a party of cowboys and hunters surrounded a sergeant from D Company, cut the chevrons from his sleeves, the stripes from his pants, and had a good laugh over his discomfiture. They did not laugh for very long. The soldier returned to the post and gathered up some fellow troopers. Armed with carbines, they went to Morris' and a blazing gunfight at close quarters followed in which one hunter was killed and two others wounded, while Private John L. Brown was killed and another trooper wounded.

Sparks's replacement, Captain G. W. Arrington, came to the post with a party of rangers intent on arresting First Sergeant George Goldsby of D Company for allowing the troopers to get their carbines, but Grierson challenged their authority on a federal post and, meanwhile, Goldsby, ironically a native of Selma, Alabama, a stormy center of civil rights controversy in recent years, had departed for parts unknown. Nine troopers of Company D were indicted for murder and one, William Mace, was given a death sentence, although he later won an appeal. There is no record of any indictment of the others who participated in this affair. The day was still far distant when justice or injustice fell equally on men regardless of race, color, or creed, and the buffalo soldiers had not seen the last of Captain Arrington.[42]

---

41 Haley, *op. cit.,* 274.

42 Galveston *Daily News,* March 1, 1878; Organizational Returns, Tenth Cavalry, February, 1878. Most accounts of this trouble give Goldsby's name as Goldsbery which is incorrect. He enlisted as a private in 1867 and by 1872 had risen to the rank of sergeant major. Discharged at the expiration of his five-year term, he re-enlisted and had become D Company's first sergeant. Register of Enlistments.

Grierson and his regiment had little time to reflect on an unsatisfactory environment, however, for with the spring of 1878 the old Río Grande troubles flared with renewed violence. So great was the upswing of revolutionary activity and Indian raiding that Mackenzie replaced Shafter in command of the District of the Nueces, and six companies of the Fourth Cavalry were moved from Indian Territory to add their strength to the border forces.[43]

This move enabled Grierson to withdraw most of his troopers, who were on the lower Río Grande, and concentrate them in his own District of the Pecos, where Lipans, Kickapoos, and Mescaleros were striking with a vengeance. However, trouble loomed at Fort Sill where the reservation Indians were growing restless and sullen over inadequate issues of rations, and it became necessary to shift Nolan's A, Lee's G, and Baldwin's I under Colonel Davidson to that post.[44]

Davidson was his usual temperamental self and soon engaged in quarreling with his company commanders. Baldwin, Nolan, and Lee were reprimanded for their dress, manner of saluting, and lack of soldierly bearing, and were constantly reminded that they could be "black booked." Finally Baldwin exploded in a letter to the Adjutant General complaining of Davidson's "tyrannical character" and harsh treatment, and asked for a full investigation. Baldwin's request was denied, and his wife took up the cudgels in her husband's behalf and wrote a letter to President Hayes detailing the mistreatment her spouse had suffered, and described Davidson as "nearly always under the influence of alcoholic stimulant."[45]

43 *H.R. Exec. Doc. No. 1,* Part 2, 45 Cong., 3 sess., 87; Organizational Returns, Tenth Cavalry, January, 1878.

44 Organizational Returns, Tenth Cavalry, January, 1878. Captain Lee was a popular officer at Fort Griffin and received a letter of tribute signed by twenty-five prominent citizens which appeared in the Fort Griffin *Echo* of January 10, 1878. Praise for an officer commanding Negro troops in Texas was rare indeed. In 1878 the Department of Texas was divided into a number of districts, namely, the Río Grande, the Nueces, the Pecos, and North Texas, commanded respectively by Colonel George Sykes, Twentieth Infantry, Colonel Mackenzie, Colonel Grierson, and Colonel H. B. Clitz, Tenth Infantry.

45 Mrs. T. A. Baldwin to President Hayes, October 13, 1878, LR, AGO; Baldwin to the AG, July 28, 1878, *ibid.;* Judge Advocate General Swain to Davidson, May 21, 1878, *ibid.;* Baldwin to the AG, September 22, 1878, *ibid.*

In the midst of this battle of words detachments of buffalo soldiers pursued their old enemies, the horse thief and bootlegger, with considerable success, but the overriding problem at Fort Sill was simply too many hungry Indians. In providing ration allotments for the tribes, the Indian Bureau had made liberal allowance for fresh meat that Indian hunters could supply from the buffalo range, but the once vast herds of buffalo had been virtually exterminated by 1877, and food from this source had dwindled to a vanishing point. There had been no corresponding increase in the ration allotment, and grafting contractors made inroads into an already inadequate supply. The result was thousands of half-starved Indians.

To alleviate this sorry situation and to avoid a possible outbreak, Indian agents permitted small parties of armed Indians, under military escort, to leave the reservation in search of game. The appearance of roving parties of Indian hunters along the northern border of Texas created alarm among farmers and ranchers who feared for their crops, cattle, and hair, although few, if any, could cite more than the loss of a few head of stock. Pleas for protection were sent to Major John B. Jones, commanding the Texas Frontier Battalion, and he ordered Captain Arrington with C Company of the rangers to the North Texas frontier with orders to kill any armed Indians he could find.

On January 15, 1879, while scouting along the Pease River, the rangers spied a party of Kiowas who fled as they approached. In a hot pursuit one Indian was killed, while the others took refuge in a village of fourteen lodges. Arrington was preparing to charge when a detachment of Nolan's A Company approached and informed him that the Indians were out hunting under their supervision. Arrington complained in his report to Jones that the Indians were not under the control of the troopers, but he admitted he had learned of no depredations except one in which a rancher had lost six head of cattle.[46]

<hr />

[46] *H.R. Exec. Doc. No. 1*, Part 2, 45 Cong., 3 sess., 40; Nolan to the PA, Fort Sill, January 8, 1879, LR, AGO; Arrington to Jones, June 20, 1879, LR, AGO; Webb, *op. cit.*, 413. The Kiowas were not guilty of depredations, but in April, 1879, they

Given the situation, friction between ranger and buffalo soldier was inevitable, and the former needed little excuse. In May a small band of Comanches fled the reservation with Nolan and A in pursuit. Close behind were two small parties of peaceful Comanches under Black Bear and White Eagle who were authorized to assist Nolan in rounding up the runaways. Nolan searched along Red River, crossed south to the headwaters of the Pease, and then into Blanco Cañon, where he halted at the store of a Mr. Jacobs. Jacobs had been robbed by white thieves of some horses, new rifles, and one thousand dollars in cash, but he had seen no Indians. Here Black Bear and White Eagle joined Nolan and assisted in scouting the Double Lakes country where the latter had so nearly lost his life in the summer of 1877. No sign of the Comanches was found, and Nolan felt certain they had gone on west across the Staked Plains, to join the Apaches.[47]

Meanwhile, Captain June Peake and a detachment of Company B, Texas Rangers, out on scout near Big Spring, came upon a party of Comanches butchering some colts and immediately attacked. The Indians fought like cornered wildcats and stood off the rangers until nightfall when they retreated westward. Peake pursued the next day but ran into an ambush that cost the life of Ranger W. G. Anglin and a serious wound to another. So hot was the Indian fire that Peake was forced to withdraw, leaving the body of Anglin on the field.

The day following Peake's fight, Lieutenant C. R. Ward with a detachment of D Company of the Tenth, scouting out of Fort Concho, struck the trail of Peake and the Indians and followed it to where Anglin's body lay. The buffalo soldiers buried Anglin where he had fallen, but they lost the trail of the Comanches.[48]

In his report Peake was quick to blame Nolan, Black Bear,

killed a Texan named Earle in retaliation for the killing of one of their tribesmen by the rangers in January. Lieutenant Colonel John Hatch to the AAG, Department of the Missouri, April 18, 1879, LR, AGO.

47 Nolan to the AAG, Department of the Missouri, July 22, 1879, LR, AGO; Lieutenant Colonel Hatch to Commanding Officer, Fort Concho, Texas, May 2, 1879, *ibid.*

48 Peake to Jones, July 5, 1879; *ibid.;* Nye, *op. cit.,* 238–39; Organizational Returns, Tenth Cavalry, June, 1879.

and White Eagle for the fight. He charged that Nolan had armed these Indians and turned them loose on their promise that they would return to Fort Sill. Instead, they had committed depredations and fought him when he overtook them. Peake's report spawned inquiries from both General Ord and General Pope, but a thorough investigation revealed that Peake was in error. The Indians he had fought were the runaway Comanches from Fort Sill under Chief Black Horse, the same party that Nolan and the Indians with him had been pursuing.[49]

Ranger headquarters remained unconvinced, however, and the stage was set for a fiery clash between Captain Arrington and Colonel Davidson. Reports of large parties of armed Indians along the Sweetwater in the Texas Panhandle brought Arrington and his company north to scout along that stream. They turned up no Indians, but they did encounter Davidson and a detachment of buffalo soldiers. Arrington told Davidson bluntly that he intended to kill any armed Indian he could find, and Davidson, hardly the man to be awed or impressed by a threat, just as bluntly told the ranger that if he or his men killed an Indian who was causing no trouble, it could create a serious situation for settlers in the area. This being the case, he proposed to keep troops in the vicinity to prevent any collision between rangers and reservation Indians.

Arrington reported that Davidson had theatened to fire on him and the air became extremely tense, but fortunately no incident arose to provoke further difficulties between two equally determined and stubborn men. Little wonder, however, that no love was lost between officers and men of the Tenth and the Texas Rangers.[50]

While three companies of the regiment were thus engaged in watching over reservation Indians and fighting verbal battles with the rangers, the remaining companies were doing their utmost to make the District of the Pecos a safe place in which to settle.

[49] Peake to the AG, State of Texas, September 3, 1879, LR, AGO; Lieutenant W. C. Manning, Twenty-fifth Infantry, to the AAG, Department of the Missouri, February 6, 1880, *ibid.*

[50] Manning to the AAG, Department of the Missouri, February 6, 1880, *ibid.;* Arrington to the AG, State of Texas, June 18, 1879; *ibid.;* Pope to the AAG, Military Division of the Missouri, February 7, 1880, *ibid.;* Webb, *op. cit.,* 413–14.

It was a task of some proportions, for in the first four months of 1878 hostile Indians killed fourteen persons in the district, and defied the best efforts of the buffalo soldiers to run them down.[51] With only one man for every 120 square miles, the lack of success was no reflection on Grierson and his regiment, a fact which General Sheridan realized fully. In his annual report Sheridan described the situation accurately:

> In all other countries, it is the custom to establish garrisons of not less than a regiment or a brigade, while we have for the performance of similar duties only one or two companies; with us, regiments are rarely if ever together, the posts are generally garrisoned by one, two, or four companies, who are expected to hold and guard, against one of the most acute and wary foes in the world, a space of country that in any other land would be held by a brigade. To do this requires sleepless watchfulness, great activity, and tireless energy.[52]

Given these circumstances, Grierson was convinced that a change in strategy was required in order to cope successfully with the old hit-and-run challenge. Beginning in May and continuing throughout the remainder of 1878 and all of 1879, Grierson kept his troopers continually in the field. Many camps and subposts were established from which the scene of a raid could be reached quickly, and with some possibility of overtaking the raiders. Underlying the effort was the determination "to make a vigorous effort to drive the Indians and other marauders out of my District, and prevent them, if possible, from returning to commit further depredations."[53]

In 1878 alone, hard-riding columns under Carpenter, Keyes, Norvell, Lebo, and others patrolled and scouted nearly twenty-five thousand miles, opened new roads, and mapped every stream, water hole, and mountain pass that came under their observant eyes. Grierson himself spent much time in the saddle gaining an intimate knowledge of the region in his charge. In October, 1878,

[51] *HR Exec. Doc. No. 1*, Part 2, 45 Cong., 3 sess., 82.
[52] *Ibid.*, 33.
[53] Organizational Returns, Tenth Cavalry, May–December, 1878; Grierson to the AAG, Department of Texas, December 28, 1878, File No. 1653.

he left Fort Concho with twenty veteran troopers and rode west to Horsehead Crossing on the Pecos. Here he turned upstream to Pope's Well on the Texas–New Mexican border and west again along Delaware Creek and Independence Spring to the Guadalupe Mountains. Wild game abounded and the command feasted on deer and antelope as the troopers explored Blue River Cañon.

The beauty of the country stirred the sensitive musician's heart:

> The Canon is situated just south of the boundary line of New Mexico, is from eight to ten miles in length, and varies in width from fifty feet or less at the head, north of Guadalupe Peak, to half a mile or more near the mouth of the Canon which opens to the east. On either side as you enter the mountains rise almost perpendicularly to the height of three thousand feet, and, besides the great variety of pine, White Oak, Post Oak, Maple, Ash, Wild Cherry, Elm, Hackberry and Mansenita, abounds . . . frost had set in and the great variety of tints and hues of foliage, from dark green to pure carmine, added greatly to the life and beauty of the magnificent scenery.[54]

From the Guadalupes, Grierson and his cheerful twenty cut southwest, skirting the Sierra del Diablo and Carrizo Mountains and on to the Río Grande at Fort Quitman. From this lonely post he moved east to Eagle Springs, where he inspected Captain Viele's C Company, and then marched on to Fort Davis for a look at Carpenter's proud H. On November 5, he set out due south, found and pushed through a gap in the Santiago Mountains, located water where none was expected, and again reached the Río Grande downriver from San Felipe, about equidistant from Davis and Stockton. After locating a number of fording places, the command marched for Fort Concho which was reached late in the month after an absence of six weeks.

The intimate knowledge Grierson gained on this long scout, when combined with that of his company commanders', provided the avenues for the tough buffalo soldiers virtually to clear their district of raiders before the year 1879 was out. Officers and men

---

[54] Grierson to the AAG, Department of Texas, December 28, 1878, File No. 1653.

of the regiment could look back on a task well done, and Grierson could reflect on the future of this rugged region. He was convinced it was destined to "become a great resort for those seeking health and enjoyment."[55] Many years were to pass before this prophecy came true, but in a few short months the men of the Tenth would be called upon to apply all the skill and knowledge they possessed to meet the greatest challenge of their lives—invasion by the cunning and deadly Apache.

[55] *Ibid.*

VII

APACHES, CIVIL BROILS, AND UTES

THE MOVEMENT of the Ninth Cavalry to the District of New Mexico in the winter and spring of 1875-76 plunged the regiment headlong into the Apache troubles that had plagued the New Mexico–Arizona region for centuries. For three hundred years these Indians fought the Spaniard and the Mexican, and they resisted fiercely the efforts of the Americans after 1846 to dispossess them of their homeland. According to one student of the subject, "In fact, from 1540 to 1886 the Apaches were the most important human element in retarding the occupation and development of the Southwest."[1]

The Civil War presented the Apaches with a rare opportunity to drive out their white tormentors, and they took to the warpath with a vengeance. Brigadier General James H. Carleton, commanding Union forces in the area, took the field for an all-out campaign against them and enjoyed some temporary success, but the ever increasing flow of settlement after the war brought a renewal of hostilities on a greater scale than ever before. Grisly atrocities were committed by both Indian and white, and "sudden death stalked every trail and lurked behind every rock or clump of cactus."[2]

Such was the state of affairs when President Grant launched his "Peace Policy." The immediate results were successive missions by special peace commissioners to the Apache country in

[1] Ralph Ogle, "Federal Control of the Western Apaches," *New Mexico Historical Review*, Vol. XIV, No. 4 (October, 1939), 309.

[2] Edward E. Dale, *The Indians of the Southwest*, 95; Bertha Blount, "The Apache in the Southwest, 1846–1886," *Southwestern Historical Quarterly*, Vol. XXIII, No. 1 (July, 1919), 24–25; Ralph E. Twitchell, *The Leading Facts of New Mexican History*, II, 428–29.

1871 and 1872. Vincent Colyer, secretary of the newly created Board of Indian Commissioners, first visited New Mexico and recommended the removal of the Warm Springs Apaches from their reserve near Ojo Caliente to a new location in the Tularosa Valley. After an extensive tour of Arizona, Colyer selected Fort Apache, Camp Grant, and Camp Verde as permanent reservations as well as three temporary ones at Camp McDowell, Beal's Spring, and Date Creek.[3]

Hard on Colyer's heels came General O. O. Howard as President Grant's personal representative. Howard made a valiant effort and achieved some success, particularly with the Chiricahuas of Cochise, and located them on a reservation in the mountains near the Mexican border. He enlarged the area selected by Colyer at Fort Apache in order to create two reservations, San Carlos and White Mountain, and he abolished the temporary asylums which Colyer had created.[4]

Despite these efforts, Apache depredations continued, and in the fall of 1872 General George Crook began an around-the-clock campaign to drive the Apaches into their reservations. A dedicated and able soldier, Crook conducted a grim and unrelenting operation that ended only when most of the hostile Apaches surrendered at Camp Verde on April 6, 1873. Meanwhile, most of the Mescaleros, constantly harassed by troops and victimized by lawless whites, were ready for peace and were settled on a reserve near Fort Stanton, New Mexico.[5]

Prospects seemed bright in 1873 for a lasting peace, although renegade bands continued to make isolated raids. These too might soon have ceased had policy been guided by those genuinely interested in Indian welfare, but, tragically, this was not the case. Scheming contractors, delivering goods to the various agencies at the same price, saw opportunities for a windfall if the Indian Bureau could be persuaded to concentrate the Apaches of Arizona on one reservation. The virtue of such a policy was not lost on miners, lumbermen, cattlemen, and homesteaders who coveted In-

3 Dale, *op. cit.,* 98; Frank C. Lockwood, *The Apache Indians,* 184.
4 Lockwood, *op. cit.,* 187; Dale, *op. cit.,* 100.
5 Lockwood, *op. cit.,* 188–202; Twitchell, *op. cit.,* 438.

dian lands. These interests coalesced into the infamous "Tucson Ring" and brought heavy pressure to bear in Washington for adoption of a policy of concentration. Success, as usual, attended their efforts, despite warnings by responsible officials and army officers on the scene that such a policy would prove disastrous.[6]

The blow of concentration to the Apaches might have been softened somewhat had a desirable site been chosen, but instead they were to be transferred to "the desolate sand waste of San Carlos," an area most Apaches detested.[7] Thus policy and point of concentration conspired to provide ample assurance of Apache hostility, and thus of many more years of additional bloodshed.

The instrument to implement the new policy was the agent at San Carlos—able but arrogant John P. Clum, who arrived in 1874, took control with a firm hand, organized an efficient cadre of Indian police, and instituted a viable system of Indian self-government for the one thousand Apaches then at San Carlos. In the spring and summer of 1875, Clum transferred more than three thousand Indians from Camp Verde and White Mountain with a minimum of difficulty. No additional transfers to San Carlos were authorized for the remainder of the year, although the Indian Bureau softened its heart sufficiently in neighboring New Mexico to permit the Warm Springs Apaches to return to their old reserve near Ojo Caliente.[8]

An uneasy quiet prevailed along the Apache frontier during the winter and early spring of 1875–76, but it was interrupted in April. Meat was scarce at the Chiricahua agency at Apache Pass, and Agent Tom Jeffords told these Indians that they must supplement the supply by hunting. Acting on these orders, a band under Taza, successor to Cochise, who had died the previous year, set

6 Lockwood, *op. cit.,* 204–207; Major General J. M. Schofield, Commanding the Military Division of the Pacific, Annual Report of Operations, File No. 1653; Colonel August V. Kautz, Commanding the Department of Arizona, to the AAG, Military Division of the Pacific, October 20, 1875, File No. 1653. Kautz placed the blame for the concentration policy squarely on contractors in Tucson and predicted the policy would lead to war.

7 Lockwood, *op. cit.,* 206.

8 John P. Clum, "Geronimo," *New Mexico Historical Review,* Vol. II, No. 3 (January, 1928), 122; E. P. Smith, Commissioner of Indian Affairs, to the Secretary of Interior, June 9, 1875, File No. 1653; Clum to E. P. Smith, July 31, 1875, File No. 1653.

out for a hunt in the Dragoon Mountains. A bitter quarrel divided the band and a majority, led by Taza, returned and encamped near their agency. A murderous few under Skinya remained in the mountains, and from this group a handful of warriors made a raid into Mexico and returned with a quantity of gold and silver.

On the morning of April 6, one of Skinya's warriors rode to the Overland Mail Station at Sulphur Spring and exchanged some of the stolen money for whisky with a Mr. Rogers, the station keeper. Next day he was back again for more whisky accompanied by another warrior. Both Apaches were drunk and Rogers, with fear overcoming greed, refused to sell them more. He was shot and killed along with the station cook, a man named Spence, and the Indians took all the whisky and ammunition they could carry, stole some horses, and returned to their camp.

Next morning some of Skinya's warriors, roaring drunk, rode into the settlements along the San Pedro River, killed a rancher named Lewis, rounded up a number of horses, and fled into the San José Mountains.[9]

News of the murders of Rogers, Spence, and Lewis led to exaggerated reports of a major Chiricahua outbreak, and troops in both Arizona and New Mexico were rushed into the field. A detachment of the Sixth Cavalry located Skinya's renegades on a peak in the Dragoons, but the troopers were unable to dislodge them and were forced to retire to Fort Bowie. Some six weeks later Skinya and his followers came in to Taza's camp in an effort to persuade the latter to take the warpath but met with a blunt refusal. A bloody fight followed in which Skinya and eight of his warriors were either killed or wounded and the "outbreak" was at an end.[10]

Despite the fact that only half a dozen renegade Chiricahuas had been involved in these troubles, Agent Clum was ordered to remove all the Chiricahuas from their reservation and take them to San Carlos, a task which the energetic agent accomplished in

9 Lockwood, *op. cit.*, 214–15; Governor A. K. Safford to the Commissioner of Indian Affairs, April 17, 1876, SDLR, 1872–76, AGO.
10 Safford to the Commissioner of Indian Affairs, April 17, 1876, SDLR, 1872–76, AGO; Schofield to the AG, April 13, 1876, *ibid.*

the early part of June. Thus several hundred Chiricahuas were uprooted and punished for the acts of a few. The "Tucson Ring" should have provided Skinya with an elaborate funeral, for he had supplied them with another easy victory, but the citizens and soldiers of Arizona and New Mexico would pay a high price in blood and terror for that triumph.[11]

Clum had by no means corralled all the Chiricahuas at San Carlos. Prior to the Skinya episode some four hundred of them under Juh and Geronimo had fled to Mexico, committed depredations there, and returned to the vicinity of the Warm Springs reservation where still other Chiricahuas had sought sanctuary to escape removal. A condition fertile for trouble had thus developed in southern New Mexico.[12]

It was this state of affairs that confronted Hatch and his buffalo soldiers newly arrived from Texas. The regiment was badly scattered and far under strength. Two companies were at Fort Bayard, one at Fort McRae, two at Fort Wingate, three at Fort Stanton, one at Fort Union, one at Fort Selden, one at Fort Garland, and one company, K, had still not transferred from Texas. With an authorized strength of 845 men Hatch could field scarcely more than half that number, and to make matters worse, neither officers nor men were familiar with the country.[13]

But Hatch wasted no time on complaints. Detachments were thrown out from the various posts scouting in all directions, while General Pope was urged to build a fire under army recruiters in order to fill the depleted ranks. Pope scarcely needed urging to bend every effort to bring the regiment to full strength, but he was more than indignant at the Indian Bureau for creating what might well become a bloody mess. He wrote angrily to Sheridan that the source of the trouble was simply lack of food which the Bureau should have supplied, and that the Ninth had been placed in the

11 Lockwood, *op. cit.*, 216–17.

12 *Ibid.*, 217.

13 Organizational Returns, Ninth Cavalry, April, 1876; *H.R. Exec. Doc. No. 1*, Part 2, 45 Cong., 2 sess., 32. Companies A and C were at Bayard, B at McRae, E and I at Wingate, H, L, and M at Stanton, D at Union, F at Selden, and G at Garland. The total enlisted strength at this time was only 456 men.

near intolerable position of forcing the Indians to starve to death
on their reservations or of killing them if they left.[14]

Meanwhile, the far-flung detachments, while playing no part
in the tragic removal of the Chiricahuas at Apache Pass to San
Carlos, found more than enough to do in pursuing small parties of
raiders from the bands of Juh and Geronimo as well as a few
Warm Springs and Mescalero Apaches who left their reservations
to depredate. Little success attended these initial efforts, although
the relentless Captain Carroll and twenty-five hard-bitten veterans
of F Company struck a renegade band in the Florida Mountains
on April 15, killed one warrior, and captured eleven horses.[15]

Hatch feared an outbreak of the Warm Springs Indians and
journeyed to Ojo Caliente late in April. He found little that was
reassuring. The "visiting" Chiricahuas had spread their fears and
restlessness among the Warm Springs people, and some truculent
Mescalero warriors had come in from Fort Stanton to enliven affairs. The warriors were heavily armed with late-model weapons,
including Springfield carbines and Smith-Wesson revolvers. The
chiefs, including the potent Victorio, were openly defiant. They
told an indignant Hatch that their people could easily live in
Sonora and raid in the United States. Securing food, guns, and
ammunition from the Mexicans posed no problem.[16]

Hatch reported to department headquarters that he would
keep detachments on constant patrol and that this would probably
curb all but the most turbulent spirits. These his troopers most
surely would have to whip.[17] Hatch proved an accurate prophet.
Virtually ceaseless patrols for the remainder of 1876 kept raiding
to a minimum, and on no more than half a dozen occasions did
the rattle of gunfire mark a brush between searching troopers and
furtive Apaches.[18]

[14] Organizaional Returns, Ninth Cavalry, April, 1876; Pope to Sheridan, April
11, 1876, SDLR, 1872–76, AGO.
[15] Organizational Returns, Ninth Cavalry, April, 1876; Hutcheson, *loc. cit.*, 285.
[16] Hatch to the AAG, Department of the Missouri, May 20, 1876, SDLR, 1872–
76, AGO.
[17] *Ibid.*
[18] In September Captain Carroll had a skirmish in the Florida Mountains in
which a dozen animals were recovered, but the few remaining encounters produced
no losses to either troopers or Indians. See Organizational Returns, Ninth Cavalry,
July–December, 1876.

It was rough work for the buffalo soldiers. In a land of extremes one day's march could bring searing desert heat that beat down mercilessly, provoking an aching thirst that often went unslaked for hours, while the night might well be spent in lonely vigil on a frosty mountaintop. Through it all, with little time for relaxation, to say nothing of entertainment, the troopers remained cheerful and uncomplaining. Indeed, desertion in the Ninth had all but reached the vanishing point.[19]

The new year opened on a decidedly different note. Outlaw Chiricahuas stepped up their raids and the more restless young men among the Warm Springs and Mescalero tribes slipped away from the reservations to depredate. Late in January, word reached Fort Bayard that a party of forty to fifty Chiricahuas had fought a detachment of the Sixth Cavalry in Arizona and had probably moved eastward into New Mexico. Lieutenant Henry H. Wright with six men of Company C and three Navaho Indian scouts left the post at once to search for these Indians.

The trail was struck and followed into the Florida Mountains where the Indian camp was located on the morning of January 24. Outnumbered badly, Wright did not attack but sought instead to persuade the Chiricahuas to surrender. Half an hour of talk proved fruitless, and Wright observed that he was completely surrounded. Breaking off the council, Wright ordered his men to push through the encircling Indians, but as they did so a deadly fight at close quarters broke out. Weapons were fired and then used as clubs. In the center of the melee Corporal Clifton Greaves fought like a cornered lion and managed to shoot and bash a gap through the swarming Apaches, permitting his companions to break free. But with five of their number dead and more wounded, the Indians fled leaving the field to Wright and his gallant nine. The troopers, suffering only minor wounds, gathered up six Indian ponies and returned to Fort Bayard. For his role in this affair, Corporal Greaves was awarded the Congressional Medal of Honor. Privates Richard

19 *H.R. Exec. Doc. No. 1,* Part 2, 45 Cong., 2 sess., 49. The Ninth suffered only 6 desertions for the year as compared with 170, 224, 172, and 174 for the Third, Fifth, Seventh, and Eighth, respectively. The Tenth Cavalry in neighboring Texas had only 18 desertions.

178

Epps, Dick Mackadoo, John Adams, and one of the scouts, José Chaves, were all commended for bravery in action.[20]

Four days later, Captain Beyer with the whole of Company C and Captain Cooney with a detachment of A Company found and followed a trail in the vicinity of Wright's engagement. Soon thereafter the command came upon a camp of about twenty-five Apaches and attacked at once. The Indians took wing and eluded Beyer but lost all their camp equipage and supplies.[21]

Upon returning to Bayard, Beyer recommended that Hatch station an officer and twenty men at Fort Cummings, which had been evacuated in 1873, for trails leaving the Warm Springs reserve "can invariably be found in the valley between Fort Cummings and the Magdelena Moutains." Further, the old post was only twenty-five miles from the Florida Mountains in which war parties rendezvoused.[22] Hatch agreed with Beyer but had no troopers to spare and wrote to General Pope requesting that D and L Companies, on duty in the Ute country of Colorado, be returned to New Mexico. Pope refused the request because "these are the only cavalry in that portion of the Department."[23]

Demands on the Ninth were so heavy that Hatch feared a possible loss of morale and asked Pope for permission to send the regimental band on a tour of the posts at which his troopers were stationed. "The various Companies of the regiment should have the benefit of the Band a portion of the year," he wrote, and Pope consented readily. An evening concert became a rare treat indeed for trail-worn troopers, but Hatch's fears regarding morale were groundless, for the men seemed to thrive on the rough work.[24]

By early March it was obvious that Geronimo and many of

20 Organizational Returns, Ninth Cavalry, January, 1877; *Army and Navy Journal*, Vol. XIV (May 12, 1877), 18; Memorandum, No. 1555B (EB), February 13, 1879, AGO, RG 94, NA. Greaves' citation in part read "for coolness and courage displayed in a hand to hand fight with the Apache Indians in the Florida Mountains of New Mexico, January 24, 1877."

21 Organizational Returns, Ninth Cavalry, January, 1877; *Army and Navy Journal*, Vol. XIV (May 12, 1877), 18.

22 Beyer to the AAG, District of New Mexico, January 30, 1877, LR, District of New Mexico, Records of United States Army Commands, RG 98, NA.

23 Pope to Hatch, March 31, 1877, *ibid.*

24 Hatch to the AAG, Department of the Missouri, March 20, 1877, LS, District of New Mexico, United States Army Commands, RG 98, NA.

his followers were constantly among the Warm Springs people, and the Commissioner of Indian Affairs ordered Clum to take the necessary steps to arrest these renegades and to call on the military for assistance if needed. Clum requested Hatch's co-operation, and the latter readily agreed to send Major James Wade with A, B, and C companies of the Ninth from Fort Bayard to Ojo Caliente to join with Clum and his Apache police in making the arrests.

The concentration of forces proved unnecessary, for Clum was able to accomplish his mission on April 21 without undue difficulty, but he took a fateful step in deciding to remove all the Warm Springs Apaches to San Carlos as well as the renegade Chiricahuas. It was to prove a costly mistake, for these Indians despised San Carlos and had no intentions of remaining there. Clum's decision marked the beginning of one of the bloodiest chapters in New Mexican history and one of the most trying for the officers and men of the Ninth Cavalry.[25]

The lull before the storm for the Ninth came in the summer of 1877 and brought a welcome respite from almost constant field duty. It was not a time to complain of monotony, however, for white cattle-thieves from Texas kept the Mescalero agency in an uproar, and Agent F. C. Godfroy was forced to call on Captain Purington and H Company at Fort Stanton for aid in recovering stolen stock.[26] Captain Hooker's E Company had its hands full with squatters who began moving into the Warm Springs reservation before the dust settled from the heels of the departing Indians, and far to the north G Company had the unpleasant task of removing unauthorized settlers from the Los Pinos reservation in southern Colorado.[27] By contrast Captain Beyer and C Company were enjoying a well-earned rest at Mesilla and gaining the plaudits of Mesilla *Independent* as having made "an enviable reputation wher-

25 *Annual Report of the Commissioner of Indian Affairs for the Year 1877*, 34–35. Clum remarks in his report that the, "Cooperation of troops under General Hatch and Colonel Wade was perfect." Organizational Returns, Ninth Cavalry, April–May, 1877. For a detailed report of the arrest and transfer of these Indians, see Woodworth Clum, *Apache Agent.*

26 *Annual Report of the Commissioner of Indian Affairs for the Year 1877*, 157; Organizational Returns, Ninth Cavalry, July–August, 1877.

27 Organizational Returns, Ninth Cavalry, April–May, 1877; *Annual Report of the Commissioner of Indian Affairs for the Year 1877*, 44.

ever stationed" and always under "perfect discipline."[28] Such un-accustomed praise must have placed the troopers in a pleasant state of shock.

The summer, however, was a time of trial for Colonel Hatch, for a quarrel of long standing broke over the regiment and was to have far-reaching consequences for both officers and men. Wesley Merritt, Lieutenant Colonel of the Ninth for a decade, was promoted to Colonel and transferred to the Fifth Cavalry in July, 1876, and the vacancy was filled with an officer whose career was checkered with controversy, Lieutenant Colonel N. A. M. Dudley.[29]

There had been no love lost between Hatch and Dudley since 1869, when they had served together on a court-martial in Jefferson, Texas. The two men had a disagreement, the nature of which was never made public, but Dudley was a petty and contentious officer, suffered from a persecution complex, and was often at odds with his superiors. It did not help matters any that he nursed a strong affection for the bottle. Dudley was assigned to command the post at Fort Union, and there is no doubt that Hatch determined to keep a close watch on his new lieutenant colonel.[30]

Running true to form, Dudley was soon embroiled in a bitter quarrel with Captain A. S. Kimball, post quartermaster at Fort Union, over the quantity and control of transportation on the post. Additional fuel was added to the controversy by a difference of opinion over repair of porches along officers' row, and the inability of Dudley, in a drunken state, to comprehend a report Kimball submitted on the amount of cordwood on hand. On May 30, 1877,

---

28 Mesilla *Independent,* August 25, 1877.

29 Organizational Returns, Ninth Cavalry, July, 1876. Merritt eventually rose to the rank of major general. See Heitmann, *op. cit.,* I, 706. Nathan Augustus Monroe Dudley was a native of Massachusetts who joined the Tenth United States Infantry in March, 1855. His career in the Civil War was undistinguished and he emerged as a major in the Fifteenth Infantry. After brief service in the Twenty-fourth Infantry, he transferred to the Third Cavalry. He was promoted to lieutenant colonel and assigned to the Ninth Cavalry on July 1, 1876. Heitman, *op. cit.,* I, 386.

30 Dudley was court-martialed at Camp McDowell, Arizona, in 1871 for drunkenness and conduct unbecoming an officer. For one explanation of the origin of the Hatch-Dudley feud, see Chris Emmett, *Fort Union and the Winning of the Southwest,* 376. Dudley's explanation was that they "simply didn't get along." Dudley to the AAG, Department of the Missouri, August 30, 1877, LR, District of New Mexico.

while Dudley was conducting an inspection of post transportation, the quarrel flamed into the open when he accused Kimball of fraud and charged that Hatch was a party to it.[31]

Dudley must have known that he was heading for serious trouble, but he plunged headlong into additional difficulties by engaging in a petty squabble with the post chaplain, Rev. George Simpson, and suspending religious services for the summer. Shortly thereafter, however, he came charging to the defense of the chaplain's daughter, Miss Lizzie, by accusing a local doctor, W. R. Tipton, of seducing her, and demanding that amends be made or at least to "restore the good name of the girl."[32]

Hatch was sorely tried and he wrote to General Pope requesting that Dudley be transferred to another post. The request was refused:

> The disposition to be troublesome evinced by Colonel Dudley at Fort Union would probably find means to evince itself wherever he might be stationed and such disposition had better be met by strictly defining his duties and requiring rigid observance of them than by removing him to some other point.[33]

Dudley might have continued to skate on thin ice at Union had he walked the straight and narrow, but he was soon charging that the post surgeon, Dr. Carvallo, was conniving with Hatch to embezzle funds donated to the post hospital. For Hatch this was the last straw. He came to Union forthwith, placed Dudley in arrest, and removed him from command of the post.[34]

Hatch wasted no time in filing an impressive list of charges against Dudley with department headquarters, and the latter was equally prompt in filing similar charges against Hatch. It was soon clear, however, that Pope wished to avoid a court-martial. Hatch was informed that such proceedings would be inordinately ex-

31 The PA to Captain A. S. Kimball, April 23, 1877, LR, District of New Mexico; E. R. Platt to Dudley, October 31, 1877, LS, Department of the Missouri, United States Army Commands, RG 98, NA.

32 Emmett, *op. cit.*, 380.

33 E. R. Platt to Hatch, August 11, 1877, LR, District of New Mexico.

34 Dudley to the AAG, Department of the Missouri, August 30, 1877, *ibid.;* Emmett, *op. cit.*, 382.

pensive and bring scandal to the service. It would be better "if the interest of the service and the requirements of discipline can be properly maintained, to avoid a trial." Pope would, however, send an experienced officer to make a thorough investigation of affairs at Fort Union.[35]

Dudley, meanwhile, remained under close arrest and in September J. T. Martin, acting assistant surgeon, U. S. Army, examined Dudley and found him very nervous, "addicted to headaches," and in declining health from confinement to his quarters. Shortly thereafter Pope ordered Hatch to release Dudley from arrest, but to permit him no functions of command until the report of his investigating officer had been received.[36]

Pope's investigation proved anything but complimentary to Dudley, and a court-martial convened at Fort Union on November 23, 1877. After weeks of testimony Dudley was found guilty of defaming Captain Kimball, of vilifying and prejudicing Hatch, and of conduct prejudicial to good order and military discipline. He was suspended from rank and command and his pay was forfeited for three months. General Pope approved the verdict, but President Hayes did not and ordered the unexecuted portion of the sentence remitted. John C. Dent, post sutler at Fort Union, was an intimate of Dudley's, as well as former President Grant's brother-in-law, and Grant was never one to disappoint his relatives.[37]

Thus the Ninth was not free of Dudley, and Hatch was forced to place him in command at Fort Stanton where he was soon involved in an affair of far more serious nature than any of those at Fort Union.

Meanwhile, the "honeymoon" of the summer of 1877 did not carry over into fall. It was rudely shattered on September 2, 1877, when Victorio and three hundred of his Warm Springs and Chiricahua followers fled the San Carlos reservation. Hatch immediately ordered every available man in his district into the field

35 E. R. Platt to Hatch, September 22, 1877, LR, District of New Mexico.

36 J. T. Martin to H. Kinzie, Surgeon General, Fifteenth Infantry, September 25, 1877, *ibid.;* Hatch to Dudley, October 15, 1877, *ibid.*

37 Emmett, *op. cit.,* 378.

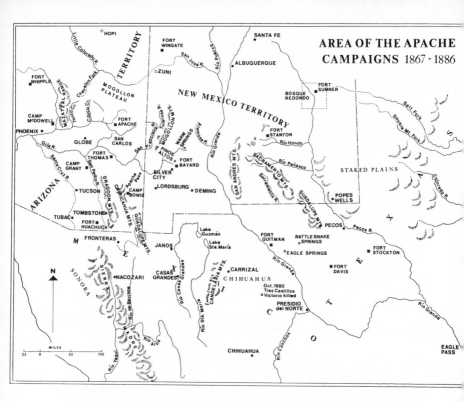

in pursuit. Four companies of the Ninth plunged into the rugged Mogollon Mountains, three more searched out of Ojo Caliente, while Hooker's E remained on the lookout in that vicinity.[38]

The Indians raided along the Upper Gila, killed a number of persons in outlying ranches, and stole a few horses and mules, but the troops were swiftly upon them and they were forced to retire to the mountains. The breakout had been ill-prepared, and Victorio had little in way of arms, ammunition, food, or clothing. Kept in constant motion by swarming detachments, the Apaches were soon in forlorn condition. Many were barefoot, others were naked, and hunger stalked their ranks. Early in October nearly two hun-

[38] Organizational Returns, Ninth Cavalry, September, 1877; Mesilla *Independent,* September 15, 1877; *Annual Report of the Commissioner of Indian Affairs for the Year 1877,* 20–21. Eight persons were killed in these raids, while troops and scouts killed thirteen Apaches.

dred of them, including Victorio, came in to Fort Wingate and surrendered. Within a few days seventy more came in, while the few remaining "outs" escaped into Mexico.[39]

Victorio told Colonel P. T. Swain, commanding at Wingate, that he and his people would not willingly return to San Carlos; that they preferred to return to Warm Springs, and that this was the place where they wished to be buried. For a time it appeared that this wish might be granted, and escorted by Captains Bennett and Moore and Companies I and L of the Ninth, they were taken to Warm Springs bereft of arms and horses. But their stay was a short one and before October was out they were back at San Carlos once more, although eighty of them, including Victorio, had managed to escape while en route.[40]

During the next few months a trickle of these Warm Springs escapees began arriving at the Mescalero reservation where Agent Godfroy permitted them to remain. In February, 1878, Victorio and a few followers came to Ojo Caliente and surrendered to Captain Hooker. They were willing to stay in their old homes but refused even to discuss a return to San Carlos. A decision was then made to join them with their kinsmen at Mescalero, but this was not to their liking and they fled to the mountains once again. In June, however, they reappeared, this time at the Mescalero agency, and received Godfroy's promise of good treatment. A short time later their wives and children were brought to them from San Carlos, and all outward signs pointed to peace at last with these divided and unhappy people.

The Ninth had been fortunate in this short campaign. Not a single man had fallen to an Indian bullet. But a fatal accident had occurred in the Mogollons and the aftermath sent a wave of bitterness through the regiment. Corporal James Betters of C Company received a mortal wound when his carbine discharged accidentally. Before his death, Betters asked that he be buried at Fort

[39] Mesilla *Independent*, September 15, 1877; Captain Horace Jewett, Fifteenth Infantry, to the AAG, District of New Mexico, October 8, 1877, LR, District of New Mexico.

[40] Swain to the AAG, District of New Mexico, November 1, 1877, LR, District of New Mexico; Pope to Colonel R. C. Drum, AAG, Military Division of the Missouri, October 18, 1877, *ibid.*; Organizational Returns, Ninth Cavalry, October, 1877.

Bayard and his wishes were carried out, but Captain Beyer, commanding C, complained bitterly about the manner of interment. The body was laid to rest in the same condition in which it arrived at the post—not even the face was washed. The coffin was placed on a police cart used for carrying garbage and driven by a military convict:

> . . . and in this manner, without a flag covering his coffin, without a formal escort, without a single mourner or friend to follow the poor fellows remains to their last resting place was all that remained of this soldier, who had served his country honestly and faithfully for the space of eleven years.[41]

Hatch ordered Major Wade to make an investigation, and he did so but absolved those responsible for the burial because of the condition of the body when it reached Fort Bayard.

The echo of gunfire had scarce died away in the Mogollons, ending the threat of a major war with the Warm Springs Apaches, when a civil dispute in El Paso suddenly erupted into small-scale civil war. For many years people on both sides of the Río Grande had gathered salt from large deposits some one hundred miles east of El Paso. The area was isolated and thinly settled and the sharing of salt occasioned no difficulty. After the Civil War, however, more people settled in El Paso and in the little river towns of Ysleta, Socorro, and San Elizario south of El Paso, and ideas of profit from the sale of salt became attractive.

The salt issue became political in the late eighteen sixties when a "Salt Ring" and an "Anti-Salt Ring" formed and supported candidates for local and state offices. Leader of the Anti-Salt Ring was an influential priest of San Elizario, Antonio Borajo, who used his great prestige among the Mexican element to elect A. J. Fountain to the state senate. Borajo's motives, however, were far from pure. He soon proposed that Fountain "locate" the salt deposits and then Borajo would advise his Mexican followers to pay the tax. The profits would be divided equally between him and Fountain. This cozy scheme fell through when Fountain flatly rejected the

41 Captain Beyer to the AAAG, District of New Mexico, October 3, 1877, LR, District of New Mexico.

186

proposal. Borajo then joined forces with two recent arrivals, Luis Cardis and Charles Howard, to prevent any legislation whatever regarding the salt deposits.

All went well with the triumvirate for a time. Cardis was elected to the state legislature and Howard became district judge, and the people continued to gather salt as before. But Howard and Cardis quarreled over political matters, and twice Howard gave Cardis beatings in fist fights. Bitter factionalism developed with Borajo and Cardis leading the Mexican element and Howard heading a small minority composed of a few Mexicans and all the Americans.

At this point Howard took the step that led to violent civil strife. In the name of his father-in-law, George B. Zimpleman of Austin, Texas, he located the salt deposits and, with the assistance of a surveyor and John E. McBride, he surveyed the deposits and put up notices that no salt was to be taken without first paying a fee. The Mexican population seethed with indignation and a mob, aroused to fever pitch by Borajo, prepared to lynch Judge Howard. He was caught at Ysleta, but his life was spared when Cardis proposed that he be set free, provided that he agree never to come back and to post a fourteen-thousand-dollar bond. On October 3, he was released and went to Mesilla, New Mexico.[42]

Americans in the area feared the fury of the mob, and reports indicated that a large body of Mexicans was gathering across the river to take action with the mob. When news of these developments reached Washington, Hatch received orders to send a detachment to El Paso to protect government property and to offer sanctuary to those who desired it. In no case were the troops to interfere in civil affairs unless United States officials were prevented from carrying out their duties, or Mexicans from Mexico intervened. Hatch promptly ordered Lieutenant Rucker and twenty buffalo soldiers to El Paso.[43]

On October 10, Judge Howard returned to El Paso armed

[42] Sol Schutz, United States Commercial Agent, El Paso, to Second Assistant Secretary of State, October 21, 1877, File No. 1653; Webb, *op. cit.*, 347–52; *Mesilla Independent*, October 6, 1877.
[43] Sheridan to Townsend, October 21, 1877, File No. 1653.

with a double-barreled shotgun and set out to find Cardis whom he regarded as the source of his difficulties and an "infamous monster."[44] He found his quarry in the store of Samuel Schultz and Brothers and, without a word, riddled Cardis with blasts from both barrels of the shotgun. Howard then climbed into his buggy and drove back to Mesilla.[45]

The Cardis slaying outraged the Mexican population, and large groups of heavily armed men roamed the streets of Ysleta, Socorro, and San Elizario. Americans feared a massacre and appealed to Governor Hubbard of Texas for protection. Major John B. Jones of the Texas Rangers came to El Paso, decided at once that the situation was explosive, and organized a ranger company of twenty men under Lieutenant John B. Tays. Apparently satisfied that Tays could keep matters under control, Jones returned to Austin.

Unfortunately, Howard learned early in December that wagons had left San Elizario for the salt deposits. He came to El Paso and, with Tays and the rangers as escorts, left for San Elizario to prosecute the trespassers. Word of Howard's intentions preceded him, and an inflamed mob of more than four hundred men prepared to kill him, rangers notwithstanding. When Howard and Tays reached ranger quarters in San Elizario on the evening of Wednesday, December 12, they were surrounded immediately and forced to hole up in the quarters. Charles Ellis, a local merchant, attempted to reason with the mob but was roped, shot, his throat cut, and his body thrown in a pool of water.[46]

Tays managed to get word of his plight to Captain Thomas Blair, Fifteenth Infantry, at Fort Bliss, and Blair marched at once with a detachment of nineteen men. Near San Elizario, however, he was stopped by a strong force of Mexicans who informed him that the trouble in town was a purely local matter and that they would fight him if he failed to turn back. Blair's nerve apparently

44 Mesilla *Independent,* October 6, 1877; Webb, *op. cit.,* 353.
45 Robert J. Casey, *The Texas Border and Some Borderliners,* 146; Webb, *op. cit.,* 353; Report of Captain Thomas Blair, Fifteenth Infantry, to the AAG, District of New Mexico, December 19, 1877, LR, District of New Mexico.
46 Webb, *op. cit.,* 355; Casey, *op. cit.,* 147; Carlysle G. Raht, *The Romance of Davis Mountains and Big Bend Country,* 210–14.

failed him and he retired to Fort Bliss. Had he pushed on, he could well have saved many lives, for it is doubtful that the Mexicans would have fired on federal troops and assured swift and decisive intervention from Washington.[47]

Meanwhile, Tays had barricaded the doors and windows of the ranger quarters and cut portholes in the walls. In the building, in addition to Howard and the rangers, were Ranger Campbell's wife and two children, John G. Atkinson who was a merchant of San Elizario, John McBride, a Mr. Loomis of Fort Stockton and his Negro servant.

On Thursday morning the battle opened and heavy firing continued until the following Wednesday. Then, with three of his rangers dead and two wounded, and with ammunition, food, and water supplies running low, Tays arranged for a parley under a flag of truce. Mob leaders told Tays they only wanted Howard, and if he was turned over to them, the others were free to leave. Tays refused but on his return informed Howard of the terms, although he also told him that he would be defended to the last man.

At Howard's insistence, he and Tays went out to the mob to talk and were at once seized and disarmed. Meanwhile, on Atkinson's instigation, the other rangers surrendered. A firing squad of nine men swiftly executed Howard, the body was horribly mutilated and thrown into a well. McBride and Atkinson were also shot and some shouted for the blood of all the Americans, but more moderate counsels prevailed. The mob then set about systematically looting towns and homes.[48]

Not until fighting was well under way did Governor Hubbard ask for federal assistance, and it was December 15 when Hatch received orders from General Pope to march with every available man to the scene of the rioting. The Ninth was badly scattered, but Hatch soon had nine companies on the march toward El Paso and reached that place himself on December 19. He issued a general field order, assuming command of all troops at El Paso and

[47] Blair to the AAG, District of New Mexico, December 19, 1877, LR, District of New Mexico.

[48] *Ibid.*; Mesilla *Independent*, December 22, 1877.

in the immedate vicinity, and then pushed on to San Elizario with fifty-four troopers and two howitzers.[49]

Hatch found about five hundred rioters "spoiling for a fight" and he was ready to oblige, but quietly waited for the rest of his command to come up at which time he intended to "clean them out." It was not necessary. As column after column of scowling, battle-toughened buffalo soldiers, also "spoiling for a fight," trotted into San Elizario, the rioters lost all enthusiasm for a fight or even an argument—they simply faded away. Eleven persons had been killed and an undetermined number wounded, but the total was not complete. The rangers, having recovered their arms with the arrival of the troops, arrested and then shot two Mexicans "for attempting to escape." Hatch investigated the shootings, minutely examined the bodies, and came to the conclusion that both men had been bound when shot. Promptly he made his position clear to all. Federal troops were there on application of Governor Hubbard to maintain order and protect the lives and property of all citizens, and "outrages in the name and under color of the law and by those who ought to be its representatives and guardians will not be tolerated."[50]

The "Salt War" ended with Hatch's statement. Most, if not all, the bloodshed and property destruction could have been avoided if a federal officer, Blair, had been less timid and state officials less tardy in requesting necessary assistance. Hatch and his troopers brought an abrupt end to the "war" and prevented a far greater loss of life. As the old year became history and the new one began, Hatch reported that citizens of San Elizario, who fled their homes during the disorders, were returning and that all was quiet.[51]

Upon his return to district headquarters in Santa Fe, Hatch found numerous complaints on his desk concerning Mescalero

[49] Pope to the AAG, Military Division of the Missouri, February 7, 1878, File No. 1653; Hatch to Pope, December 22, 1877, *ibid.;* Organizational Returns, Ninth Cavalry, December, 1877. Concentration of the Ninth at El Paso all but stripped the District of New Mexico of cavalry. Only E, I, and K companies remained at strategic posts.

[50] Hatch to Pope, December 22, 1877, File No. 1653; Hatch to Pope, December 27, 1877, *ibid.;* Mesilla *Independent*, December 26, 1877.

[51] Sheridan to Townsend, January 2, 1878, File No. 1653.

raids into West Texas and across the border into Mexico. Agent Godfroy insisted that his Indians were not depredating, but that there were hostile bands in the Guadalupe Mountains who should be on some reservation. Dudley, commanding at Fort Stanton, reported that he had investigated conditions at the Mescalero agency and that a few reservation Indians might be raiding, but he placed the blame on renegades or "cut-offs" who were living off the countryside and making mescal.[52]

In June Captain Carroll left Fort Stanton to search the Guadalupes for these Indians with Lieutenant G. W. Smith, fifty-two men of F and H companies, and nineteen Navaho scouts under Lieutenant Wright. The command carried forty days' rations and 150 rounds of ammunition per man. Carroll worked his way through the Guadalupes to Pine Spring, where he met Captain Norvell, scouting out of Fort Davis with M Company of the Tenth Cavalry. Norvell had marched along the Pecos and as far west as Hueco Tanks before coming in to Pine Spring and had seen no Indians or any fresh trails.[53]

Convinced that the Guadalupes were "clean," Carroll turned west to search the Sacramentos, and near the head of Dog Cañon he flushed a small party of Apaches. In sharp skirmishing three warriors were killed and fourteen horses captured. Moving on up the cañon, the troopers struck a larger party with the warriors fighting a strong rear-guard action to save their women, children, and property. The ascent was very steep, the August heat like a furnace, and a few of the troopers collapsed with heatstroke.

The Indians took refuge on a ledge some eight hundred feet high, fired down at the struggling soldiers, and heaved large rocks at them. Carroll reached the ledge just at nightfall, but the hostiles had fled and scattered. Pursuit proved futile and Carroll turned back to scout Alamo Cañon, and when no Indians were found, he marched back to Fort Stanton.[54]

---

[52] Godfroy to Dudley, April 22, 1878, SLR, AGO; Dudley to the AAAG, District of New Mexico, May 24, 1878, *ibid.*

[53] Dudley to the AAG, District of New Mexico, July 12, 1878, LR, District of New Mexico; Norvell to the AAAG, District of the Pecos, July 25, 1878, File No. 1653.

[54] Carroll to the PA, Fort Stanton, August 12, 1878, LR, District of New Mexico.

While Carroll scoured the Guadalupes and the Sacramentos, detachments of the Ninth from Forts Bayard, Wingate, Stanton, and Bliss were contending with hit-and-run raids by Warm Springs and Chiricahua outlaws. Chasing these crafty renegades was a tedious and frustrating task, for they skipped nimbly into Mexico when hotly pressed. Often reports of a raid were two or three days in reaching a post, and by that time pursuit was all but useless. Saddles scarcely cooled in the undermanned Ninth, and Captain Beyer at Bayard wrote Hatch that so few cavalry were left at the post he wished permission to mount the regimental band. Hatch approved and by early August members of the band had exchanged their instruments for Springfield carbines and were scouting in the Hatchet and Florida Mountains.[55]

The Mexican government complained bitterly that raids by American Apaches amounted to an invasion, and lodged an official protest that United States troops were not doing enough to stop them—a charge that must have caused many a bone-weary buffalo soldier to shake his head and wonder just how much he had to do to earn a few words of praise. But Hatch was not prepared to accept such criticism and complained officially to General Pope. The Indians were obtaining guns and ammunition with ease from Mexican citizens, and co-operation on the part of the Mexican government in the campaigns against these outlaws was conspicuous by its absence. Major Morrow had gone to Janos in Chihuahua in an effort to co-ordinate operations, and, in effect, had been run out of town. Vigorous co-operation on the part of Mexico could have brought an end to these raids in short order.[56]

And while officials of both countries bickered over their respective responsibilities for Indian troubles, restive Mescaleros left the reservation to add their bit to the toll of death and destruction along the turbulent border. They could scarcely be blamed for these forays. Conditions in Lincoln County, adjoining

55 Beyer to the AAAG, District of New Mexico, July 31, 1878, File No. 1653; Hatch to the AAG, Department of the Missouri, August 14, 1879, *ibid.*
56 John W. Foster to Miguel Ruelas, Minister of Foreign Affairs, March 16, 1879, *ibid.*; M. de Zamacoma to William Evarts, June 18, 1879, *ibid.*; Morrow to the AAG, District of New Mexico, August 4, 1879, *ibid.*; Hatch to the AAG, Department of the Missouri, May 28, 1879, *ibid.*

their reserve, had reached the stage of anarchy, and the activities of lawless white men so disturbed the Mescaleros that some of them abandoned their crops and scattered into the mountains; others yielded to the temptation to depredate. The violence in Lincoln County, meanwhile, involved the already overburdened Ninth in one of the most sanguinary civil broils in the history of the West.[57]

For many years Lincoln County had enjoyed the unenviable reputation of having at least as many crooks, thieves, and murderers per square foot as any other county in the West. Late in 1873, civil war was narrowly averted when a number of hard-eyed Texans, including five brothers named Herrold, arrived on the scene to engage in ranching. Shortly thereafter one of the brothers had the misfortune to quarrel with a deputy sheriff and was killed in the gunfight that followed. The surviving brothers were quick to take revenge. On the night of December 20, 1873, they rode into Lincoln, shot up a wedding reception, and killed four men.[58]

The citizens of Lincoln, headed by L. G. Murphy, J. J. Dolan, and William Brady, organized a vigilante committee and requested the assistance of federal troops at nearby Fort Stanton. The request was denied, however, for General Pope telegraphed headquarters, District of New Mexico:

> Instruct the Commanding Officer, Fort Stanton, to take no action, whatever, in any disturbances among the citizens near Stanton, and not on the reservation, until summoned by U. S. officers as a posse, to execute the mandates of the U. S. courts.[59]

Fortunately for all concerned, the Herrold brothers decided for reasons of health and longevity to migrate back to Texas.

Far more serious trouble was just over the horizon. The economic life of Lincoln County was dominated by L. G. Murphy and James J. Dolan, who operated a general store in the town of Lincoln and engaged in small-scale banking and large-scale ranching.

---

[57] Dudley to the AAG, District of New Mexico, January 23, 1879, *ibid.*; Louis Scott, American Consul, Chihuahua, to Honorable W. Hunter, Assistant Secretary of State, July 20, 1879, *ibid.*; *Annual Report of the Commissioner of Indian Affairs for the Year 1878*, 107.

[58] William A. Keleher, *Violence in Lincoln County*, 13–15.

[59] Pope to the Commanding Officer, District of New Mexico, December 30, 1873, LR, AGO, RG 94, File No. 554–1874, NA; Keleher, *op. cit.*, 15.

They also held a lucrative contract to supply the Mescalero agency with beef and flour—mercilessly and systematically cheating the Indians—and were on intimate terms with Agent Godfroy and with the officers at Fort Stanton. Apparently, however, Murphy and Dolan were actually little more than agents for the politically potent Thomas B. Catron, attorney general of New Mexico Territory and president of the First National Bank of Santa Fe.[60]

Storm clouds loomed over this cozy and profitable arrangement in 1876 with the appearance on the Pecos River of a Texas cattle baron, John S. Chisum. Chisum represented formidable competition in the ranching business and, further, in his far-flung operations had encountered legal difficulties with Catron. Chisum soon joined forces with a Lincoln lawyer, Alexander McSween, onetime legal council for Murphy-Dolan. McSween had broken with the partners over disposition of a ten-thousand-dollar life insurance policy upon the death of the insured, Emil Fritz. The firm claimed to be the creditor of the deceased and demanded settlement of the account, while McSween, as executor of the Fritz estate, refused payment on the grounds that the claim was fraudulent. Murphy-Dolan charged that McSween was an embezzler, and at the time of Chisum's arrival the dispute had become a no-quarter legal battle.

Events took an ominous turn in 1877 with the arrival in Lincoln of a wealthy young Englishman, John H. Tunstall, who allied himself with Chisum and McSween and proposed to compete with Murphy-Dolan on all fronts and replace them as the dominant business combine of the county. The stakes were high, feelings bitter, and in the prevailing climate of Lincoln County both sides resorted to the employment of accomplished gunmen to further their interests. The inevitable result was a rapid increase in the

60 Keleher, *op. cit.*, 15; Harwood P. Hinton, Jr., "John Simpson Chisum, 1877–1884," *New Mexico Historical Review*, Vol. XXXI, No. 3 (July, 1957), 191–92. It should be noted that the firm was known as L. G. Murphy and Co., with Dolan as principal partner. On April 20, 1877, Murphy sold his share of the business, which then was known as James J. Dolan and Co. Murphy maintained his ranching and live-stock activities in Lincoln County. Thus, although the partnership was dissolved, the Murphy-Dolan faction continued to wield influence in the county.

mortality rate as trigger-happy partisans shot it out with little or
no excuse.

So long as only the small fry were involved, this state of affairs
could have continued indefinitely, but in February, 1878, events
took a decisive turn. The legal squabble over the Fritz estate resulted in the issue of attachments on McSween's property. Sheriff
William Brady of Lincoln attached the McSween holdings in town,
including goods in the new Tunstall store. In the meantime, a deputy, with a large posse of known gunmen, attached other property
in the outlying countryside. While returning to Lincoln, the posse
encountered Tunstall riding with a few companions and murdered him in cold blood. The other members of the Tunstall party,
including William Bonney, known as Billy the Kid, fled for their
lives and made good their escape.[61]

Passions ran high in Lincoln County over the Tunstall killing
and mounted to a fever pitch when Sheriff Brady proved unwilling
or unable to arrest the slayers. Fearing civil war, Governor Samuel B. Axtell hurried to Lincoln and wasted no time in asking
President Hayes for military assistance, but his sympathies were
with Murphy-Dolan, and his message placed full blame for the
troubles on Alexander McSween.

Axtell's request was approved at once, and Captain George
Purington at Fort Stanton was ordered to support the proper civil
authorities in the conduct of their duties. Purington hurried a detachment of twenty-five troopers of Company H to Lincoln but
found the situation so confusing he was temporarily at a loss as to
how to proceed. Justice of the Peace John B. Wilson issued warrants for the arrest of members of Sheriff Brady's posse, while
Brady demanded assistance in rounding up members of the Mc-
Sween faction, and a deputy United States marshal named Weide-
man argued that he had first claim on the troops. Purington eventually decided that duty demanded only that he protect the women

---

61 Hinton, *loc. cit.*, 194–95; Keleher, *op. cit.*, 82–91; Mesilla *Independent*, September 8, 1877; Frederick W. Nolan, *The Life and Death of John Henry Tunstall*, 220.
Tunstall's friends were some distance away engaged in a hunt when he was halted
and killed by the posse. Billy the Kid's real name was Henry McCarty.

and children, and he so notified the leaders of both factions, adding that if they were "spoiling for a fight," they could "withdraw to the mountains and fight to their hearts content."[62]

Apparently neither side was prepared at this point for open warfare and decided upon a waiting game. Meanwhile, Purington's dilemma as to the appropriate authorities in Lincoln was solved by General Pope, who telegraphed Hatch:

> Until this conflict of authority ceases, the Sheriff will be con-
> sidered by you the proper powers to render assistance to when
> required by him to preserve the peace and sustain the laws.[63]

Pope's message thrust the officers and men of the Ninth squarely into the Lincoln County conflict and, at the same time, placed a potent weapon in the hands of Sheriff Brady and indirectly into those of Murphy-Dolan, for Brady almost invariably followed their wishes.

Since a roundup of Tunstall's killers would have required Brady to arrest members of his own posse, he made no effort to do so, and it was not long before Tunstall's friends took matters into their own hands. In March, Richard Brewer, a neighbor of the slain man, organized a posse which included Billy the Kid and, with the warrants issued by Justice of the Peace Wilson, set out in search of the murderers. They soon found and arrested Frank Baker and William Morton, known to have been in the party that killed Tunstall. En route to Lincoln with their prisoners, the posse apparently decided Brady would release the captives, and both were shot along with a member of the posse who had proven to be a spy. The Lincoln County War was on in earnest.[64]

[62] Purington to the AAAG, District of New Mexico, March 6, 1878, LR, AGO, File No. 1405–1878, RG 94, NA (hereinafter cited as File No. 1405–1878). Axtell to President Hayes, March 4, 1878, *ibid*. George A. Purington, a native of Ohio, rose through the ranks during the Civil War to the rank of lieutenant colonel, Second Ohio Cavalry. He accepted a commission as captain, Ninth Cavalry, in July, 1866, and served continuously with the regiment until October, 1883, when he transferred in the rank of major to the Third Cavalry.

[63] Pope to Hatch, March 24, 1878, *ibid*.

[64] Keleher, *op. cit.*, 97–98; Sheridan to Sherman, April 5, 1878, File No. 1405–1878; Purington to the AAAG, District of New Mexico, March 29, 1878, File No. 1405–

On the morning of April 1, while Sheriff Brady and two deputies, George Hindman and J. B. Matthews, were walking along Lincoln's main street, a volley of shots from behind an adobe wall in the rear of Tunstall's store killed Brady and Hindman instantly, and Matthews narrowly escaped the same fate. Billy the Kid and three other members of the McSween faction immediately were accused of the shooting.

The killings brought Captain Purington, Lieutenant G. W. Smith, and Company H to Lincoln, and with George W. Peppin, a tool of the Murphy-Dolan crowd, they made a number of arrests and, without a warrant, searched McSween's home for weapons. Up to this time the officers at Fort Stanton, outwardly at least, had acted impartially, but Purington's actions on April 1 indicated leanings toward Murphy-Dolan, a preference that soon became obvious.[65]

April 5 brought still more killings. The Lincoln county commissioners offered a reward of two hundred dollars for the assassins of Brady and Hindman "dead or alive." The offer stimulated Andrew "Buckshot" Roberts, a Murphy-Dolan partisan, to go bounty hunting. At Blazer's Mill, on the Mescalero reservation, he encountered far more than he had bargained for in the form of Richard Brewer, Billy the Kid, and several others. In an instant guns were flaming, and when the shooting stopped, Roberts lay mortally wounded and Brewer was dead.[66]

The county commissioners elected John S. Copeland, a McSween sympathizer, as Brady's successor, in the hope that he could restore order. Copeland appealed to the new commander at Fort Stanton, the eccentric N. A. M. Dudley, for assistance, and a detachment of twenty troopers of H Company under Lieutenant Smith accompanied Copeland in his efforts to disarm and arrest roving armed bands. The new sheriff apparently made an honest

1878. For one story of Billy the Kid, see Pat F. Garrett, *The Authentic Life of Billy the Kid.*

65 Organizational Returns, Ninth Cavalry, April, 1878; Nolan, *op. cit.*, 130–311; Keleher, *op. cit.*, 110.

66 Keleher, *op. cit.*, 113.

effort, but he was removed from office by Governor Axtell at the instigation of Murphy-Dolan and George Peppin was appointed in his place.[67]

The increasing demands for troops in the bloody feud caused grave concern in Washington. Pope undoubtedly was uncomfortable over the presence of the unpredictable Dudley at Fort Stanton, and Hatch received orders to require the former to submit "full and frequent reports" on all matters connected with the use of troops in civil matters in Lincoln County. On May 30, Hatch received a telegram from Governor Axtell requesting troops be sent to the vicinity of Roswell, New Mexico, where rustlers were active and had stolen horses belonging to Attorney General Catron. In addition, Axtell desired sufficient troops sent to Lincoln to "disarm all bands of men found there, whether they claim to be sheriffs posse or otherwise."[68]

Hatch honored Axtell's request by sending Company H to Roswell and ordering Captain Carroll with Company F to Lincoln, but he wrote department headquarters a review of the troubles in Lincoln County and asked for immediate clarification of the extent of military participation required. At the same time he telegraphed Dudley to co-operate with Sheriff Peppin and to furnish escorts for contractors' cattle being driven to the Mescalero reservation, as he feared they might be stolen.[69]

For the moment, however, a deadly calm had settled over Lincoln County, but no one was deceived; all knew it to be a period of preparation for the final showdown between Murphy-Dolan and McSween. On June 7, Dudley reported cheerfully that

[67] *Ibid.*, 124; Dudley to the AAAG, District of New Mexico, May 4, 1878, File No. 1405–1878. It cannot be proved, but there is some evidence to indicate that Dudley, with his penchant for meddling, connived with Murphy-Dolan in the removal of Copeland. See Statement of Corporal Thomas Dale, Co. H, 9th Cavalry, May 1, 1878, Fort Stanton, New Mexico, on the Conduct of Sheriff John N. Copeland, File No. 1405–1878.

[68] Axtell to Hatch, May 30, 1878, LR, District of New Mexico; Pope to Hatch, April 24, 1878, File No. 1405–1878.

[69] Hatch to Dudley, June 1, 1878, File No. 1405–1878; Hatch to the AAG, Department of the Missouri, June 1, 1878, *ibid*. The strife in Lincoln County had disorganized transportation, and the delivery of beef and flour had been disrupted. Reports had also reached Hatch that outlaws planned to burn the agency buildings and steal stock from the Indians. Small wonder that some of the Mescaleros left the reservation to depredate.

all was quiet. The only request for troops had come from Agent Godfroy for the purpose of stopping the sale of whisky to his Indians in Tularosa.[70]

The calm was ruffled somewhat on June 18 when Sheriff Peppin appeared at Fort Stanton and asked Dudley for troops to assist in making arrests in Lincoln. The request was granted and Peppin set out with Lieutenant M. F. Goodwin and twenty-seven troopers. En route, however, they were joined by twenty heavily armed citizens, among them John Kinney, a notorious gunman, and Lieutenant Goodwin informed Peppin he had no intentions of entering Lincoln in such company. The troopers, therefore, remained on the outskirts of town, while Peppin, Kinney, and the others searched for the wanted men. None were found, and Goodwin returned to Fort Stanton. Peppin's effort was plainly designed to break up a suspected concentration of McSween's forces.[71]

On June 25, Hatch received the clarification he had asked for three weeks earlier. Adjutant General Townsend telegraphed Pope, who in turn informed Hatch that no further assistance by the troops at Fort Stanton was to be given to civil authorities in Lincoln County. Meanwhile, Peppin again came to Dudley for assistance, which was denied, but the Sheriff persisted, and when he signed an affidavit that his deputy had been unable to serve warrants, Dudley acquiesced. Captain Carroll, Lieutenant Goodwin, and thirty-five buffalo soldiers accompanied Peppin to the Coe Ranch, some twenty-five miles south of Stanton. It was here that a courier reached them with orders to return to the post in obedience to orders from district headquarters.[72]

Early in July tension in Lincoln had become nearly intolerable. The showdown was near and fear was the constant companion of men, women, and children. Dudley visited Lincoln and learned that both McSween and Dolan were in the field with their forces engaged in a deadly game of hide-and-seek. On July 6 a delegation

[70] Dudley to Hatch, June 7, 1878, LR, District of New Mexico.
[71] Dudley to the AAAG, District of New Mexico, June 22, 1878, File No. 1405–1878; Lieutenant Goodwin to Dudley, June 19, 1878, *ibid.*
[72] The AG to Pope, June 25, 1878, *ibid.;* Dudley to the AAAG, District of New Mexico, June 29, 1878, *ibid.;* Carroll to the PA, Fort Stanton, New Mexico, July 1, 1878, LR, District of New Mexico.

of twenty-seven Mexican women came to Stanton and begged Dudley for protection "in the name of God and the Constitution," and Dudley informed Hatch that the officers and men of the garrison were embarrassed that they had to stand idly by unable to give assistance.[73]

Dudley must have been embarrassed still further when informed that R. C. Drum, assistant adjutant general of the army, had issued General Orders No. 49, dated July 7, which forbade the use of federal troops in aiding civil authorities as a *posse comitatus,* or in executing the laws without the specific consent of the President obtained through military channels. The policy was crystal clear, or it should have been, but, as events soon proved, N. A. M. Dudley was hardly the man to let policy interfere with sentiment for very long. And his actions caused a storm of criticism to break over the officers and men of the Ninth Cavalry.

On July 15, Alexander McSween, with forty-one followers, rode into Lincoln and prepared for battle. He stationed some of the men in his home, while others took positions in the houses of sympathizers and at other strategic places. A short time later Peppin, Dolan, and a posse of more than fifty men converged on Lincoln and also took up points of vantage. Then Peppin sent his deputy, John Long, to the McSween house to serve warrants on a number of men there, but he was fired on as he neared the place and was forced to take cover.[74]

Both sides "dug in" during the night, and when morning came the battle was joined. A literal rain of lead whistled across and down the streets of Lincoln with neither side able to gain an advantage, and Peppin tried to borrow a howitzer from Dudley. The latter refused, but the exchange caused him to send Private Berry Robinson of H Company to Lincoln as a courier.

Robinson arrived on the edge of town just before dark and was stopped by four armed and mounted men who inquired as to his business. He replied that he was on "government business" and

<hr />

[73] Dudley to the AAAG, District of New Mexico, July 6, 1878, LR, District of New Mexico.
[74] Nolan, *op. cit.,* 374–75; Keleher, *op. cit.,* 142; Statement of Deputy Sheriff John Long, July 22, 1878, LR, District of New Mexico.

was told he was damned saucy, to which he replied, "I talk no more damned saucy than you do."[75] The men drew revolvers and Robinson chambered a slug in his carbine, but they let him pass. As he neared the McSween house, bullets zipped dangerously close, but he reached Peppin safely.

This minor episode proved decisive in the war. It is to be doubted that the McSween people fired deliberately at a federal trooper. They were more likely shooting at members of the posse who were in his vicinity, but Dudley charged the shots were aimed at Robinson. It was all the excuse he needed to intervene, and his intervention broke the stalemate and gave victory to Murphy-Dolan.

With almost uninterrupted firing, the battle in Lincoln raged into its fourth day, while Dudley conferred with his officers and decided to march into Lincoln, so he later wrote, "for the sole purpose of giving protection to women and children." But he also added that he believed the McSween faction was wrong in defying Sheriff Peppin and, further, some of its members had fired at Private Robinson.[76]

Having satisfied himself that intervention was warranted, and in the face of General Orders No. 49, Dudley saddled every man of F and H companies, a howitzer, Gatling gun, two thousand rounds of ammunition, and three days' rations, and marched into Lincoln on July 19. Cautioning his troopers to pay no attention to catcalls and jeers, he rode down the main street and went into camp at the lower end of town. Here he issued an invitation to terrified women and children to take shelter with the troops and many did. This action would seem to have completed Dudley's announced purpose for coming to Lincoln, but it proved to be only a preliminary step.

Summoning Justice of the Peace Wilson, Dudley forced that frightened but reluctant official to issue warrants for the arrest of McSween, Billy the Kid, and others and then assisted the posse

[75] Proceedings of a Board of Officers Convened at Fort Stanton, New Mexico, July 18, 1878, LR, District of New Mexico.
[76] Dudley to the AAAG, District of New Mexico, July 20, 1878, File No. 1405–1878.

in attempting to serve them. The tide of battle turned at once. McSween's home was set ablaze, and as the defenders fled the smoke and flames, four were shot down, among them McSween who died in his own back yard. Six of the men in the house made their escape, including Billy the Kid. The Battle of Lincoln was at an end.

Next day Dudley went to the smoldering ruins of the Mc-Sween home with an escort of troopers. McSween's body lay where it had fallen, and chickens were pecking at the dead man's face and eyes. Two buffalo soldiers shooed the chickens away, but a dazed Mrs. McSween vehemently refused Dudley's belated offer of assistance and ordered him off the premises. The corpse "was placed unwashed in a blanket and box and buried without ceremony."[77] Meanwhile, the drunken and triumphant victors pillaged the Tunstall store and carried off thousands of dollars in merchandise. Dudley made no effort to protect the property, and, apparently satisfied that he had done his duty, returned to Fort Stanton.[78]

At district headquarters in Santa Fe, Hatch digested reports of the affair in Lincoln and sent a tart telegram to Dudley that his actions had been illegal and should cease at once. For the next few weeks activities of the troopers at Stanton were restricted to providing protection for the Mescalero agency from attacks by roving bands of outlaws, but killing, stealing, and general lawlessness continued to plague Lincoln and neighboring Dona Ana County. On October 2, a band known as the Wrestlers attacked the ranch of a man named Bartlett below Fort Stanton, took the wives of two employees, "forced them into the brush, stripped them naked and used them for their pleasure."[79] Dudley sent Captain Carroll

77 *Ibid.* This is Dudley's official report in which he limits his activities to protecting noncombatants and says nothing of any active role in the fighting. A well-researched and objective study of these events can be found in Keleher, *op. cit.,* 143–44. See also Nolan, *op. cit.,* 378–79. A detailed report can be found in "Charges and Specifications Against Lieutenant Colonel N.A.M. Dudley, Commander at Fort Stanton, New Mexico," May 3, 1879, LR, District of New Mexico.

78 Nolan, *op. cit.,* 379.

79 Dudley to Hatch, October 3, 1878, File No. 1405–1878; Organizational Returns, Ninth Cavalry, August-September, 1878.

and twenty troopers of F Company to the Bartlett Ranch, but they were unable to apprehend the outlaws.

Governor Axtell's partisanship in the Lincoln County troubles had, meanwhile, brought a drumfire of criticism, and on September 30, 1878, he was removed from office and replaced by the celebrated General Lew Wallace. The new governor at once applied to Hatch for troops to restore order in Lincoln County, and the latter telegraphed Pope for instructions. On October 8, Hatch received an answer in the form of a presidential proclamation ordering those responsible for the lawlessness in Lincoln County and other parts of New Mexico Territory to disperse peaceably to their homes before noon on October 13, or else military force would be invoked and continued so long as resistance lasted.[80]

Troopers moved swiftly to assist civil officials, and before the month was out, violence had subsided to the point that Wallace issued a general amnesty but did not include the officers at Fort Stanton. Dudley's talent for controversy led him to write Wallace an insulting letter, while at the same time engaging in a bitter quarrel with Mrs. McSween and Huston Chapman, a lawyer and friend of Wallace whom the widow had employed to settle her late husband's tangled affairs. Mrs. McSween blamed Dudley for the unfortunate outcome of the fight in Lincoln, and Chapman charged, in a letter to Wallace, that Dudley was "criminally responsible" for McSween's death. Dudley, never at a loss for words, replied by maligning the character of Mrs. McSween.

All this was too much for Wallace, and on December 7 he formally requested Hatch to remove Dudley as commanding officer at Stanton, remarking that the latter had "excited the animosity of parties in Lincoln County to such a degree as to embarrass the administration of affairs in that locality."[81] Hatch forwarded the request through channels, and it received the approval of both Pope and Sheridan but was denied by General Sherman. Dudley, apparently, still had loyal friends in Washington.[82]

---

[80] The Secretary of War to General Sherman, October 8, 1878, File No. 1405–1878.

[81] Wallace to Hatch, December 7, 1878, *ibid.;* Keleher, *op. cit.,* 192.

[82] Keleher, *op. cit.,* 200–201.

On February 18, 1879, lawyer Chapman was shot and killed by two gunmen of the Murphy-Dolan faction in front of the Lincoln County Courthouse. Chapman was unarmed and the killing was without provocation. George Kimball, who had succeeded the discredited Peppin, was at Fort Stanton at the time, requesting assistance in arresting Billy the Kid and a few companions who were roaming the streets. Kimball had been unable to find anyone with courage enough to join a posse. Lieutenant Dawson, with a detachment drawn from F, H, and M companies, accompanied Kimball to Lincoln, but Billy and his friends had departed. They did find the body of Chapman, still lying where he had fallen, for local citizenry were too intimidated even to approach the corpse. Dawson located a trembling justice of the peace to whom he gave the necessary assistance "and the body was removed to the Courthouse."[83]

Chapman's murder brought both Wallace and Hatch to Lincoln. The governor remained in town with a bodyguard of buffalo soldiers while Hatch went on to Stanton. Here, at Wallace's request, he removed Dudley from command and ordered him to Fort Union to await formal charges, primarily that he had conspired to murder Alexander McSween. Captain Carroll replaced Dudley as the commanding officer at Stanton.[84]

On April 14, a grand jury convened at Lincoln and returned some two hundred indictments, most of them against members of the Murphy-Dolan crowd, and one against Dudley, charging him with arson in the burning of the McSween home. Two days later a court of inquiry assembled at Fort Stanton to review a host of charges against Dudley, growing out of his action in Lincoln on July 19–20 and later. Once again Dudley's luck and influence held. He was acquitted by a jury in Mesilla on the arson charge, and after protracted hearings of more than seven weeks, the court of

83 Dudley to Hatch, February 19, 1879, File No. 1405–1878; Dawson to Dudley, February 19, 1878, *ibid*.

84 Dudley to the AG, March 13, 1879, *ibid.;* Dudley to General Sherman, March 18, 1879, *ibid*. In this personal letter to Sherman, Dudley makes much of the fact that Wallace and Hatch came to Lincoln together.

inquiry cleared him of all charges. His attorney telegraphed exult-antly to United States Attorney General Charles Devens:

> General Dudley triumphantly acquitted yesterday after long fierce trial. Jury out but a moment, great applause by people. It is time prosecutions against him eased. Inform Adj. General.[85]

It mattered little that Wallace, Hatch, and Pope all felt there had been a whitewash, for Dudley was soon commanding the post at Fort Cummings.

For many months small detachments of the Ninth continued to aid civil officials in running down desperadoes in Lincoln and Dona Ana counties, despite Hatch's protest to department head-quarters: "Unquestionably the troops find this duty disagreeable, as it must expose them to more or less odium and obloquy from the community."[86] He might have added that his obedient and tire-less troopers rarely encountered anything other than "odium and obloquy" from the public, no matter how faithfully they carried out the orders of their officers.

With the close of the Dudley court of inquiry, the Lincoln County War might properly be said to have ended, except for running down the remaining hardened outlaws. The energies of the Ninth, however, had never been fully directed toward paci-fying that strife-torn county. No more than three companies were ever at Stanton, for others were needed to combat continual Apache raiding, and trouble with the Colorado Utes diverted still more strength to that area. Officers and men of the Ninth might die, but it is doubtful that monotony killed any of them.

The background of the Ute troubles of 1878–79 is grimly similar to those of other tribes who held lands the white man found desirable. For many years the Colorado Utes—White River, Uncompahgre, and Southern Ute bands—were not in the direct

---

85 Sidney M. Barnes to Charles Devens, November 30, 1879, *ibid.;* Carroll to the AAG, District of New Mexico, May 3, 1879, LR, District of New Mexico. Carroll's letter contains a summary of affairs in Lincoln County for the week ending May 3 and includes the work of the grand jury.

86 Hatch to the AAG, Department of the Missouri, December 17, 1878, File No. 1405–1878.

line of white advance, but the discovery of gold in 1859 and the Pikes Peak rush brought the inevitable white influx, and a treaty in 1863. The terms were not ungenerous and the Utes were left all the territory west of the Continental Divide. Typically, they did not long remain undisturbed, and in 1868 they were forced to make additional cessions and to accept Ouray, an Uncompahgre, as chief of all the Utes.[87]

By the time the Ninth Cavalry moved to New Mexico in 1876 the Utes were served by three agencies: a northern on White River, a middle on the Gunnison and later on the Uncompahgre, and a southern near the New Mexican border. White pressure was mounting and bold squatters were encroaching on Indian lands. Ute retaliation was inevitable. Cabins were burned, stock stolen and sometimes killed or maimed, and by March, 1878, Agent F. H. Weaver was concerned about an outbreak and fearful for his life. Lieutenant Valois with a detachment of troopers from D Company of the Ninth came to Los Piños to investigate.

Valois was at the agency when the Utes came in for rations and annuities and sullenly insisted on a four-week supply. After discussing the matter with Valois, Weaver made the issue. The Indians did not return until the full time had elapsed and then made the same demands. Once more Weaver yielded, but when the Utes came in and wanted still another four-week issue, the agent closed the storehouse and sent for troops.

Major Morrow with D, G, I, K, and M companies marched to the La Plata River and encamped. Here he was joined by Hatch and Captain A. S. Kimball, who came north from Santa Fe. Hatch arranged a council with Ignacio, the Southern Ute war chief, and a number of his warriors. All were insolent and the warriors told Hatch "we have no ears to hear unless Ignacio agrees."[88] Hatch did not dally. He told Ignacio the troops had come in peace to protect Indians as well as whites, but if the Utes

---

87 *Annual Report of the Commissioner of Indian Affairs for the Year 1868*, 16; Robert Emmitt, *The Last War Trail: The Utes and the Settlement of Colorado*, 23–24.

88 Captain A. S. Kimball to the Quartermaster General, U.S. Army, Washington, D.C., June 1, 1878, LR, District of New Mexico; *Annual Report of the Commissioner of Indian Affairs for the Year 1878*, 17.

wanted war, it might as well begin immediately. There would be no gifts except bullets from gun muzzles, if necessary. Then, adopting a more conciliatory tone, Hatch indicated that if the Indians desired peace, he would return with a commission to negotiate an acceptable treaty. This proposal satisfied Ignacio and, after a scout along the La Plata, Hatch returned to Santa Fe.[89]

On May 24, 1878, a Ute Commission was appointed consisting of Hatch, N. C. McFarland of Kansas, and William Stickney of Washington, D.C., although the latter was soon replaced by Lot M. Morrill of Maine. Tedious negotiations were conducted during the summer and the Southern Utes agreed to move to the headwaters of Chama, Navajo, Blanco, Piedra, and San Juan rivers, thereby relinquishing claim to a strip occupied by settlers. Efforts at a more comprehensive settlement with all the Colorado Utes failed. But in Southern Colorado, at least, a possible war had been averted and peace prevailed.[90]

Serious trouble was not avoided with the White River Utes, however. N. C. Meeker, who became agent to this band early in 1879, quickly aroused bitter resentment when he made strenuous efforts to educate the Utes and convert them into farmers. A crisis came in September, 1879, when Johnson, a brother-in-law of Ouray, quarreled with the elderly Meeker and gave him a bad beating. With the atmosphere at the agency ominous, Meeker appealed for troops.

In response to this appeal, Major T. T. Thornburgh, Fourth Infantry, left Fort Frederick Steele in Wyoming on September 21 with three companies of cavalry, one of infantry, and a train of twenty-five wagons. Meanwhile, aware that Captain Dodge and Company D of the Ninth were encamped on Grand River, Meeker also messaged Dodge for aid.

Thornburgh's command reached Milk River near the agency on September 29, crossed that stream after watering, and had

[89] Kimball to the Quartermaster General, June 1, 1878, LR, District of New Mexico.

[90] William Leeds, Acting Commissioner of Indian Affairs, to Hatch, May 24, 1878, *ibid.*; *Annual Report of the Commissioner of Indian Affairs for the Year 1878,* 170–72.

proceeded only a short distance when several hundred Utes, well concealed on ridges overlooking the trail, opened a withering fire. Several men were killed and Thornburgh ordered a retreat to the wagons which had been hastily corralled about two hundred yards from the river. During the retreat Thornburgh was killed along with a number of his men.

Under heavy attack the troops unloaded the wagons, made breastworks of the contents, and fought off the swarming Utes, but fighting continued until nightfall. The troops used the respite to dig trenches around the wagons and a pit in the center of the corral for a hospital. Nearly all the horses had been killed and their carcasses were used to strengthen the breastworks. When this work had been completed, couriers were sent out to seek aid.

At daybreak the Utes opened a galling fire that made any movement about the corral suicidal, and there was no letup on this or the following day. Suffering became acute, but a measure of relief was near at hand. Captain Dodge, Lieutenant M. B. Hughes, and thirty-five buffalo soldiers, after a hard ride, reached the Yampa River before dawn on October 2 and halted briefly. Each trooper was issued three days' rations and ample ammunition, the train was parked, and with only one pack mule Dodge pushed on to the embattled command on Milk River. The corral was reached at daybreak without loss, accompanied by the cheers of the defenders.[91]

The battle continued unabated throughout the day, and that night veteran buffalo soldier Sergeant Henry Johnson left his rifle pit under heavy fire and made the rounds of the trenches to see that all was well. On the evening of the fifth day of fighting Johnson once more climbed from his pit, shot his way to the river, and returned with a supply of water. This intrepid soldier became another individual in a growing list of the Ninth Cavalry to wear the Medal of Honor.[92]

91 Elmer R. Burkey, "The Thornburgh Battle With the Utes on Milk Creek," *The Colorado Magazine*, Vol. XIII, No. 3 (May, 1936), 96–108; Organizational Returns, Ninth Cavalry, September–October, 1879.

92 Captain M. B. Hughes to the Adjutant, Ninth Cavalry, July 26, 1893, LR, AGO, File No. 5993–PRD–1890, RG 94, NA.

A deadly fire from Ute sharpshooters continued, but the couriers, sent out on the first night of the battle, had gotten through. Colonel Wesley Merritt marched from Fort D. A. Russell with five companies of the Fifth Cavalry and reached Milk River on the morning of October 5. As he approached, the Utes retreated, ending the ordeal of the men in the corral. Fourteen were dead, forty-three were wounded, and of all the horses and mules only a handful were still alive. In Dodge's company only two animals were left. Ute casualties were uncertain, but the Indians were well concealed and their losses were undoubtedly light.

Merritt rode on to the agency to find nothing but death and devastation. Meeker and eleven employees had been murdered and all the women and children taken captive. Their release was soon obtained, and the White River Utes faced removal for their deeds, but Captain Dodge and a weary Company D were already marching south. Apaches were on the rampage in New Mexico and Colonel Hatch was in desperate need of every buffalo soldier in the regiment.[93]

[93] Burkey, *loc. cit.,* 108–109; Walter F. Beyer and Oscar F. Keydel, *Deeds of Valor,* II, 253–59.

VIII

THE VICTORIO WAR

THE POLICY of Apache concentration paid a frightful and inevitable dividend in late August, 1879. Victorio and his Warm Springs Apaches, along with a few restless Mescaleros, fled the Fort Stanton reservation resolved to die before submitting to the white man's yoke. The immediate cause of the breakout was the appearance on the reservation of a hunting party, among them a judge and the Grant County prosecuting attorney. Under indictment for murder, and fearing either arrest or another forced return to the hated San Carlos reserve in Arizona, Victorio chose to run and to fight. At root, however, the Victorio War was a direct result of white greed coupled with mistaken policy which denied the right of the Warm Springs Indians to live on land they loved and required that they dwell on a reservation where time and again they had sworn never to remain.

It was not the role of the buffalo soldiers and their officers to make Indian policy, but to carry out that policy and contend with its results regardless of merit. General Pope summarized their duty succinctly. He deplored the concentration policy as a tragic mistake, but there was now a war to be fought against Victorio and his people and, "The capture is not very probable, but the killing (cruel as it will be) can, I suppose, be done in time."[1] It was a grim prophecy and it fell the lot of the Ninth and Tenth Cavalry to be the prime instruments in its realization.

Victorio had scarcely left the reservation before he cut a swath through sheepherders and their flocks, and he was quick to leave his calling card with the Ninth. On September 4, with

[1] *Annual Report of the Secretary of War for the Year 1880*, I, Part 2, 88.

sixty warriors, he struck like a lightning bolt at the horse herd of Captain Hooker's Company E at Ojo Caliente. In a matter of minutes eight troopers guarding the herd were either dead or wounded and E was minus forty-six mounts. Hooker had been all but unhorsed at one fell swoop, and General Pope was quick, and perhaps unfair, to charge him with "carelessness."[2]

In the next six days the Apaches killed nine citizens and Hatch put every company of his regiment into the field. It was the beginning of more than a year of concerted effort by the buffalo soldiers to run Victorio to earth—as grueling a campaign as United States cavalry ever was called upon to undertake.

Victorio's trail was found on September 16 by scouts from a column under Lieutenant Colonel Dudley consisting of Captain Dawson's B Company and Hooker's E. A pursuit of two days brought them to the cañons at the head of the Las Animas River, and here a strongly entrenched Victorio awaited them. The troopers found themselves virtually trapped under a withering fire. Dudley was in another mess and one which all his Washington influence could hardly solve for him. His luck held to some degree, however, for the heavy gunfire echoing and re-echoing along the cañon walls was heard by Captain Beyer and Lieutenant Hugo who were searching nearby with Companies C and G.

Beyer and Hugo galloped to the scene and joined the fight, but all four companies were unable to dislodge the Apaches, and, after an all-day fight, Dudley ordered a withdrawal at nightfall. Five troopers and three scouts were dead as well as thirty-two horses. The Ninth's first head-on encounter with Victorio had been a near disaster, and thereafter Dudley's name was conspicuous by its absence from field reports. Major Morrow, a far abler soldier, took command of operations in southern New Mexico.[3]

Morrow, with detachments from B, C, and G and a body of Apache scouts, found Victorio's trail and stuck like glue for

---

2 *Ibid.,* 86.

3 Pope to the AAG, Military Division of the Missouri, September 24, 1879, Selected Documents Relating to the Activities of the Ninth and Tenth Cavalry in the Campaign against Victorio, 1879–80, File No. 6058–1879, AGO, RG 94, NA (Hereinafter cited as File No. 6058–1879).

eleven days until the chief turned at bay on the Cuchillo Negro. Morrow launched his attack at once and fighting raged from mid-afternoon of September 29 until ten o'clock in the evening when both sides let their rifles cool and got some rest. Next morning, while the troopers were swallowing their hardtack and coffee, an Apache sharpshooter killed a sentinel on post overlooking the camp. Fighting broke out immediately with the troopers pressing their antagonists, and finally dislodging them. A two-hour running fight followed, but near two in the afternoon Morrow was forced to break off the action and return to the head of the Cuchillo Negro for water. Three Apaches were known to have been killed, while Morrow lost two troopers and a number of horses.

Pursuit was again taken up on the morning of October 1, and near sundown the scouts reported that Victorio's camp had been located some four miles to the front. Morrow halted and waited until midnight before moving up in order to strike at day-break, but when the attack was ordered the Indians had fled. Victorio's position was so strong that Morrow reported had he been forced to take the camp, it would have "cost the lives of half the command."[4]

The Apaches had fled into the Mogollons, and Morrow moved in to Ojo Caliente for rations and ammunition and sent to Fort Bayard for reinforcements. He moved out again on October 5 and was joined on the march by Captain Purington with H Company, Captain Beyer with the rest of C, a detachment of A Company, Sixth Cavalry, and about two dozen Indian scouts. Three weeks of twisting, turning, grinding pursuit followed that took its toll of men and horses and eventually brought the column to Palomas Lake some four miles south of the Mexican border.

The dogged Morrow, reduced to eighty-one leather-tough buffalo soldiers and eighteen Indian scouts, continued the pursuit although "horses were dropping every mile." His bulldog tenacity was finally rewarded on October 27 when he overtook Victorio near the Corralitas River, but he could not drive him from very strong positions. With his troopers in tatters, rations gone, and

4 Morrow to the AAG, District of New Mexico, November 5, 1879, *ibid.*

most of his animals dead, Morrow had no choice other than to retire to Fort Bayard where he arrived on November 2. He had been unable to bring off a decisive action, but he had at least driven Victorio from the country.[5]

Colonel Hatch wrote to General Pope at this point describing the difficulties involved in fighting such an enemy:

Major Morrow's command shows that the work performed by these troops is most arduous, horses worn to mere shadows, men nearly without boots, shoes and clothing. That the loss in horses may be understood when following the Indians in the Black Range the horses were without anything to eat five days except what they nibbled from piñon pines, going without food so long was nearly as disastrous as the fearful march into Mexico of 79 hours without water, all this by forced marches over inexpressably rough trails explains the serious mortality among the horses. . . . Morrow has over exerted himself to such an extent as to produce a dangerous hemorage [*sic*], long night marches have been made on foot by the troops in their efforts to surprise the Indian camp. Morrow deserves great credit for the persistency with which he has kept up the pursuit and without foot Indians and constant vigilance must have fallen into ambuscades resulting in the destruction of his command. The Indians are certainly as strong as any command Major Morrow has had in action. We always fight in extended skirmish line, the Indian line is always found to be of same length and often longer extending in some actions more than two miles hence the efforts to extend his flanks with the object of surrounding them fails.

The Indians select mountains for their fighting ground and positions almost impregnable usually throwing up stone rifle pits where nature has not furnished them and skilfully devising loopholes.

The Indians are thoroughly armed and as an evidence they are abundantly supplied with ammunition their fire in action is incessant and nearly all their horses and mules they abandon on the march are shot. It is estimated they have killed 600 to 1,000 since the outbreak. . . . It is impossible to describe the exceeding

5 *Ibid.* Morrow had high praise for the courage and devotion to duty of Sergeants Thomas Fredericks of H Company and David Badie of B, Corporal Charles Parker of G, and Privates Isaac Holbrook and William Jones of H and L respectively.

roughness of such mountains as the Black Range and the San Mateo. The well known Modoc Lava beds are a lawn compared with them.[6]

After shaking off Morrow, Victorio holed up in the Candelaria Mountains for a time. Here he rested amidst plenty of wood, water, and grass. His warriors, however, found easy prey upon which to improve their marksmanship. A party of fifteen Mexicans from the little town of Carrizal went out in search of cattle thieves and had the misfortune on November 7 to come upon Victorio's trail. They followed it and rode straight into an Apache ambush. Not a single man survived. When they failed to return, thirty-five of their fellow citizens set out to find them, were also ambushed, and eleven of their number killed. The desperate Mexicans sought the aid of Lieutenant G. W. Baylor, who was stationed at Ysleta, Texas, with Company C, Texas Rangers. Baylor responded with ten men and marched with the Mexicans to the scene of the ambush. All they accomplished was the burial of twenty-six bodies.[7]

The devastating blow to the people of Carrizal did, however, stir a lethargic Mexican government to action. General Trevino, commanding in Chihuahua, raised a large force to fight the Apaches and telegraphed Hatch that the movement of Mexican troops would probably serve to drive Victorio back into New Mexico, and he pledged his full co-operation. Trevino was right —January, 1880, found Victorio on another slashing raid into New Mexico and the Ninth once more took to the field.[8]

On January 9, Morrow closed with Victorio near the head of the Puerco River, but the cunning chieftain slipped from his grasp

[6] Hatch to Pope, February 25, 1880, *ibid.* It is noted here that many writers in describing these campaigns stress the large number of troops in the field against Victorio. At this period the Ninth and Tenth Cavalry constituted most of the soldiers in the field and thus added up to twenty-four companies with a normal strength of about 2,000 men, and this is the figure commonly used. This information ignores the fact, however, that both regiments were far under strength and that Hatch had not more than 400 effectives and Grierson about 550. Thus the combined strength of both regiments was fewer than 1,000. See Organizational Returns of the Ninth and Tenth Cavalry for the months of September, 1879, to February, 1880.

[7] Lieutenant G. W. Baylor, Company C, Texas Frontier Battalion, to General John B. Jones, AG, Austin, Texas, December 3, 1879, File No. 6058–1879.

[8] Pope to the AAG, Military Division of the Missouri, January 9, 1880, *ibid.*; Hatch to Pope, January 13, 1880, *ibid.*

and then, like a chain of exploding firecrackers, Morrow pursued, caught up, and was fought off on January 17 in the San Mateos, on January 30 and again on February 3 in the San Andrés Mountains. None of these engagements was decisive and Morrow's loss was three men killed, including Lieutenant Hansell French, and seven men wounded. A month of continuous marching and fighting had exhausted Morrow's command. Forage, rations, and ammunition were also dangerously low, and he turned back to Ojo Caliente to rest and refit. Meanwhile, Victorio seemed to vanish in thin air, though leaving a trail of dead and dying New Mexicans in his path.[9]

Victorio's success thus far in fending off all forces sent against him brought new recruits to his ranks, including several score fighting men from the Mescalero reservation. Believing that the Mescaleros were not only joining but feeding and arming Victorio's renegades, General Pope issued orders to Hatch to march on the Mescalero reservation and disarm and dismount these Indians.[10]

On February 23, Hatch formed all the troops at his disposal into three battalions under Morrow, Captain Hooker, and Captain Carroll. Believing that Victorio was in Hembrillo Cañon in the San Andrés Mountains, Hatch decided on a two-phase operation. His battalions would descend on Victorio from the west, east, and north, and having, he hoped, inflicted a decisive defeat on the elusive chief, he would then march on to the Mescalero reservation and attend to his assigned task there.[11]

Morrow left Fort Bayard on March 29 with Companies H, L, and M, Ninth Cavalry, about seventy-five men, a detachment of the Fifteenth Infantry, and a few San Carlos Indian scouts. He marched to Palomas where he was joined by reinforcements from Arizona—Captain C. B. McClellan, Lieutenants Gatewood and

[9] Morrow to Hatch, January 18, 1880, *ibid.;* Hatch to Pope, February 3, 1880, *ibid.*

[10] Secretary of the Interior to the Secretary of War, February 11, 1880, *ibid.;* *Annual Report of the Secretary of War for the Year 1880,* I, Part 2, 93–98.

[11] *Annual Report of the Secretary of War for the Year 1880,* I, Part 2, 109–10; General Field Order No. 1, Headquarters, District of New Mexico, February 23, 1880, File No. 6058–1879.

Mills with eight-five troopers of the Sixth Cavalry, and about forty Indian scouts. The battalion then marched to Alemán on the Jornada del Muerto near the west slope of the San Andrés. Carroll, with Companies A, D, F, and G of the Ninth, about one hundred men, moved westward from Fort Stanton to attack from the east, while Hooker with detachments of buffalo soldiers from E, I, and K, twenty men of the Fifteenth Infantry, and some Navaho scouts came down the west slope from the north.

The plan was well conceived and just might have worked, but a water pump spoiled Hatch's strategy. Carroll was on the march on April 4 and Hooker two days later. Morrow was scheduled to reach Hembrillo Cañon by daybreak on April 8, but the water pump at Alemán, the only source of water at that desert station, had broken down and Morrow had great difficulty watering his command. On the evening of April 7, Morrow ordered McClellan and his scouts to make a night march in order to reach the cañon at the appointed time. Meanwhile, he would follow with the main column as rapidly as it could be watered. It proved a costly delay.

Early on the morning of April 8, McClellan reached Hembrillo Cañon to the sound of heavy gunfire and found Carroll pinned down and virtually surrounded. McClellan and his scouts swarmed to the attack, but Victorio and his warriors scattered among the rocks and vanished. It had been a close call for Carroll's diminutive battalion. Eight men were wounded, including Carroll, and twenty-five horses and mules had been killed. Indian losses were uncertain. Carroll believed at least three had been killed, while the scouts claimed that twenty had been bagged. Whatever the actual score, only one dead warrior was found on the field. A scout through the hills by the entire command on April 9—Morrow had arrived at sundown the previous day—found no sign of the Apaches. Hatch, who had come up with Morrow's battalion, took command of the united forces and set out for the Mescalero reservation to disarm and dismount the Indians at that agency.[12]

Meanwhile, General Ord had received orders from Sheridan

[12] Captain C. B. McClellan to the PA, Fort Bowie, Arizona Territory, May 16, 1880, File No. 6058–1879; Hatch to Pope, April 10, 1880, *ibid.*

216

to send the Tenth Cavalry to assist Hatch at the Mescalero agency. Grierson received his instructions on March 20 and began preparations at once. Officers and men were eager to carry out the assignment, for small parties of Warm Springs and Mescalero Apaches had been causing more than a little difficulty. Between July, 1879, and March, 1880, Captain Viele's C Company alone had chased raiding Mescaleros more than two thousand miles, while Carpenter, Keyes, and Lebo with H, D, and K amassed the amazing total of six thousand miles. They had been unable to inflict much damage on these flitting bands but had successfully screened the frontier from significant depredations.[13]

Grierson swiftly completed arrangements to protect his district and then set out with Companies D, E, F, K, and L, and a small detachment of the Twenty-fifth Infantry to guard his train. Scouting parties were thrown far out in order to cover a fifty-mile front and two strikes were made en route. Lieutenant Calvin Esterly, with troopers from D and L, found a trail that led northward through the White Sand Hills, and after a three-day pursuit of two hundred miles, ninety of which were without water, he overtook a band of raiders, killed one, and recovered eight head of stolen stock. Captain Lebo with K found a camp at Shakehand Spring, some forty miles south of the Peñasco River, killed one warrior, captured four squaws, and recovered a captive Mexican boy, Cayetano Segura, and more than twenty head of animals.[14]

On April 10 the entire command rendezvoused on the Peñasco after finding many trails that "invariably" led toward the Mescalero reservation. From the rendezvous the march was to the Tularosa where a number of Indian camps were found and Grierson prepared to attack, but a courier arrived from Agent S. A. Russell, who had replaced Godfroy, with the information that these Indians were friendly and were under instructions to move to the agency. After making certain that the Indians were actually

[13] Grierson to the AAG, Department of Texas, May 21, 1880, *ibid.;* Expeditions and Scouts Between August 31, 1879, and September 1, 1880, in *Annual Report of the Secretary of War for the Year 1880*, 134–47; Organizational Returns, Tenth Cavalry, July, 1879–March, 1880.

[14] Grierson to the AAG, Department of Texas, May 21, 1880, File No. 6058–1879.

on the move, Grierson moved on to the Mescalero agency where he joined Hatch on April 12.[15]

After some discussion with Agent Russell, Hatch and Grierson decided to wait another day until all the Indians had come in before disarming and dismounting them. If the delay was agreeable to Grierson, the disposition of troops and the location of the Indian camps were not. The former were at the agency, while the latter were across the Tularosa on a timbered ridge at the base of the mountains and a good half mile from the troops. Grierson reported:

> I advised the surrounding and complete disarming and dismounting of all the Indians at the Mescalero Agency, and their removal to Fort Stanton, where they would be under direct control of the military authorities. The agency had, for a long time, been simply a sort of hospital for old, infirm Indians, a commissary for Indian women and children, and a safe refuge and convenient place for the younger and more active Indians to obtain supplies to enable them to continue their raiding and depredations in Texas and elsewhere. The agency, too, had also become virtually a supply camp for Victorio's band, who, in addition to such means of subsistence, were, by a most remarkable manifestation of generosity on the part of the Interior Department, having their families fed and kindly cared for at the San Carlos Agency.[16]

Hatch, however, preferred to leave the Indians alone as long as Agent Russell felt he could handle them. This bit of leniency Hatch could ill afford, as he was soon to learn, and had Grierson's advice been taken, the lives of many Indians as well as whites would have been spared.

For two days stormy weather delayed any action and the Apaches came in slowly. The time was set forward to April 15, but a count on that day showed only 320 Indians present, and Russell believed another day would bring the total to four hundred. To this delay Hatch also assented, and April 16 was agreed upon for the disarming and dismounting.

15 *Ibid.*
16 *Ibid.*

On the morning of April 16, everything seemed to be in order and Hatch moved his command west of the agency, while Grierson and his troopers, along with Captain Steelhammer and Company G, Fifteenth Infantry, remained in camp. About ten o'clock in the morning firing was heard south of the agency, and Grierson mounted his command on the double but soon learned that some of the scouts had intercepted a small party of Indians running off some stock, had killed two of them, and returned the animals. Agent Russell was much upset. He claimed the Indians whom the scouts had killed were simply obeying his orders to go out and drive in some strays and that the scouts had made a terrible mistake.

Meanwhile, Hatch and Russell had agreed on a plan of procedure. Captain Steelhammer with his company, along with the agent, would carry out the actual disarming beginning precisely at two o'clock. Grierson and Hatch would hold their troopers in readiness in the event of trouble. If assistance was needed, Steelhammer was to fire three quick shots.

At the appointed time Steelhammer and Russell left to collect the arms and horses, and all seemed to go well until Grierson noticed a number of Indians, mounted and on foot, ascending the mountain behind their camp. Shortly thereafter came three quick shots. The troopers charged immediately and after lively skirmishing rounded up most of the runaways, but fourteen had been killed and about thirty had made their escape. The remaining Indians, about 250, were quickly disarmed and their animals taken from them. Then they were marched to the agency corral and placed under close guard.[17]

With duties completed at the Mescalero agency, Grierson and his command scouted "very thoroughly" in the Sacramento and Guadalupe Mountains, rounded up several small parties of Mescaleros, and drove them back to their reservation. Then with detachments ranging over a wide front he set out for Fort Concho where he arrived on May 16. The Concho column had marched

[17] Sheridan to Townsend, April 20, 1880, *ibid.;* Grierson to the AAG, Department of Texas, May 21, 1880, *ibid.; Annual Report to the Commissioner of Indian Affairs for the Year 1880*, 130.

fifteen hundred miles, killed five Indians, and captured five women, two children, and fifty head of stock. Young Cayetano Segura had been returned to his family.[18]

Victorio had not been idle in the meantime. After the fight in Hembrillo Cañon, he moved westward across the Río Grande and into the Mogollons, killing sheepherders, miners, and anyone else who had the misfortune to cross his path. Among the slain was a miner, James C. Cooney, brother Captain Cooney, commanding A Company, Ninth Cavalry. The latter had the sad task of burying personally his dead brother.[19]

Hatch and his Ninth were once again embarked on their seemingly unending pursuit of Victorio. At the time of the Mescalero breakout, Morrow's battalion was encamped southwest of the agency to prevent any flight in that direction. When news of the trouble reached him, Morrow moved toward Alamo Cañon and on April 17 overtook a small party, killed three warriors, and captured twenty animals. After a futile scout through Alamo and Dog cañons, Morrow moved in to Tularosa where he was joined by Lieutenant Cusack, commanding Carroll's battalion while the latter recuperated from his wounds.

Morrow marched southwest by way of White Sands and San Nicolás Spring into the San Andrés Mountains, but his scouts could find no sign of hostiles. The command watered at San Agustín Spring and then turned west to the Río Grande, and at last the elusive foe was sighted, but the horses were so broken down that the gap could not be closed and Morrow was forced to give up the chase and turn toward Ojo Caliente.[20]

Meanwhile, Hatch, with Hooker's battalion, cut Victorio's trail and pursued him into Arizona, but the Apaches doubled back into New Mexico and headed in the direction of Old Fort Tularosa, some fifty miles northwest of Ojo Caliente. On the evening of May 13, a lone rider on a lathered horse galloped into the Barlow and Sanders Stage Station with the news that Victorio, at that

18 Grierson to the AAG, Department of Texas, May 21, 1880, File No. 6058–1879.
19 Twitchell, *op. cit.*, 11, 439.
20 Morrow to the AAG, District of New Mexico, May 21, 1880, File No. 6058–1879.

moment, was probably wiping out the small settlement adjacent to Old Fort Tularosa. Fortunately, Sergeant George Jordan and a detachment of twenty-five buffalo soldiers of K Company were at the station and preparing to turn in for the night.

Jordan saddled his detachment at once and marched throughout the night, arriving at the Old Fort early on the morning of May 14. Victorio had not attacked, but Jordan set his troopers to work at once building a stockade. Once this task was completed, Jordan carefully stationed his troopers, sent out vedettes, and moved the frightened citizens into the stockade. Courage and fast work saved a slaughter. At dusk the Apaches struck but were met with a curtain of fire that drove them back. They again attacked and were fought off with equal vigor. This was enough for Victorio. He turned southwest toward the Mexican border, leaving Sergeant Jordan in full control of the stockade. Hatch rode in the following morning, paused only long enough to learn the details, and then pushed on after the fleeing Apaches. For gallantry and courage at Old Fort Tularosa, Sergeant Jordan was awarded the Congressional Medal of Honor.[21]

Hatch reached Ojo Caliente on May 21 and the next day Morrow also came in. Both commands were badly used up and Hatch telegraphed Pope that "the trails in the Mogollon and in Arizona are fearfully rough. There is no grass . . . and no forage to be obtained."[22] In fact, some of the detachments were still straggling in—their back trails littered with the dead animals of pursuer and pursued. Captain H. K. Parker and the Indian scouts were, however, still clinging doggedly to the trail, and on May 23 their persistence was rewarded—Parker located Victorio's camp near the head of the Palomas River.

Moving with the utmost caution and stealth, the scouts managed to creep within fifty yards of the unsuspecting Indians. At daybreak next morning Parker opened fire. The first volley killed a number of men, women, and children, but the Apaches were quick to recover from the surprise and returned shot for shot. It

21 Hatch to the AAG, Department of the Missouri, May 17, 1880, *ibid.;* Hutcheson, *loc. cit.,* 286; Beyer and Keydel, *op. cit.,* II, 273–76.
22 *Annual Report of the Secretary of War for the Year 1880,* I, Part 2, 109.

was a bitter, desperate little struggle which ended when Parker ran out of ammunition and water. He withdrew with seventy-five captured animals and left thirty dead Indians at the campsite.[23]

When Hatch received word of Parker's fight, he sent Morrow out at once to take up the trail. Pushing horses and men to their limits, Morrow caught up with Victorio's rear guard on May 30, killed three warriors, and wounded several more. The pursuit continued to the Mexican border where the troopers were forced to halt and in helpless rage watch their old enemy slip from their grasp—pressure from a vacillating Mexican government had once again caused Washington to issue orders forbidding violations of the international boundary.

Six days later, however, Morrow dealt the Apaches a sore blow. He intercepted a small party making its way to Mexico and his troopers killed two and wounded three others. One of the dead was Victorio's son.[24]

This may have been something of a consolation prize, but the main body of Indians had escaped, and a frustrated Hatch telegraphed General Pope to inquire if something could be done to lift restrictions on crossings into Mexico, particularly if the trail was "hot." In ten days he had the answer—the Mexican government refused to give its consent. Despite the fact that his foe had escaped, Hatch's campaign was hardly a failure, for he had again forced Victorio to take a Mexican vacation and had inflicted serious losses in men and animals. The chieftain's effective strength had been reduced to fewer than two hundred men.[25]

The brunt of the fighting thus far had fallen on the troopers of the Ninth, and late in May, General Sheridan ordered the Tenth sent to New Mexico. Grierson protested the move. It would leave the West Texas frontier wide open to attack, and he was convinced that Victorio's next move would be into Texas. Ord agreed with

23 Hatch to the AAG, Department of the Missouri, May 27, 1880, Military Division of the Missouri, Special File, Victorio Papers, 1880, United States Army Commands, RG 98, NA (hereinafter cited as Victorio Papers).

24 Hatch to Pope, June 1, 1880, File No. 6058–1879.

25 Hatch to Pope, June 12, 1880, Victorio Papers; Pope to Hatch, June 22, 1880, *ibid.*; Pope to the AAG, Military Division of the Missouri, June 21, 1880, File No. 6058–1879.

him and prevailed upon Sheridan to rescind the order. As it turned out Grierson had predicted the next phase of the campaign perfectly.[26]

Grierson was not clairvoyant. There were clear indications that Victorio might be looking with some favor on a tour of West Texas. On May 12 a party of eight Mescalero warriors, armed with late-model Winchester carbines, ambushed a party of citizens in Bass Cañon west of Fort Davis, killed James Grant and Mrs. Margaret Graham, wounded Harry Graham and a Mr. Murphy, and stripped their wagons of everything of value. Carpenter with H pursued to the Río Grande and reported that he was convinced the warriors were on their way to join Victorio.

In mid-June a party of Pueblo Indian scouts en route to Fort Davis was hit while passing through Viejo Cañon in the Chinati Mountains, and the chief scout, Simón Olguin, was killed along with most of the horses. Extensive scouting by detachments of the Tenth failed to turn up anything, but the surmise was that the Pueblos had run afoul of hawk-eyed spies from Victorio's camp.[27]

Grierson, meanwhile, had profited from Hatch's experience and decided on a change in tactics. Instead of wearing down his command in long and probably unprofitable pursuits, he proposed to guard the mountain passes and water holes. In this way he could block the movement of the Apaches through the passes, or failing in that, he could deny them water—and even an Apache had to stop for a drink.

Posting his troopers accordingly, Grierson left Fort Concho on July 10 and headed west with a small escort and his son Robert, who had arrived for a visit and a bit of excitement. He could hardly have chosen a better time. At Fort Davis on July 18, Grierson received word that Colonel Valle and four hundred Mexican troops were on Victorio's trail and believed the Apaches were headed for Eagle Springs, Texas. Continuing west, Grierson reached Eagle

[26] Sheridan to Townsend, May 26, 1880, File No. 6058–1879; Grierson to Hatch, May 29, 1880, Victorio Papers; Colonel William Whipple, AAG, Military Division of the Missouri, June 11, 1880, Victorio Papers.

[27] Grierson to the AAG, Department of Texas, May 18, 1880, LR, AGO; Carpenter to the AAG, District of the Pecos, June 2, 1880, *ibid.*; Lieutenant Robert Reed, Tenth Cavalry, to the PA, Fort Davis, Texas, June 28, 1880, *ibid.*

Springs on July 23 and learned that Victorio was near Ojo del Pino some fifty miles to the southwest in Mexico, that he had skirmished with Mexican scouts, and that he was on the move to the Río Grande. Grierson and his party proceeded to Fort Quitman where he was surprised to find that Valle and his troops were just across the river and badly in need of supplies. Grierson sent provisions to Valle but was fearful that the concentration of Mexican troops had given Victorio easy access to Texas.[28]

Grierson left Quitman on July 29 and headed for Eagle Springs, hopeful that he could intercept the Indians before they could do much damage. While en route an Indian was seen who fled when fired upon, and it was believed that he was a member of Victorio's advance. A short time later couriers from Captain J. C. Gilmore at Eagle Springs informed Grierson that Victorio had crossed into Texas. Gilmore had received the news from couriers sent by Captain Nolan, on the river near Quitman. Led by Lieutenant Henry Flipper, the first and only Negro officer in the regiment, the couriers had carried the dispatches ninety-eight miles in twenty-two hours.[29]

Faced with this information, Grierson decided to make camp at Tinaja de los Palmos, some fifteen miles west of Eagle Springs and "the only waterhole for a long distance north." Victorio would undoubtedly seek to water here and Grierson would be directly in his path. But Grierson had only eight men with him including his son Robert, hardly enough to fight Victorio and scarcely enough to detain him for long. Nevertheless, Grierson and his little band entrenched themselves as best they could high on the side of a ridge near the road. When the eastbound stage came by, Grierson sent word to Gilmore at Eagle Springs to send reinforcements immediately. About midnight couriers reached Grierson and informed him that the Indians were encamped not more than ten miles from his position. The couriers were hastened off

28 Grierson to Ord, July 24, 1880, File No. No. 6058–1879; Grierson to Pope, July 24, 1880, Victorio Papers.

29 Henry Flipper, *op. cit.*, 16. Flipper, the first Negro graduate of West Point, joined the Tenth in 1878.

to Fort Quitman with orders for Captain Nolan to come up with A Company as rapidly as possible.[30]

About four in the morning Lieutenant Leighton Finley of G Company, with ten troopers, arrived to escort Grierson to Eagle Springs. Instead Grierson posted Finley and his men lower down on the ridge and sent a courier to Gilmore with orders to bring every available man at Eagle Springs to Tinaja, and on the double. This done, Grierson settled down to await the sunrise.

At nine o'clock the Indian vanguard came into view, spied Grierson's position, and turned eastward so as to cross the road without a fight. Grierson would have none of this; he ordered Lieutenant Finley and ten men to charge the Apaches and hold them up until the other troops arrived. Finley carried out his orders "handsomely" and managed to hold the Indians in check. Near ten o'clock the advance guard of Captain Viele and C Company came up but in the smoke and dust mistook Finley's men for Indians and fired into them. Finley beat a hot retreat with the Indians in pursuit, but fire from the camp drove them off. Viele came up and entered the fight, and with the odds narrowing, the Apaches withdrew to a ridge south of Grierson's position, but Viele charged and dislodged them. The warriors then attempted to cross to the north but were driven back in some confusion, and at this point dust clouds from the west signaled Nolan's rapid approach. In danger of being cornered, Victorio turned and fled south toward the Río Grande. It had been a four-hour fight which cost the life of Private Martin Davis of C Company. Lieutenant S. R. Colladay was wounded and ten horses were killed. The Indian loss was placed at seven killed and an undetermined number wounded.[31]

Grierson sent out scouting parties immediately to find the Indian camp, and it was located on the Mexican side of the river about sixty miles below Fort Quitman. Colonel Valle was notified at once, but instead of marching downriver to attack, he turned northward toward El Paso and away from the scene of action.

[30] Grierson to Ord, July 30, 1880, File No. 6058–1879.
[31] *Ibid.*

Grierson believed Victorio was certain to make another attempt to move northward, and it came on August 3 when a patrol under Corporal Asa Weaver of H Company engaged the Indians in a fifteen-mile running fight near Alamo. During the action the mount of Private Willie Tockes of C Company suddenly bucked and ran squarely into a swarm of Apaches. When last seen, Tockes had dropped the reins and was firing his carbine right and left before going down under an avalanche of warriors.[32]

Grierson believed Victorio would attempt to get through one of the passes east of Van Horn's Wells, and with every available man from Eagle Springs he marched to that point only to discover that his wily foe had gone northwest of Van Horn's on the evening of August 4. Grierson knew how to march, he had proved that in his raid of 1863, and he proved it again on a torrid August 5, 1880. He was on the move at three in the morning for Rattle-snake Springs some sixty-five miles northwest, keeping a range of mountains between his command and the Indians. He covered the distance in twenty-one hours, arrived ahead of Victorio, and had ample time to prepare an ambush. Few, if any, commanders and their troops could boast of having outmarched a band of Apaches.

Early on August 6, Grierson placed C and G companies under Captain Viele in Rattlesnake Cañon to await Victorio's approach. It was a long wait, but near two in the afternoon the Indians were seen approaching. The troopers withheld their fire, hoping to volley at point blank range, but Victorio was cautious and perhaps sensed a trap, for he halted. Viele opened on them, causing considerable consternation in the Indian ranks, and they swiftly withdrew out of range. But Victorio needed water, and seeing only a few troopers, he regrouped his warriors and moved to attack. Grierson countered by sending Carpenter forward with H and B, and the Indians were thrown back and scattered among the hills and ravines.

At four in the afternoon Grierson's train, guarded by Company H, Twenty-fourth Infantry, and a detachment of troopers, rounded a point of the mountains to the southeast and headed for the spring.

---

32 Bigelow, "Sketch"; Organizational Returns, Tenth Cavalry, August, 1880.

Typical Apache Country. (Courtesy U.S. Signal Corps, National Archives)

Captain Thomas C. Lebo, Tenth Cavalry. (Courtesy National Archives)

Captain A. S. B. Keyes, Tenth Cavalry. (Courtesy National Archives)

"Tenth Cavalry at the Battle of Rattlesnake Springs," *original painting by Nick Eggenhofer.* (Courtesy of the artist, the National Park Service, and the Fort Davis National Historic Site)

Colonel Edward Hatch, commander of the Ninth Cavalry. (Courtesy National Archives)

Captain Henry Carroll, Ninth Cavalry. (Courtesy National Archives)

Lieutenant P. H. Clarke, Tenth Cavalry. (Courtesy National Archives)

A strong force of warriors rode to cut off the wagons, but they were beaten off by Captain Gilmore. Near dusk the Apaches made a final effort to reach water but were thrown back in confusion and fled with Carpenter in close pursuit.[33]

Victorio suffered a decisive defeat at Rattlesnake Springs, but this was not the only blow. Three days earlier Captain Lebo and K Company on scout in the Sierra Diablo struck pay dirt in the form of Victorio's supply camp. He routed the warrior guards, captured twenty-five head of cattle, a quantity of maguey bread, a supply of beef on pack animals, and some berries.

Grierson gave Victorio no time to rest. Companies of the Tenth guarded the water holes and closed the mountain passes to the north, while others pushed the search for Victorio, and on August 11, Carpenter and Nolan found his trail west of Fresno Spring and set out in pursuit. Carpenter's horses gave out, but Nolan hung on and chased the fleeing Apaches to the Río Grande where they crossed into Mexico. It was Victorio's last appearance on American soil.[34]

Grierson reported that his troopers had killed and wounded at least thirty warriors and more than seventy-five animals. Victorio had been stripped of his supplies and driven from the country. Scouts sent to follow the chief into Mexico had returned with the information that the Indians were making their way slowly to the Candelaria Mountains, hampered by many wounded, and with most of their stock broken down. Grierson's losses were three men killed, three seriously wounded, and a number with minor injuries, and one trooper, Private Wesley Hardy, was missing in action.[35]

Meanwhile, Mexican and American governments had at last agreed on a co-operative campaign to destroy Victorio. A powerful force was assembled under Colonels George Buell and Eugene

---

[33] Grierson to the AAG, Department of Texas, August 3, 1880, Victorio Papers; Grierson to the AAG, Department of Texas, August 4, 1880, *ibid.*; Grierson to Ord, August 14, 1880, *ibid.*

[34] Grierson to Ord, August 14, 1880, *ibid.;* Nolan to the Commanding Officer, Fort Bliss, Texas, August 15, 1880, *ibid.*

[35] Grierson to the AAG, Department of Texas, August 19, 1880, *ibid.;* Organizational Returns, Tenth Cavalry, August, 1880.

Carr to cross into Mexico and take combined action with Mexican troops commanded by Colonel Joaquin Terrazas. Ten companies of Grierson's buffalo soldiers were posted along the Río Grande to prevent a break into Texas.[36]

During the first days of October the troops of Buell, Carr, and Terrazas converged on Victorio, and scouts reported that he had taken refuge in the Tres Castillos Mountains. Avenues of escape were quickly closed off and plans for a final assault were made, but on October 9, Terrazas informed his American counterparts that the presence of their troops in Mexico was objectionable, and Buell and Carr reluctantly withdrew to the border. Terrazas then moved up, surrounded Victorio's camp, and on the morning of October 14 attacked from all sides. The battle was over by nine o'clock. Victorio was dead. Sixty warriors and eighteen women and children were also killed and sixty-eight women and children taken prisoner. One hundred and eighty animals were captured. Terrazas reported that only a handful of warriors had escaped his net and thrown off pursuit.[37]

Mexican troops had killed Victorio and most of his warriors and brought an end to the war. In a very real sense, however, they had only delivered the *coup de grâce*. The real victors were the buffalo soldiers of the Ninth and Tenth Cavalry. They had pursued and fought the great chief over thousands of blood-spattered miles in an unrelenting contest of courage, skill, endurance, and attrition. Twice Hatch had forced Victorio into Mexico and with a modicum of co-operation from Mexican troops could have ended the struggle. When Victorio turned into Texas, he marched into the jaws of disaster. Grierson's campaign was a model of its kind, a masterpiece of guerrilla warfare. Not an Indian penetrated the settlements, the Apaches were outfought and outmarched, denied access to food and water, and driven pell-mell into Mexico. Beaten, dispirited, and sapped of the will to fight, Victorio was an easy target for the final thrust.

Despite these achievements the buffalo soldiers received vir-

---

[36] Pope to Sheridan, September 10, 1880, Victorio Papers.
[37] Buell to Hatch, October 18, 1880, File No. 6058–1879; Terrazas to Buell, October 22, 1880, *ibid.*

tually no credit at the time and precious little since. Hatch and Grierson were objects of bitter criticism, and the latter has sometimes been pictured as little more than a buffoon. The men in the ranks more often than not were and have been tailored to fit the stereotype of grinning, fumbling, misfits, incapable of independent thought or action. But General Pope knew better and at the close of the campaign remarked:

> It is my duty, as it is my pleasure, to invite the special attention of the authorities to the meritorious and gallant conduct of Col. Edward Hatch, commanding the District of New Mexico, and to Major A. P. Morrow, Ninth Cavalry, and the officers and soldiers under their command, in the difficult and trying campaign against the Southern Apaches. Everything that men could do they did, and it is little to say that their services in the field were marked by unusual hardships and difficulties. Their duties were performed with zeal and intelligence and they are worthy of all consideration.[38]

And General Ord, who lost no love on Negro troopers, wrote:

> I trust that the services of the troops engaged will meet with that recognition which such earnest and zealous efforts in the line of duty deserve. They are entitled to more than commendation. . . . In this connection I beg to invite attention to the long and severe service of the Tenth Cavalry, in the field and at remote frontier stations, in this department. Is it not time that it should have relief by a change to some more favored district of the country?[39]

Rare praise and a worthy recommendation, but General Sheridan did not agree with his subordinate on a change to a "more favored district"—there were still more Apaches to fight and the Tenth faced five more years on the Texas frontier.

[38] *Annual Report of the Secretary of War for the Year 1880,* I, Part 2, 93.
[39] *Ibid.,* 111.

IX

THE FINAL YEARS

THE DEATH of Victorio and the near annihilation of his Warm Springs band at Tres Castillos on October 14, 1880, did much to bring peace along the Texas–New Mexican border, but a remnant had survived that was still capable of a painful if not fatal sting. A party of thirty warriors, en route to Victorio's stronghold, tarried long enough on the Río Grande to escape the fate of their people, and its members were quick to exact revenge. At dawn on October 28 they ambushed one of Grierson's patrols under Sergeant Charles Perry on the river below Ojo Caliente, Texas. Firing at point-blank range, they killed Corporal William Backus and Privates Jeremiah Griffin, James Stanley, Carter Burns, and George Mills. When reinforcements arrived, the Indians had departed and in so doing made off with four horses and two mules.[1]

For the next few months small parties of these inveterate raiders, ranging in number from eight to ten, were active enough in southern New Mexico to keep Hatch and most of his regiment in the field. In January, 1881, the stage was attacked near Fort Cummings, the driver, Thomas White, and a passenger were killed, and the mail scattered to the winds. Detachments of C, D, F, and I were unable to run down the renegades who fled back and forth across the international boundary. Repeated raids in February, March, and April brought the same results.[2]

More serious trouble was forthcoming. Nana, one of Victorio's lieutenants, had not been at Tres Castillos. More than

[1] Organizational Returns, Tenth Cavalry, October, 1880; Bigelow, "Sketch."
[2] Hatch to the AAG, Department of the Missouri, January 15, 1881, File No. 6058–1879; Organizational Returns, Ninth Cavalry, February–April, 1881.

seventy years old, bitter, implacable, and able, he nursed a burning desire to avenge his kinsmen. Carefully he collected a few warriors, guns, ammunition, and by July, 1881, he was ready. Nana with fifteen warriors left his nest high in the Sierra Madres of Mexico and General Pope later described what followed: "[they] rushed through the country from one mountain range to another like a pack of hungry wolves, killing everybody they met and stealing all the horses they could get their hands on."[3] Nana stopped long enough to recruit about two dozen war-hungry Mescaleros and with a force of forty warriors he gave the buffalo soldiers a nightmarish four months of campaigning.

Nana served notice on July 17 when he struck the pack train of Company L near the mouth of Alamo Cañon, wounded one trooper, and made off with three mules. Lieutenant John Guilfoyle with twenty men of L and a body of Apache scouts set out in pursuit. The chase led through Dog Cañon, across the inferno of White Sands, where the renegades killed three Mexicans, and on into the rugged fastnesses of the San Andres. And here on July 25 Guilfoyle caught up and attacked. The Indians fled leaving two horses and twelve mules behind, and Guilfoyle believed he had killed or wounded two warriors.[4]

Nana rode west, crossed the Río Grande, killed three more citizens, and headed into the San Mateos. Ranchers in the area formed a posse of thirty-six men in the naïve belief they could do better than regular troops and marched into the San Mateos to beard the Apaches. They found the trail and followed it into Red Cañon and into an ambush. When the firing was over, one rancher was dead, seven were wounded, and Nana had all their horses. Guilfoyle, following rapidly, caught up again on August 3 at Monica Springs, captured eleven horses, and wounded two warriors, but the rest of the band got away.[5]

Guilfoyle's horses broke down and it was nine days and two

---

[3] *Annual Report of the Secretary of War for the Year 1881*, 117.

[4] *Ibid.*, 126; Organizational Returns, Ninth Cavalry, July, 1881; Hutcheson, *loc. cit.*, 286.

[5] Organizational Returns, Ninth Cavalry, August, 1881; *Annual Report of the Secretary of War for the Year 1881*, 127; C. L. Sonnichsen, *The Mescalero Apaches*, 192.

dead citizens later before the Ninth found Nana again. Captain Parker and nineteen troopers of K Company intercepted him about twenty-five miles west of Sabinal. The Indians entrenched themselves in near impregnable positions, but Parker, outnumbered two to one, attacked at once. In a bitter fight of an hour and a half the gallant buffalo soldiers were beaten off and Nana escaped. Privates Charles Perry and Guy Temple were dead, three other troopers were wounded, and nine horses were killed. Parker cited Sergeant Thomas Shaw for extraordinary courage in action.[6]

On August 16, a hysterical Mexican dashed into the camp of Lieutenant Valois and I Company near Cuchillo Negro to report that Nana and his warriors had butchered his family on a ranch nearby. Lieutenant George Burnett and a detachment of fifteen men saddled immediately and set out for the ranch, while Valois and the rest of I prepared to follow. Burnett reached the ranch to find the horribly mutilated bodies of a woman and three children. The trail was easily found, and reinforced by a few Mexicans, Burnett took up the pursuit. The Indians were overtaken in the foothills of Cuchillo Negro, but as usual they had taken strong positions among the rocks and crevices.

Burnett deployed in three wings with himself leading the center, First Sergeant Moses Williams the right, and the Mexicans taking the left. Unable to dislodge the Indians, Burnett attempted to flank them with a handful of men and was nearly surrounded. Trumpeter John Rogers volunteered to go for aid and under a hail of bullets managed to get away unhurt and reach Valois. The latter marched swiftly to Burnett's right to flank the Indians from that side, but they shifted quickly and poured a volley into I Company killing ten horses.

Burnett charged, fought his way to Valois, and the united command fell back to stronger positions. Four troopers failed to hear the order to retreat and the Apaches moved to cut them off. Burnett, Sergeant Williams, and Private Augustus Walley

<hr>

[6] *Annual Report of the Secretary of War for the Year 1881*, 127; Organizational Returns, Ninth Cavalry, August, 1881; Hutcheson, *loc. cit.*, 286–87.

dashed to their rescue with leaden slugs cutting the air all around. Two of the imperiled men were wounded and unable to move. Burnett and Walley carried these, while Williams and the remaininw two troopers covered the retreat. Fighting continued until nightfall when Nana broke off the engagement and disappeared in the hills. For conspicuous gallantry in action Lieutenant Burnett, Sergeant Williams, and Private Walley were awarded the Congressional Medal of Honor—three more in the growing list of heroes among the officers and men of the Ninth Cavalry.[7]

From Cuchillo Negro Nana's trail led south, and Captain Cooney with A and Valois with I struggled to close with the fiendishly clever old warrior and his band. But another blow was in store for the Ninth. In an effort to cut off Nana's escape to Mexico, Hatch ordered Lieutenant G. W. Smith to march from Fort Cummings with a detachment of forty-six men of B and H. For reasons never explained, Smith moved out with only seventeen men. A party of cowboys under rancher George Daly joined him near McEver's ranch and the trail was followed to Gavilan Cañon.

Smith, fearing an ambush, called a halt, but Daly and his untrained crew plunged ahead, and the gallant Smith would not let them go alone. They had hardly entered the cañon before a crashing volley killed both Smith and Daly, and the latter's followers took to their heels, leaving seventeen buffalo soldiers to carry on the fight as best they could. Sergeant Brent Wood of B Company took command and held his ground until a detachment of H under Sergeant Anderson arrived. The combined command put the Apaches to flight, and Anderson pursued "carrying his dead and wounded with him."[8]

Nana and most of his warriors returned to the Sierra Madres after the fight in Gavilan Cañon, but some of them lingered on —too long as it turned out. On the morning of October 4, Apachewise Captains Carroll and Parker, with F and K companies, hit

[7] Hutcheson, *ibid.,* 287; Organizational Returns, Tenth Cavalry, August, 1881; Beyer and Keydel *op. cit.* II, 277–81.

[8] *Annual Report of the Secretary of War for the Year 1881,* 127; Beyer and Keydel, *op. cit.,* II, 281; Hutcheson, *loc. cit.,* 287; Organizational Returns, Ninth Cavalry, August, 1881.

the trail of these renegades on the eastern slopes of the Dragoon Mountains and followed it until late afternoon when the Apache rear guard was sighted. A fifteen-mile running fight brought the Indians to bay among the rocks and a sharp engagement of an hour was required to drive them out. The hostiles then scattered like a covey of quail and made for the Mexican border. F and K had three men and a horse wounded, while Indian losses, though believed heavy, were uncertain.[9]

Nana's raid capped six years of arduous service for the Ninth in New Mexico, Colorado, and Texas. They had fought effectively and almost continuously against Apaches, lawless whites, and Mexicans—this on the heels of eight demanding years on the Texas frontier. General Pope felt the Ninth was entitled to a much-needed rest, and in November Hatch was ordered to transfer regimental headquarters from Santa Fe to Fort Riley, Kansas. Five companies garrisoned this post with the others taking station at Fort Elliott, Texas, Fort Hays, Kansas, and Forts Sill, Reno, and Supply in Indian Territory.[10]

Meanwhile, Grierson and the Tenth were encountering problems of a different kind. The defeat of Victorio and the growing power of the Díaz regime in Mexico had gone far toward bringing unprecedented peace to the West Texas frontier. This favorabe turn of events permitted concentration of the regiment at Forts Concho, Stockton, and Davis, although small detachments maintained patrols along the Río Grande and in the Guadalupe Mountains.

Grierson was proud of his buffalo soldiers and with good reason. Their performance against Victorio could scarcely be faulted. They had marched, fought, and scouted in the best traditions of the service. Equally their behavior in camp and station left little to be desired. Desertions in 1880, despite the most rigorous campaign in the regiment's history, reached an all-time low of five— the best record by far of any regiment in the country. Other violations of the military code were also few in number: four cases

9 Organizational Returns, Ninth Cavalry, October, 1881; Hutcheson, *loc. cit.,* 287.
10 *Annual Report of the Secretary of War for the Year 1881,* 118; Organizational Returns, Ninth Cavalry, November–December, 1881.

of theft, one "neglect of duty," one assault and battery, three A.W.O.L., one "sleeping on post," one "leaving post as sentinel," one "selling of clothing," and two lesser offenses. By contrast the Eighth Cavalry, stationed adjacent to the Tenth, had exactly twice this number of offenses.[11]

A combat record that saved many lives and thousands of dollars in property, as well as excellent behavior, made little or no impression on the citizens of tough little Saint Angela [San Angelo after about 1880–81] and tensions between the town and the Fort Concho garrison remained high. Late in January, 1881, an incident occurred that finally broke the dam of trooper restraint. Impecunious soldiers sometimes danced or sang for drinks in the saloons, and on the night of January 31 Private William Watkins of E Company was so engaged in McDonald's Saloon. Tom McCarthy, a sheepman on the San Saba River, was enjoying the show and buying drinks. When Watkins finally tired and expressed a desire to stop, McCarthy insisted that he continue. Watkins protested politely, but this was enough to offend McCarthy. He pulled his pistol and killed the unarmed trooper with a shot through the head.

McCarthy fled the saloon, but on his way out of town he was apprehended by post guards at Fort Concho. He was held until the following morning when he was released in the custody of Sheriff Jim Spears. Instead of jailing the prisoner, Spears permitted him the freedom of the town, pending an examining trial. Feeling ran high at the garrison, and on Thursday, February 3, a handbill appeared on the streets of Saint Angela:

FORT CONCHO, TEXAS, FEB. 3, 1881
We, the soldiers of the U. S. Army, do hereby warn the first and last time all citizens and cowboys, etc., of San Angelo and vicinity to recognize our right of way as just and peaceable men. If we do

11 Organizational Returns, Tenth Cavalry, November, 1880; *Annual Report of the Secretary of War for the Year 1880,* I, Part 2, 152. Offenses for troopers of the Eighth included one discharge for worthlessness, three for neglect of duty, one for disobedience of orders, four for drunkenness on guard duty, one for quitting the guard, four for sleeping on post, four for being A.W.O.L., four for being drunk and disorderly, and six for minor offenses—not a bad record, but not as good as the Tenth.

not receive justice and fair play, which we must have, some one will suffer—if not the guilty the innocent.

"It has gone too far, justice or death."

SIGNED U. S. SOLDIERS[12]

On the evening the handbill appeared, a group of troopers left the post and searched for McCarthy, but Spears managed to hide that worthy behind the boardinghouse of a Mrs. Tankersley. Grierson, meanwhile, sent a strong detachment into town to round up the enraged troopers and at the same time promised to see to it that McCarthy was lodged in jail where he properly belonged.

The examining trial was held on February 4, and McCarthy was ordered held without bond, pending action by a grand jury. A detachment from the post accompanied civil authorities to Ben Ficklin, the county seat, to make certain McCarthy was safely lodged in jail. The matter might well have ended here except for an unfortunate stroke of fate. McCarthy, had a brother, Dave, a near twin in appearance, who picked that very evening to ride into Saint Angela. He was sighted almost at once and news reached the men at Fort Concho that Tom McCarthy had been turned loose.

Their rage knew no bounds and a large number of troopers armed themselves, marched into town, and relieved their feelings by firing into a number of buildings, including the Nimitz Hotel. According to local sources, more than 150 shots were fired, although no one was killed and only one man was slightly wounded. The troopers dispersed quickly when bugle calls and the roll of drums from the post indicated Grierson was preparing to send a sufficient force into town to preserve order.

Thereafter Grierson kept his men under rigid control, but on February 5 he received a caller, Captain Bryan Marsh of the Texas Frontier Battalion, who had just arrived with twenty-one rangers. Marsh is said to have informed Grierson that any soldier crossing the North Concho into town in the next ten days would be carried back feet first, and that if necessary he and his rangers

12 San Saba *News*, February 12, 1881; Organizational Returns, Tenth Cavalry. February, 1881.

would storm the post. Grierson's reply is not a matter of record, but Bryan Marsh, brave man that he undoubtedly was, faced an old soldier whose courage had never faltered in more than twenty years in uniform. Marsh's threat to storm the post was sheer braggadocio. Twenty-one rangers thrown at two hundred veteran buffalo soldiers would have been more in the nature of pouring sausages into a meat grinder than a fight.

Tom McCarthy was indicted for murder in the first degree and transferred to Austin, Texas, for trial. The jurors had scarcely left their seats before returning with a verdict of "not guilty." The cause of justice may have been served, but poor William Watkins and more that a few officers and men at Fort Concho would not have agreed. However, tempers and tensions soon subsided— when payday came around, according to one chronicler—and the "matter passed into history."[13]

If there had been a whitewash in Austin, the surgeon at Fort Concho made certain there was plenty of it at that post. In May he recommended:

> . . . a thorough cleaning of the back yards to officers quarters and damp wet places covered with lime, all out buildings should be carefully cleaned and limed. . . . The privies should be thoroughly disinfected with sulfate of Iron (which can be supplied from the hospital) and white-washed. If any stables are used in back yards they should be likewise cleaned, disinfected and white-washed. Indeed I should recommend that the quarters occupied by the officers be white-washed. . . . The privies attached to the barracks should be white-washed and disinfected. . . . The slop barrels should be white-washed on the outside and should have a piece of sacking thrown over them which should be . . . disinfected with Carbolic acid or permanganate of Potash.[14]

Fatigue details spent many a weary hour in the hot summer of 1881 seeing to it that Fort Concho was properly whitewashed.

The summer also found Lieutenant Flipper in major trouble. The only Negro officer in the Tenth, and for that matter in the

---

[13] Marguerite E. Kubela, "History of Fort Concho, Texas," 96; San Saba *News*, February 19, 1881.
[14] Medical History, Fort Concho, Vol. 404.

United States Army, Flipper had been assigned to Nolan's A Company. He was well received by officers and men and proved an excellent soldier. His services in the Victorio War had won plaudits from both Nolan and Grierson and a bright career seemed assured. Clouds appeared on the horizon when A Company came in to Fort Concho. Flipper found a riding companion in one of the few eligible young ladies at the post, and his attentions aroused the resentment of some of his fellow officers.

Lieutenant Charles Nordstrom, who had previously enjoyed the lady's undivided attention, was particularly incensed, and Flipper soon found the atmosphere about Fort Concho increasingly cool. When A Company transferred to Fort Davis, Flipper was appointed post commissary and within a short time was arrested for embezzling some two thousand dollars and confined in the post guardhouse. On June 30, 1882, a court-martial cleared Flipper of embezzlement but convicted him of "conduct unbecoming," and he was dismissed from the service. To the end of his days Flipper maintained that he was the victim of a plot hatched by Colonel Shafter, Lieutenant Nordstrom, and Lieutenant Louis Wilhelm.[15]

In July, 1882, headquarters of the Tenth was shifted to Fort Davis which was home of the regiment for nearly three years. It was a period of quiet for the buffalo soldiers, punctured only occasionally by pursuit of a band of horse or cattle thieves, or the arrest of an outlaw who defied civil authorities. Such activity seldom reached the newspapers or required lengthy official reports but was found in the terse phraseology of the *Organizational Returns*:

Troop M–Peña Colorado, Texas. Saddler Ross mortally wounded, Sgt. Winfield Scott and Pvt. Augustus Dover wounded in line of duty while attempting to arrest desperado on military reservation —desperado W. A. Alexander was killed resisting arrest.

Troop C.–Sergeant Pratt and 9 men encamped at Peña Colorado,

[15] Flipper, *op. cit.*, 15–20; Organizational Returns, Tenth Cavalry, August, 1881, and July, 1882.

Texas went in pursuit of horse thieves who stole 14 horses. Sergeant recovered nine head.[16]

Sometimes the stark sentences of the surgeon's report revealed much of the loneliness and tragedy that accompanied garrison life at an isolated post: "Died, John Wesley Wiggins 9 10/30 mos— male–negro–a son of Pvt. John Wiggins, Band, 10 Cav." Grierson undoubtedly shared Trooper Wiggins' bereavement, for his own daughter, thirteen-year-old Edith, lay in the post cemetery, a victim of typhoid fever.[17]

By 1885 the Tenth was no longer needed on the Texas frontier. Settlement, law, and order, which the regiment had done so much to further, had arrived, but far to the west there was trouble. Geronimo and his Chiricahua Apaches were on the loose and troops were badly needed. In March came orders transferring the Tenth to the Department of Arizona. Officers, men, and equipment were concentrated at Fort Davis, and on April 1, for the first time in the history of the regiment, all twelve companies—38 officers and 696 enlisted men—marched together along the tracks of the Southern Pacific Railroad.[18]

At Bowie Station, Arizona, the regiment split up once more. Grierson established headquarters at Whipple Barracks, while the various companies took station at Forts Grant, Thomas, Apache, and Verde. The Apaches had been troublesome recently, but at the moment all was quiet on the Arizona frontier and the troopers could look forward to acquiring a leisurely acquaintance with their new stations and the surrounding country. So it seemed in early May, 1885, but the men of the Tenth had scarce warmed their bunks before they were in the saddle and riding hard to overtake fugitive Apaches.

The Apache problem in 1885 centered around the Chiricahuas. Years of campaigning had driven a majority of the Apaches into the reservations at San Carlos and Fort Apache, although many renegades remained at large. Serious outbreaks occurred

16 Organizational Returns, Tenth Cavalry, September, 1882, and January, 1884.
17 Medical History, Fort Davis, Vol. 12; Medical History, Fort Concho, Vol. 404.
18 Bigelow, "Sketch"; Organizational Returns, Tenth Cavalry, March–April, 1885.

in 1881–82, however, and General Crook returned to Arizona in the summer of the latter year. With his customary skill, patience, and resourcefulness, Crook soon restored peace, but there remained a grave source of concern—some five hundred Chiricahua and Warm Springs outlaws, old Nana among them, who were still holed up in the mountains of northern Mexico, ever ready to launch devastating raids into Arizona.

In March of 1883 a small band of these Indians under Chatto struck like a hurricane in southern New Mexico and Arizona. In just six days twenty-five persons were killed, one young boy captured, and a number of ranches looted and burned. Then like wraiths the Apaches disappeared across the border, leaving citizens and troops alike in a state of shock.[19]

Crook reacted swiftly. He gathered a powerful force, including a large body of Apache scouts, crossed into Mexico, and invaded the Sierra Madres. In a three-week campaign of alternate fighting and deft diplomacy, Crook forced the surrender of the Chiricahua irreconcilables. Chatto, Geronimo, Nachez, Loco, Benito, Mangus, and their followers, as well as Nana and his Warm Springs Apaches, agreed to march to the San Carlos reservation where they were to remain under control of the army.[20]

The Indians were slow to come in, but by the spring of 1884 they were on the reservation a few miles southwest of Fort Apache. Peace had come at last, but it proved ephemeral. Bickering over Indian policy was quick to develop between the War and Interior departments, and Crook asked to be relieved of any responsibility for control over the Apaches in Arizona. Ultimately Crook was sustained and the military remained in control, but the quarrel had penetrated, as it always did, to the lower echelons and the reverberations reached the wary tribesmen. Nervous and uneasy,

[19] Twitchell, Leading Facts, II, 441–43. An interesting account of Crook's campaigns is in John G. Bourke, *On the Border With Crook*. See also, by the same author, *An Apache Campaign in the Sierra Madre*. Whipple Barracks was located on Granite Creek near Prescott, Arizona. It was named in honor of Major General A. W. Whipple, who was mortally wounded at the battle of Chancellorsville in May, 1863. Frazer, *op. cit.*, 14. Grierson's headquarters remained here until July, 1886, when they were moved to Fort Grant.

[20] Report of Brigadier General Crook in *Annual Report of the Secretary of War for the Year 1886*, I, 147; Lockwood, *op. cit.*, 279.

many of them were ready to listen to Geronimo, Nana, and others, who were urging a return to the Sierra Madres and the old way of life.

On the night of May 17, 1885, after a "tiswin drunk," Geronimo, Nachez, Chihuahua, Nana, and Mangus, with nearly 150 followers, broke from the reservation. Troopers at Fort Apache were in the saddle within an hour but failed to overtake or even to ascertain the direction taken by the runaways. Crook threw every available man into the field to hunt them down, and by May 20 Grierson had his buffalo soldiers searching in the Black Range, the Mogollons, and the Chiricahua Mountains. Units of the Third, Fourth, and Sixth Cavalry, accompanied by Apache Scouts, swarmed in all directions, yet not a trace of the Indians could be found.[21]

The puzzle of their whereabouts was solved on June 10. The hostiles appeared with startling suddenness in Guadalupe Cañon, surprised a detachment of Fourth Cavalry encamped there, killed four troopers, and crossed into Mexico. The trail pointed toward the Sierra Madres and Crook sent Captains Emmet Crawford, Third Cavalry, and Wirt Davis, Fourth Cavalry, in pursuit with two companies of cavalry and nearly two hundred Apache scouts. To cut off a return to the United States, Crook stationed detachments "at every water-hole along the border" and established a "second line" paralleling the Southern Pacific Railroad. For most of the buffalo soldiers these dispositions meant seemingly endless days and nights of staring at a waterhole.[22]

For three months Crawford and Davis toiled across the peaks and cañons of the Sierra Madres but were unable to bring off a decisive encounter. Their pressure was unrelenting, however, and on September 28 the Chiricahuas fled back across the border, eluded patrols in Guadalupe Cañon, and headed into the Chiricahua Mountains with Crawford and Davis in close pursuit. The constant harassment was telling on the renegades. Their animals

---

[21] Report of General Crook, 148; Organizational Returns, Tenth Cavalry, May, 1885.

[22] Report of General Crook, 149; Organizational Returns, Tenth Cavalry, June–September, 1885.

were breaking down, and they might well have been cornered had Arizona ranchers not unwittingly provided a convenient means of escape. They were engaged in a roundup and had a large *remuda* at a ranch in White Tail Cañon. The Apaches descended on the herd and "made off with some of the best stock in the country."[23] The Indians, now superbly mounted, easily shook off pursuit and regained the border. Captain Viele with C and G of the Tenth followed their trail all the way to Ascensión in Chihuahua where his animals gave out.[24]

By the end of November, Crawford and Davis were again in the Sierra Madres and after weeks of grueling cat-and-mouse, the former located the Indian camp on the Aros River sixty miles below Nácori. On the night of June 10, Crawford attacked and captured all the stock and supplies, but the hostiles escaped to nearby peaks. During the night Apache couriers came in to inform Crawford that their people desired a conference on the following morning to discuss terms of surrender.

At daylight, however, Crawford's camp was attacked by Mexican forces who mistook the scouts for hostiles. Before the ensuing confusion could be cleared up, Crawford was mortally wounded and Tom Horn, an interpreter, was shot through the arm. Fortunately the hostiles remained in the vicinity and arrangements were made for a meeting with General Crook in the Cañon de los Embudos on March 25.[25]

The conference was held at the appointed time, and after lengthy discussions the hostiles agreed to surrender and return to the reservation. Crook set out for the border on March 27 with Geronimo, Nachez, Chihuahua, Nana, and 111 men, women, and children, but on the night of March 29, Geronimo and Nachez stole away and fled into the mountains. Twenty warriors and sixteen women and children accompanied them. The remaining Apaches, seventy-seven in all, were taken to Fort Bowie and entrained for Fort Marion, Florida, as prisoners of war.[26]

23 Report of General Crook, 150.
24 *Ibid.;* Organizational Returns, Tenth Cavalry, October, 1885; Post Returns, Fort Thomas, October, 1885.
25 *Annual Report of the Secretary of War for the Year 1886,* I, 9–10.

The escape of Geronimo and Nachez upset General Sheridan, as did Crook's extensive use of Apache scouts. Crook asked to be relieved, and on April 2, 1886, he was replaced by General Miles. The task before Miles was clear—to capture or destroy Geronimo, Nachez, and their thirty-six followers, as well as the shadowy Mangus and his small band who appeared to have vanished. Miles made careful preparations, including the establishment of twenty-seven heliograph stations for the rapid transmission of messages, but Geronimo struck before plans had been completed.[27]

On April 27, he crossed the border and swept through the Santa Cruz Valley, killed a number of cowboys, captured the Peck Ranch, butchered Mrs. Peck and one of her children, and took her husband and thirteen-year-old daughter as captives. Peck, temporarily insane, was soon released, but the Apaches still held the girl as they turned and headed for Mexico. News of the raid reached Captain Lebo who was scouting in the vicinity with Company K. Lebo was an able and seasoned commander and at his back were many veterans of the Victorio War. They found Geronimo's trail and clung like leeches. The Apaches tried every trick in their plentiful bag to throw off these pursuers, but to no avail. For two hundred miles the chase continued, and at last Lebo brought his quarry to bay on a rocky slope in the Piñito Mountains, thirty miles south of the border in Sonora. On the back trail were thirty horses the Indians had ridden to death.

K Company dismounted and started up the slope, but the men were met with a curtain of lead that killed Private Hollis, severely wounded Corporal Scott, and forced the troopers to take cover. A vicious, short-range rifle duel developed and Scott lay exposed to enemy fire. Young Lieutenant Powhattan Clarke rose from behind a boulder, and ignoring a hail of bullets, raced to the trooper's side and carried him to safety. Presently the Indian fire slackened and then ceased—Geronimo was on the move again. Lebo hung on for four days until pursuit was taken up by a com-

---

[26] Report of General Crook, 152; *Annual Report of the Secretary of War for the Year 1886*, 11.

[27] Bourke, *On the Border with Crook*, 474; *Annual Report of the Secretary of War for the Year 1886*, 12.

pany of Fourth Cavalry. For the rescue of Corporal Scott, Lieutenant Clarke was awarded the Congressional Medal of Honor.[28]

Miles gave the Chiricahuas no rest. Companies of the Tenth and Fourth kept them constantly on the move. On May 15, Captain C. A. P. Hatfield, Fourth Cavalry, with a strong detachment struck the hostile camp near Santa Cruz in Sonora. The blow caused the Apaches to turn northward into Arizona where they sought refuge in the Dragoon Mountains. There was no respite. Detachments of buffalo soldiers under Captain Norvell and Lieutenants Read, Hunt, Hughes, and Shipp pursued without letup, and in desperation the Indians fled toward Fort Apache to seek aid from their kinsmen on the reservation. As they came near, however, they were intercepted by Captain J. T. Morrison and A of the Tenth, stripped of all their horses, and driven back.[29]

Sorely beset, the hostiles turned toward Mexico and were hastened in their flight by troopers working in relays. Once the Indians were over the border, the chase was taken up by troops and scouts under Captain H. W. Lawton, Fourth Cavalry. For months Lawton trailed his slippery foes but was unable either to capture or to destroy them. His work was not in vain, for it finally convinced the Apaches of the utter hopelessness of ever finding a safe retreat, and word reached Miles that they were willing to discuss terms of surrender.

Miles sent Lieutenant Charles B. Gatewood, Sixth Cavalry, to Mexico as a special emissary, and Gatewood made contact with Geronimo on the Bavispe River near the end of August, 1886. Arrangements were made for a meeting between Geronimo and Miles in Skeleton Cañon, and here on September 3 the Apaches formally surrendered. They were taken to Fort Bowie and sent by train to Fort Marion as prisoners of war.[30]

---

[28] Glass, *op. cit.*, 24; Organizational Returns, Tenth Cavalry, May, 1886; General Nelson A. Miles, *Personal Recollections of General Nelson A. Miles*, 489. Lebo joined the Tenth in June, 1867, and remained with the regiment until 1893 when he transferred to the Sixth Cavalry. He retired in 1901 as colonel of the Fourteenth Cavalry. Heitman, *op. cit.*, I, 622.

[29] *Annual Report of the Secretary of War for the Year 1886*, I, 167–69; Organizational Returns, Tenth Cavalry, May–June, 1886.

[30] *Annual Report of the Secretary of War for the Year 1886*, I, 169; Miles, *op. cit.*, 529; Lockwood, *op. cit.*, 301–306.

The buffalo soldiers played no role in these final months, although Lieutenant Leighton Finley of the Tenth was in command of the scouts under Lawton. They were, however, destined to be principals in drawing the final curtain on the Apache wars.

The vast majority of the Chiricahuas had remained peacefully on the reservation during the breakout, but Miles wished these people removed from the state and Washington officialdom agreed. It fell the lot of Lieutenant Colonel Wade, commanding at Fort Apache, and more than half the companies of the Tenth to arrest and transport more than four hundred men, women, and children to Holbrook, Arizona, where they were entrained for Fort Marion. These Apaches had been well behaved since General Crook placed them on the reservation in 1884 and they deserved a better fate, but it was not for the buffalo soldiers to reason why.

One hostile chief remained at large. Mangus and his small band had separated from Geronimo and managed to avoid efforts to run them down. The search continued, however, and on September 18 a detachment of H Company under Captain Charles Cooper found a trail in the White Mountains. A pursuit of more than forty miles over rough and broken country brought Cooper upon a small party of Apaches. After a running fight of fifteen miles the troopers cornered the Indians and forced their surrender. The net had finally closed over the last holdouts—Mangus, two warriors, and eight women and children. The Arizona frontier was at peace.[31]

While the Tenth fought the "battle of Saint Angela," pursued horse thieves, and then the Chiricahua Apaches, Hatch and the Ninth were hardly getting the much-needed rest that General Pope had recommended. In fact, they had their hands full trying to clear Indian Territory of invading and ingenious "Boomers." It proved to be four years of near-unremitting and frustrating labor at the end of which the Ninth could point to a mountain of abuse as the sole monument to their efforts.

Intruders had long been a sore problem to Indian agents and

[31] Organizational Returns, Tenth Cavalry, September, 1886; Bigelow, "Sketch"; Miles, *op. cit.*, 528–30.

the military. As early as 1870 Grierson found it necessary to keep patrols on the lookout, and two years later he moved his headquarters from Fort Sill to Fort Gibson, partly in response to growing intruder activity in that vicinity. By 1876 the problem was serious enough to require attention from Secretary of War George W. McCrary and General Sherman. Three years later intruders were crossing the Kansas line in sufficient numbers to occupy virtually the full attention of a battalion of buffalo soldiers under Captain Nolan. Many of these troopers undoubtedly breathed a sigh of relief when the demands of the Victorio War occasioned their transfer to West Texas in June, 1880.[32]

Intruder or Boomer activity had been on the upswing since the spring of 1879. The immediate source of inspiration apparently stemmed from an article, widely circulated, that appeared in the *Chicago Times* of February 15. Written by a Cherokee, Colonel Elias C. Boudinot, the article pointed to fertile and unoccupied lands in the heart of Indian Territory and went on to argue that these potentially productive millions of acres were public domain and therefore subject to settlement under existing homestead laws. Boudinot's message was all that hordes of land-hungry citizens and railroad promoters needed to hear, nor were the possibilities of fat profits from increased trade lost on entrepreneurs in the towns bordering the Territory. The goal of these groups was simply to force settlement with or without federal authority.[33]

Rumors of a Boomer invasion in April, 1879, led by "Colonel" Charles C. Carpenter, caused President Hayes to issue an official warning that the lands in question were not open to homestead entry and any invaders would be expelled by force if necessary. Carpenter breathed fury and defiance, and border merchants did a land-office business in firearms with prospective homesteaders. In considerable numbers they crossed the Kansas line near Wichita

---

[32] W. Sherman Savage, "The Role of Negro Soldiers in Protecting the Indian Frontier From Intruders," *The Journal of Negro History,* Vol. XXXVI, No. 1 (January, 1951), 26–28.

[33] Edwin C. McReynolds, *Oklahoma: A History of the Sooner State,* 281–82; Gaston Litton, *History of Oklahoma,* I, 358.

and Coffeyville, but the sight of Nolan's scowling troopers was enough for most of them, and Carpenter's movement collapsed.[34]

His place was taken by a far abler and more persistent leader, David L. Payne. Payne had served with the Nineteenth Kansas Cavalry in Sheridan's winter campaign of 1868–69 and was much impressed with the possibilities of the country he traversed. Later he served as a member of the Kansas legislature and as an assistant doorkeeper of the United States House of Representatives. He appeared in Wichita, Kansas, in August, 1879, and immediately assumed leadership of the Boomer movement, probably with financial assistance from the Atlantic and Pacific Railroad. In the next five years Payne launched no fewer than nine attempts to colonize in Indian Territory.[35]

The target area for Boomer efforts was in the vicinity of present Oklahoma City, and Payne's initial efforts at establishing a colony were on a comparatively small scale. In April, 1880, and again in July of the same year, he managed to elude patrols and reach the chosen site but in each case was arrested swiftly and ejected from the Territory. Payne had little to show for a year of effort except a charge of trespass lodged against him at Fort Smith, Arkansas. Yet Payne thrived on failure, redoubled his activities, and the movement continued to grow.

In the summer of 1881 small parties of Boomers filtered in from various points along the border in sufficient numbers to require the constant attention of six companies of cavalry, and Pope had to borrow D, E, I, and M of the Tenth from Ord. In November the ubiquitous Payne made a third effort, this time from the Texas line, but was caught on Cache Creek and expelled with little ceremony. Such was the situation when Pope transferred the Ninth from New Mexico.[36]

Hatch was keenly aware that his regiment faced a tedious and unpopular task. He also knew that bloodshed was a distinct possi-

---

[34] Litton, *op. cit.*, I, 360–61; Organizational Returns, Tenth Cavalry, April–May, 1879.

[35] Litton, *op. cit.*, I, 363–69.

[36] Fort Griffin *Echo*, May 21, 1881; Organizational Returns, Tenth Cavalry, June, 1881.

bility in which case he and his troopers could not escape a wave of national indignation. He nevertheless set about an unpleasant duty with his customary efficiency and energy. Ceaseless patrols were maintained out of Forts Sill, Reno, and Supply, and from the border town of Arkansas City. Four times in 1882 Payne led his followers into the Territory, and four times he was promptly arrested and ejected.

Persuasion proved successful at first, but the Boomers, imbued with the justice of their cause, became increasingly stubborn and resentful. In August, 1882, Lieutenant C. W. Taylor ordered Payne to reload his wagons and move out. When the order was refused, Taylor instructed his troopers, "Yellow Legs" as the Boomers called them, to hitch the teams and load both goods and home-steaders into them. Fists flew before the Boomers were over-come, bound hand and foot, and tossed into the wagons as if "they were sacks of shelled corn."[37]

In January, 1883, the irrepressible Payne was back again, this time with nine hundred settlers, some of them heavily armed. The long column was sighted near the North Canadian on February 7 by young Lieutenant Stevens and a dozen troopers. Stevens attempted to place Payne under arrest, but the latter failed even to slow his pace. Stevens then sent a courier to Captain Carroll at Fort Reno and fell in beside the wagons. By midafternoon of the following day Payne's column reached a valley near the North Canadian and the men set to work at once constructing "Camp Alice."

About five o'clock, however, Payne had far more to contend with than a nervous and uncertain young lieutenant. Captain Car-roll arrived with ninety veterans of F and I companies and came to the point at once. The Boomers could get out of their own accord or they would be "helped out." At the same time Carroll made it clear that he had nothing to do with the laws. He and his troopers were simply performing their duty. Resistance melted be-fore Carroll's gentle firmness. Payne and ten old offenders were

---

[37] Carl Coke Rister, *Land Hunger: David L. Payne and the Oklahoma Boomers,* 111–12; Savage, *loc. cit.,* 32.

arrested and taken to Fort Reno, while the others were escorted to the Kansas line by the weary buffalo soldiers who were not totally unsympathetic toward Boomer ambitions.[38]

Carroll held Payne and his companions for a few days, treated them kindly, and then sent them under escort to Caldwell, Kansas. Kindness did not stop the Boomers. Payne's principal lieutenant, William L. Couch, forced Hatch's troopers to escort him from the Territory three times between August, 1883, and the end of the year. And Couch could scarcely complain of the treatment he received at the hands of the buffalo soldiers, for they often shared their beans, bacon, and hardtack with him and his followers.[39]

The era of good feeling, if such it was, came to an abrupt end in the spring of 1884. Couch brought more than a thousand Boomers to the site of Oklahoma City in April, and four large camps were established along the North Canadian. The men were soon hard at work erecting cabins, building a schoolhouse, and plowing the soil. On April 24, Lieutenant M. H. Day with seven troopers arrived, found Couch's father plowing a field, and placed him under arrest. The old man resisted and Day was forced to have him bound and placed in a wagon.

Day proceeded to the main Boomer camp and arrested nine leaders, including J. D. Odell. The latter, incensed over the treatment of the elder Couch, put up a fight, and two troopers had the unpleasant duty of subduing and binding him. Next morning, as Day prepared to take his prisoners to Fort Reno, Odell refused to climb into a wagon. Day was in no mood to argue and had the recalcitrant Boomer tied to the vehicle. He could take his choice —either walk or be dragged all the way to the post. The tempers of Boomers and soldiers were beginning to run thin.

By May 7, Day was back with a detachment of twenty troopers and six Indian scouts. He attempted to arrest a number of men at work on the schoolhouse but met with angry resistance. Efforts

38 "Tribute to Captain Payne," *Chronicle of Oklahoma,* Vol. VIII, No. 1 (March, 1930), 13–14; Rister, *Land Hunger,* 127–29; Organizational Returns, Ninth Cavalry, February, 1883.

39 Rister, *Land Hunger,* 145; Organizational Returns, Ninth Cavalry, October–November, 1883.

to seize the workmen touched off a flurry of fisticuffs and Day momentarily lost his head. He ordered his troopers to fire, but fortunately the buffalo soldiers refused to obey, and Day quickly regained his composure. The Boomers were also sobered and quietly submitted to arrest, for they realized, as did Day, that a blood bath had been narrowly avoided. Good feeling was gone, however, and only bitterness remained. *War Chief,* organ of the Boomer movement, revealed the depth of feeling with a blast at an old nemesis, Lieutenant C. W. Taylor. The officer was "one of a litter of mud turtles born of a Negro woman."[40]

Boomer determination was stronger than ever, however, and in June, 1884, David Payne made his final effort. More than fifteen hundred homesteaders crossed the line and settled at Rock Falls. Activity on such a scale brought Hatch in person to the scene. Many of the Boomers were belligerent and ready to fight, and Payne warned Hatch not to bring up troops. The atmosphere was so explosive that Hatch telegraphed his superiors outlining the situation and indicating he felt reinforcements were necessary. He received unequivocal orders to remove the Boomers, and on August 5 he delivered an ultimatum—leave before the day was over or he would drive them out. It was enough for all but a hard core of about 250. These were quickly removed by Captain Francis Moore with L and M companies, and all cabins and other buildings were burned.[41]

Payne died suddenly on November 28, 1884, and the mantle of leadership fell to William L. Couch. This activist was soon on the move with three hundred settlers and on December 12 encamped on Stillwater Creek. Hatch sent Lieutenant Day and thirty troopers to evict these Boomers, but they ignored his demand for surrender. Day's force was far too small to contend with such numbers and he withdrew. When Hatch was notified, he hastened to the scene and sent for reinforcements. By January 24, seven companies of the Ninth were on hand and all were under veteran

[40] Rister, *Land Hunger,* 149; "Publishing a Newspaper in a 'Boomer' Camp," *Chronicles of Oklahoma,* Vol. V, No. 4 (December, 1927), 368; Litton, *op. cit.,* I, 373.
[41] Organizational Returns, Ninth Cavalry, August, 1884; Rister, *Land Hunger,* 165–70.

commanders. Two howitzers and a company of infantry were in support of the cavalry.

Captain Carroll rode to the Boomer camp and demanded a surrender, which was refused, and Couch sent word to Hatch that his settlers would defend their rights. A lesser man might well have begun a battle, but Hatch was equal to the occasion. On the morning of January 25, he surrounded the camp and cut off all hope of supplies. Couch's position was untenable and five days later the wagons were loaded and he led his settlers back to Arkansas City.[42]

The disagreeable and thankless task of driving Boomers from the "Promised Land" ended for Hatch and his buffalo soldiers in June, 1885. Regimental headquarters was transferred to Fort Mc-Kinney, Wyoming, while the companies were assigned to that post and to Forts Robinson and Niobrara in Nebraska and Fort Du-Chesne in Utah. The long-promised rest had come at last after eighteen years of distinguished service in the Southwest. The Indian wars on the Plains were over, and the white man's civilization had taken a firm and lasting hold. The frontier army was faced with little more than the routine of garrison life.[43]

In the next few years many of the officers and men on the Ninth's roll of honor were no longer found on the Organizational Returns. Transfer, retirement, and death took their toll. Morrow, Carroll, Cooney, Dodge, and Parker no longer led their faithful and near-worshipful buffalo soldiers. One looked in vain at the Returns for Emanuel Stance, George Jordan, Henry Johnson, Clifton Greaves, and Brent Wood. And on April 11, 1889, Edward Hatch, colonel of the regiment for twenty-three years, breathed his last at Fort Robinson, Nebraska.[44]

His successor, Colonel Joseph G. Tilford, could, however, review his new command with considerable satisfaction. Many of his company commanders—Day, Guilfoyle, Hughes, Wright, Taylor, Loud, and Stedman—were soldiers of proven ability. Major Guy Henry, with the regiment since 1882, was one of the

[42] McReynolds, *op. cit.*, 286–87; Rister, *Land Hunger*, 190–92; Organizational Returns, Ninth Cavalry, December–January, 1884–85.
[43] Organizational Returns, Ninth Cavalry, June–July, 1885.
[44] *Ibid.*, April, 1889.

most distinguished officers in the army. In the ranks every company had a core of tough, battle-wise veterans, with whom the Apache, Comanche, Kiowa, Cheyenne, outlaw, and Boomer were well acquainted. It was a proud regiment, at least the equal, and perhaps the best, of any in the army. And ahead was one last moment of glory in the waning days of the Plains frontier.[45]

The once proud Sioux, former overlords of the Northern Plains, enclosed on reservations in South and North Dakota, were poverty-ridden, hungry, and despondent in the cruel winter of 1889–90. Many were ill and in need of medical attention, but "no one seemed to care."[46] Then came a whisper of hope—a messiah had arrived far to the West. There was great excitement in the Sioux camps and emissaries rode westward seeking the truth. They found and talked with the messiah, a Paiute named Wovoka, and learned that ghosts would return in the spring bringing with them the buffalo and all other game the white man had slaughtered. When the emissaries returned with this message, it was all that the Indians wanted to hear, and the Ghost Dance Religion swept like a prairie fire among the Sioux.[47]

Indian agents at the Pine Ridge, Rosebud, Cheyenne River, and Standing Rock reservations were inclined at first to ignore the ghost dancers, but by the summer of 1890 thousands of Indians were in a state of near frenzy. In August, Agent Gallagher at Pine Ridge attempted to break up a dance on White Clay Creek. He was an able man and not unpopular with his charges, but they defied him. At Standing Rock, Agent McLaughlin blamed Sitting Bull for the troubles and wanted him arrested. According to the agent,

45 *Ibid.*, Major Henry, a New Yorker, graduated from West Point in 1856 and was initially assigned to the artillery. During the Civil War he rose to the rank of colonel in the Fortieth Massachusetts Infantry. He served as Captain in the First Artillery from December, 1865, until December of 1870 when he transferred to the Third Cavalry. He joined the Ninth as a major in June, 1881, and remained with the regiment until January, 1892, when he was appointed lieutenant colonel of the Seventh Cavalry. At the end of his military career in 1898 he was a major general of volunteers. Henry was a brilliant officer with seven citations for gallant and meritious conduct and held the Congressional Medal of Honor for his bravery at Cold Harbor in June, 1864. Heitman, *op. cit.*, I, 523.

46 George E. Hyde, *A Sioux Chronicle*, 238; *Annual Report of the Commissioner of Indian Affairs for the Year 1890*, 123.

47 James Mooney, "The Ghost-dance Religion," *Fourteenth Annual Report, 1892–1893*, Bureau of American Ethnology, 816–21.

the old chief was the "high priest and leading apostle of this latest Indian absurdity."[48] Agents Palmer and Reynolds at the Cheyenne River and Rosebud reservations reported that many of their Indians were armed and defiant.

The Ghost Dance craze and accompanying unrest were also disturbing to the military, and in early November, Brigadier General Thomas H. Ruger, commanding the Department of Dakota, made an investigation of conditions on the reservation which he found to be unsatisfactory but not explosive. General Miles, commanding the Division of the Missouri, was sufficiently alarmed to send military observers to the agencies.[49]

The craze might well have passed without major difficulty, but two events apparently did much to trigger the flow of blood. Agent Gallagher fell victim to Indian Bureau politics and was replaced by the totally inexperienced Dr. D. F. Royer. The latter was soon unnerved by milling, well-armed ghost dancers, and on November 15 he telegraphed the commissioner of Indian Affairs, T. J. Morgan:

> Indians are dancing in the snow and are wild and crazy. I have fully informed you that employés and government property at this agency have no protection and are at the mercy of these dancers. Why delay further investigation? We need protection, and we need it now. The leaders should be arrested and confined in some military post until the matter is quieted, and this should be done at once.[50]

Three days after Royer's call for troops, General Miles ordered Brigadier General John R. Brooke, commanding the Department of the Platte, to hasten a strong force to Pine Ridge and to station most of his remaining command along the rail and telegraph lines south and west of the reservations. At dawn on November 20, Brooke reached Pine Ridge with Companies F, I, and K of the Ninth, brought up from Fort Robinson, five companies of infan-

48 *Annual Report of the Commissioner of Indian Affairs for the Year 1891*, 125.
49 Robert M. Utley, *The Last Days of the Sioux Nation*, 110.
50 *Annual Report of the Commissioner of Indian Affairs for the Year 1891*, 128; Hyde, *op. cit.*, 254.

253

try, a Hotchkiss cannon, and a Gatling gun. On the same day Lieutenant Colonel A. T. Smith, Eighth Infantry, reached the Rosebud
agency with three companies of his regiment, Companies A and
G of the Ninth, and a Hotchkiss gun.[51]

Miles wished to avoid bloodshed, and to achieve that end he
concentrated half the entire United States Army on or near the
reservations. Major Henry, with D Company of the Ninth, and two
companies of infantry were sent to Pine Ridge on November 25,
and on their heels came Colonel James W. Forsyth and eight
companies of the Seventh Cavalry. A formidable screen was
thrown around the reservations by units of the First, Second, Fifth,
Sixth, and Eighth Cavalry along with supporting infantry. Such a
force should have been sufficient to overawe even the most belligerent Sioux.[52]

The appearance of so many troops, however, frightened the
Indians, who feared a massacre was imminent, and they stampeded away from the agencies. Fanatics among them, virtually
beyond reason, fled to a stronghold in the badlands some forty
miles northwest of the Pine Ridge agency and prepared to fight.
Miles launched a campaign of pressure and persuasion to induce
the runaways to return and assemble in the vicinity of Pine Ridge,
and he met with some success, but the presence of his troops was
the first step toward tragedy.

Major trouble might still have been avoided except for Sitting
Bull. Agent McLaughlin had long urged his arrest as a perennial
troublemaker and believed his removal from the reservation would
go far toward ending the ghost dance craze. After considerable
vacillation, the Indian Bureau authorized the arrest, and plans
were made to seize Sitting Bull in late December when he came to
the Standing Rock agency for rations. But the chief had a nose
for trouble, and word reached McLaughlin that he planned to
slip away.

The original plan was discarded at once and the agent sent
forty of his Indian police, supported by two companies of the

[51] *Annual Report of the Secretary of War for the Year 1891*, 179.
[52] *Ibid.*, 147–48.

Eighth Cavalry, to make the arrest. The police arrived at Sitting Bull's lodge on Grand River at dawn on December 15. They took the chief into custody without difficulty and were preparing to take him away when they were attacked by more than one hundred of his followers. A vicious, bloody fight at close quarters ensued in which Sitting Bull was killed. Howitzer fire from the supporting troops was necessary to rescue the Indian police.[53] Sitting Bull's death was a strong push toward a serious clash, for it compromised Miles's efforts to persuade the Indians that they had nothing to fear and strengthened the hands of the fanatics.

Meanwhile, Miles instructed his commanders to push the Indians slowly toward Pine Ridge, avoiding contact, but staying close enough to keep them on the move. These tactics were proving successful, but the whereabouts of Big Foot's band, known to contain a number of Sitting Bull's followers, was uncertain and a source of concern. At length Miles ordered Brooke at Pine Ridge to find and apprehend these people, and on December 24, Major Henry, with D, F, I, and K of the Ninth, set out to find them.

Henry searched toward the northwest for fifty miles without success and took station at Harney Springs in order to scout the badlands. It was rough work at best and in bitter cold weather. Private Charles Creek recalled later, "You late [*sic*] out in the cold like a dog, [often] not in a tent because the Indians gonna sneak up on you. It was so cold the [tobacco] spit froze when it left your mouth."[54] Private Creek suffered unnecessarily, for the missing Big Foot, his band torn by dissension between fanatics and those favoring peace, had wavered and then turned resolutely south toward Pine Ridge.

When Henry failed to find Big Foot, Brooke sent out Major S. M. Whitside with four companies of the Seventh Cavalry and a platoon of Battery E, First Artillery, with two Hotchkiss guns. Whitside marched northeast and on the night of December 27 went into camp on Wounded Knee Creek. The next morning he

---

[53] Hyde, *op. cit.*, 286–89. Sitting Bull was killed by Sergeant Bullhead who was himself also killed. In all, six police and eight of Sitting Bull's warriors were killed. *Annual Report of the Commissioner of Indian Affairs for the Year 1891*, 129.

[54] Rickey, "The Negro Regulars," 10.

sent out scouts and they soon located the incoming Big Foot. When told he must surrender, the chief offered no resistance and his band was escorted to the Wounded Knee and encamped. Whitside sent word of the roundup to Brooke, and he was soon joined by Colonel Forsyth with four more companies of the Seventh and two additional pieces of artillery.

Forsyth had orders to disarm Big Foot's band, and on the morning of December 29 he so informed the chief. After some hesitation, a few antiquated arms were turned over voluntarily, but Forsyth was not satisfied and a detachment of troopers was ordered to search the lodges. Rifles and revolvers were found in quantities, and as the hunt continued a medicine man harangued the warriors. Some of these began their death chant, and suddenly one of them pulled a rifle from under his blanket and opened fire.

In a matter of seconds Wounded Knee became a slaughterhouse. Many Indians and troopers died in desperate hand-to-hand combat, while others were killed by point-blank gunfire. The deadly Hotchkiss guns opened, tore the Indian camp to shreds, and then sought out those who chose to flee. It was all over in a matter of minutes. One hundred and forty-six Indian men, women, and children were dead, and half a hundred more were wounded. Forsyth's loss was twenty-six men killed and thirty-nine wounded.[55]

The roar of the Hotchkiss guns was heard at Pine Ridge where more than six thousand Sioux had gathered as a result of Miles's drive. Swift Indian horsemen rode to investigate and soon returned with the news of Big Foot's fate. In minutes the Indian camps were a bedlam, and before the day was over four thousand of them had stampeded, and many were heading for the badlands where hostile ghost dancers were in hiding. Forsyth and the Seventh, returning from the blood bath at Wounded Knee, encountered knots of angry warriors who skirmished with them. It was an ugly situation and Brooke hastened to send off a courier to Major Henry.

55 Hyde, *op. cit.*, 301–305; Utley, *op. cit.*, 227–28; *Annual Report of the Commissioner of Indian Affairs for the Year 1891*, 130; *Annual Report of the Secretary of War for the Year 1891*, 150–51.

Henry received Brooke's message just as his troopers were turning in after a fifty-mile scout through the badlands. The command saddled immediately and set out in extremely cold weather. As they neared the agency, Henry left his train, escorted by Captain Loud and I, and pushed on with all possible speed to Pine Ridge with D, F, and K. He arrived just at dawn after an astonishing march of one hundred miles in a single day. Yet hardly had the half-frozen and bone-weary troopers started fires to warm themselves, when they were in the saddle again—Loud was under attack and needed assistance. The Indians were beaten off and the train brought safely into camp, but one buffalo soldier had lost his life.[56]

The following morning, December 30, watchers at Pine Ridge saw columns of smoke rising in the direction of Drexel Mission four miles below the agency. Forsyth and eight companies of the Seventh moved out to investigate. The command reached the mission where the Indians had fired a small building, but they drew away as the troopers approached. Forsyth followed and marched down a narrow valley with steep bluffs to the east and west, but for some unaccountable reason he failed to throw out flankers. Suddenly he found himself penned down by a leaden rain from Sioux riflemen who commanded the bluffs. Efforts to break out were thrown back and Forsyth faced disaster. Fortunately relief was near at hand.

The sound of gunfire alerted Major Henry, and although his buffalo soldiers had managed no more than two hours sleep, they were quickly in the saddle and forcing their feeble mounts to a trot in the direction of Forsyth's engagement. At one-thirty in the afternoon Henry reached the mouth of the valley, surveyed the terrain at a glance, and went into action. Captain Wright with I and K spurred jaded animals and charged the east slope, while D and F under Loud and Captain C. S. Stedman dismounted and swept up the bluffs to the west. The warriors were thrown back and driven off to the great relief of embattled Seventh cavalrymen who

---

[56] Brady, *op. cit.*, 353; Hyde, *op. cit.*, 305–306; Hutcheson, *loc. cit.*, 287; Utley, *op. cit.*, 235–36.

raced to embrace their rescuers. Corporal William O. Wilson of I received the Congressional Medal of Honor for conspicuous gallantry during the fight.[57]

After Drexel Mission, Miles returned to his campaign of steady pressure combined with assurances of safety, decent treatment, and a redress of their grievances. Within two weeks more than four thousand Indians had returned to Pine Ridge and surrendered, and all danger of a war had passed. On January 21, Miles held a grand review, and when Henry and his buffalo soldiers passed, the general raised his gloved hand in salute.[58] No soldiers could ask for more.

The Sioux troubles of 1890–91 and the fight at Drexel Mission capped the long career of the Ninth Cavalry on the frontier. This performance was in keeping with the record of the regiment since its departure from San Antonio twenty-four years before. Four companies marched an incredible 108 miles under blizzard conditions, fought two engagements, and saved a command twice their strength from grievous loss. They received little official recognition, but perhaps this was not important, for their worth was recognized clearly where it counted most—in the hearts of their white comrades of the Seventh Cavalry.

Far to the southwest the buffalo soldiers of the Tenth had marched and fought in the last Apache war in a manner that left nothing to be desired. Their final effort, the capture of Mangus, ended Apache resistance. They, too, received the customary scant attention, but soldier-musician Benjamin Grierson knew the quality of his regiment, and on this subject, at least, he had the solid agreement of Mangus and Geronimo.

The experiment with Negro troopers launched in 1866 proved a success by any standard other than that of racial prejudice. By 1891 the combat record spoke for itself. They had fought on the

57 Beyer and Keydel, *op. cit.*, II, 326; Brady, *op. cit.*, 354; Utley, *op. cit.*, 240; *Annual Report of the Secretary of War for the Year 1891*, 153–54.

58 Utley, *op. cit.*, 269; *Annual Report of the Secretary of War for the Year 1891*, 155.

plains of Kansas and in Indian Territory, in the vast expanse of West Texas and along hundreds of miles of the Río Grande and in Mexico, in the deserts and mountains of New Mexico and Arizona, in Colorado, and finally in the rugged grandeur of the Dakotas. Few regiments could match the length and sweep of these activities.

Inevitably there were individual failures, but one can search the dusty archives in vain for an instance where a detachment, company, battalion, or regiment bolted under fire or failed to do its duty. This in spite of the knowledge that their efforts would receive little or no attention, official or otherwise. It was a record, too, built on generally second-rate equipment and the worst horseflesh in the army.

Their labors were not limited to the battlefield. They built or renovated dozens of posts, strung thousands of miles of wire, and escorted stages, trains, cattle herds, railroad crews, and surveying parties. Civil officials, particularly in Texas and New Mexico, could not have performed their duties without them. Their scouts and patrols opened new roads, mapped vast areas of uncharted country, and pinpointed for oncoming settlers the location of life-giving water.

They were lusty men on an untamed frontier, but their behavior in garrison was little different from that of other regiments in comparable circumstances. Desertion, high at first, steadily declined until the rate was the lowest in the army. Major and minor violations of the military code compared favorably with any units on the frontier. Chronic drunkenness, a source of real concern in other regiments, was almost unknown among the buffalo soldiers. They were not all "angels," as the records amply show. There were murderers and thieves among them and worse. These were not representative, although many frontier editors would have had it so.

Prejudice was an ever-present obstacle and often hampered their effectiveness. Trouble with civilians in the tough little frontier towns was frequent but often exaggerated. White regiments, never immune from similar difficulties, were seldom castigated as severely in the press or in public discussion. To many the word Negro was sufficient for indictment, trial, and conviction.

In the last analysis, however, the records reveal a simple fact. The Ninth and Tenth Cavalry were first-rate regiments and major forces in promoting peace and advancing civilization along America's last continental frontier. The thriving cities and towns, the fertile fields, and the natural beauty of that once wild land are monuments enough for any buffalo soldier.

LIST OF ABBREVIATIONS
USED IN FOOTNOTES

FOR MANUSCRIPT MATERIAL FROM THE NATIONAL ARCHIVES

AG: Adjutant General
AGO: Adjutant General's Office
AAG: Assistant Adjutant General
AAAG: Acting Assistant Adjutant General
LR: Letters Received
LS: Letters Sent
NA: National Archives
PA: Post Adjutant
RG: Record Group
SDLR: Selected Documents, Letters Received
SLR: Selected Letters Received

BIBLIOGRAPHY

I. MANUSCRIPT MATERIALS

A. *National Archives, Washington, D.C.*

1. Records of the Office of Indian Affairs
   a. Letters Received by the Office of Indian Affairs, Kiowa Agency, 1864–80.
2. Records of the War Department, Adjutant General's Office, Record Group 94
   a. Annual Report of the Department of Texas for 1873.
   b. Correspondence, Adjutant General, Document File, 1876.
   c. Medical History of Posts.
   d. Letters Received, 1875–81.
   e. Selected Documents from Letters Received, 1872–76.
   f. Selected Letters Received Relating to the Ninth and Tenth Regiments, United States Cavalry.
   g. Selected Letters Received, 1870–74.
   h. Selected Letters Received Relating to Texas, 1875–76.
   i. Selected Letters Received, 1875–80.
   j. Organizational Returns, Tenth Cavalry, 1866–86.
   k. Organizational Returns, Ninth Cavalry, 1866–93.
   l. Post Returns.
      1) Camp Supply.
      2) Fort Concho.
      3) Fort Davis.
      4) Fort Dodge.
      5) Fort Grant.
      6) Fort Griffin.

7) Fort Harker.

8) Fort Hays.

9) Fort Larned.

10) Fort McKavett.

11) Fort Richardson.

12) Fort Sill.

13) Fort Stockton.

14) Fort Thomas.

15) Fort Wallace.

m. Letters Received, File No. 554–1874.

n. Letters Received, File No. 1405–1878.

o. Letters Received, Affairs on the Río Grande and Texas Frontier, 1875–81. File No. 1653.

p. Letters Received, File No. 1305–1871.

q. Letters Received, File No. 2815–1874.

r. Letters Received, File No. 3144–1874.

s. Letters Received, File No. 3300–1874.

t. Letters Received, File No. 3490–1874.

u. Letters Received, File No. 4447–1873.

v. Letters Received, Selected Documents Relating to the Activities of the Ninth and Tenth Cavalry in the Campaign Against Victorio, 1879–80. File No. 6058–1879.

w. Letters Received, File No. 5993–PRD–1890.

x. The History of the Fifth United States Cavalry from March 3, 1855, to December 31, 1905. File No. 1102491.

y. Tabular Statement of Murders, Outrages, Robberies, and Depredations Committed by Indians in the Department of Missouri and Northern Texas in 1868 and '69 (exclusive of military engagements) and officially reported to Headquarters, Department of the Missouri.

3. Records of United States Army Commands, Record Group 98

a. Letters Received, District of New Mexico, 1876–81.

b. Selected Letters Received Relating to the Tenth United States Cavalry, 1873–76.

   c. Tenth United States Cavalry, Historical Sketch, 1866–92, by Major John Bigelow, Jr.
   d. Military Division of the Missouri, Special File No. 6181–1875.
   e. Military Division of the Missouri, Special File, Victorio Papers, 1880.
   f. Letters Sent, Department of the Missouri, 1876–81.
   g. Letters Sent, District of New Mexico, 1876–81.
   h. Letters Sent, Department of Texas, 1873–74.
   i. Letters Sent, Tenth United States Cavalry, 1866–83.
   j. Registers of Enlistments in the United States Army, 1798–1914. Microcopy No. 233.

   B. *Illinois State Historical Society, Springfield, Illinois*
1. The Papers of Benjamin H. Grierson
2. Brigadier General Benjamin H. Grierson, *The Lights and Shadows of Life, Including Experiences and Remembrances of the War of the Rebellion,* manuscript autobiography

   C. *Oklahoma Historical Society, Oklahoma City, Oklahoma*
1. Indian Archives Division
   a. Cheyenne-Arapaho Files
      1) Agents and Agency.
      2) Battles.
      3) Depredations.
      4) Military Relations.
      5) Murders.
      6) Prisoners and Warfare.
   b. Kiowa Files
      1) Agents and Agency.
      2) Depredations.
      3) Military Relations.
      4) Trial of Satanta and Big Tree.

   D. *The University of Oklahoma, Norman, Oklahoma*
1. The Phillips Collection
   a. Forsyth, George A., to Brevet Brigadier General C. M.

McKeever, Assistant Adjutant General, Department of the Missouri, March 31, 1869, MS. "Report of the Organization and Operations of a Body of Scouts Enrolled and Equipped at Forts Harker and Hays, Kansas, August 24, 1868."

b. Extracts From Inspector General R. B. Marcy's Journal of an Inspection Tour While Accompanying the General in Chief During the Months of April, May, and June, 1871. University of Oklahoma copy.

c. The Sherman-Sheridan Papers. University of Oklahoma Transcript.

II. GOVERNMENT PUBLICATIONS

A. *Federal*

Annual Report of the Commissioner of Indian Affairs for the Years 1866–91.

Annual Report of the Secretary of War for the Years 1866–91.

Heitman, Francis B. *Historical Register and Dictionary of the United States Army.* Washington, Government Printing Office, 1903.

Hodge, Frederick W. *Handbook of American Indians North of Mexico, Bulletin 30,* Bureau of American Ethnology. Washington, Government Printing Office, 1912.

Kappler, Charles J. *Indian Affairs: Laws and Treaties,* Vol. II. Washington, Government Printing Office, 1903.

Mooney, James. "Calendar History of the Kiowa Indians," *Seventeenth Annual Report of the Bureau of American Ethnology,* 1895–1896. Washington, Government Printing Office, 1898.

Mooney, James. "The Ghost-dance Religion," *Fourteenth Annual Report of the Bureau of American Ethnology,* 1892–1893. Washington, Government Printing Office, 1896.

United States Army, Military Division of the Missouri, *Record of Engagements With Hostile Indians Within the Military Division of the Missouri from 1868–1882.* Washington, Government Printing Office, 1882.

United States Congress, House. *H.R. Exec. Doc. No. 97,* 40 Cong., 2 sess.

————. *H.R. Misc. Doc. No. 139,* 41 Cong., 2 sess.

————. *H.R. Exec. Doc. No. 13,* 42 Cong., 3 sess.

————. *H.R. Resolution No. 96,* April 4, 1876, 44 Cong., 2 sess.

————. *H.R. Exec. Doc. No. 1,* 44 Cong., 2 sess.

————. *H.R. Exec. Doc. No. 1,* Part 2, 45 Cong., 2 sess.

————. *H.R. Exec. Doc. No. 1,* Part 2, 45 Cong., 3 sess.

————. *H.R. Exec. Doc. No. 10,* 45 Cong., 1 sess.

————. *H.R. Exec. Doc. No. 13,* 45 Cong., 1 sess.

————. *H.R. Exec. Doc. No. 18,* 45 Cong., 1 sess.

————. *H.R. Exec. Doc. No. 14,* 45 Cong., 2 sess.

————. *H.R. Misc. Doc. No. 64,* 45 cong., 2 sess.

United States Congress, Senate. *Sen. Exec. Doc. No. 13,* 40 Cong., 1 sess.

————. *Sen. Exec. Doc. No. 7,* 40 Cong., 3 sess.

————. *Sen. Exec. Doc. No. 13,* 40 Cong., 3 sess.

————. *Sen. Exec. Doc. No. 18,* 40 Cong., 3 sess.

————. *Sen. Exec. Doc. No. 36,* 40 Cong., 3 sess.

————. *Sen Exec. Doc. No. 40,* 40 Cong., 3 sess.

————. *Sen. Misc. Doc. No. 59,* 41 Cong., 2 sess.

————. *Sen. Misc. Doc. No. 16,* 45 Cong., 2 sess.

United States Statutes at Large. Vol. XV.

The War of the Rebellion: A Compilation of the Official Records of the Union and Confederate Armies. Washington, Government Printing Office, 1891–98.

B. *State*

Day, James M., and Dorman Winfrey (eds.). Texas Indian Papers, 1860–1916. 4 vols. Austin, Texas State Library, 1961.

III. PUBLICATIONS OF LEARNED SOCIETIES

Blount, Bertha. "The Apache in the Southwest, 1846–1886," *Southwestern Historical Quarterly,* Vol. XXIII, No. 1 (July, 1919).

Burkey, Elmer R. "The Thornburgh Battle With the Utes on

Milk Creek," *The Colorado Magazine,* Vol. XIII, No. 3 (Denver, 1936).

Cahill, Luke. "An Indian Campaign and Buffalo Hunting with 'Buffalo Bill,' " *The Colorado Magazine,* Vol. IV, No. 4 August, 1927).

Campbell, C. E. "Down Among the Red Men," *Collections of the Kansas State Historical Society,* Vol. XVII (Topeka, 1929).

Carroll, H. Bailey. "Nolan's 'Lost Nigger' Expedition of 1877," *Southwestern Historical Quarterly,* Vol. XLIV (July, 1940).

Clum, John P. "Geronimo," *New Mexico Historical Review,* Vol. II, No. 3 (January, 1928); Vol. III, No. 2 (April, 1928); Vol. III, No. 3 (July, 1928).

Crimmins, Colonel M. L. "Captain Nolan's Lost Troop on the Staked Plains," *West Texas Historical Association Yearbook,* Vol. X (October, 1934).

————. "Colonel Buell's Expedition into Mexico," *New Mexico Historical Review,* Vol. X (April, 1935).

————. "Shafter's Explorations in West Texas," *West Texas Historical Association Yearbook,* Vol. IX (October, 1933).

————. "Fort McKavett, Texas," *Southwestern Historical Quarterly,* Vol. XXXVIII, No. 1 (July, 1934).

Doran, Thomas F. "Kansas Sixty Years Ago," *Collections of the Kansas State Historical Society,* Vol. XV (Topeka, 1923).

Garfield, Marvin. "Defense of the Kansas Frontier, 1864–1865," *The Kansas Historical Quarterly,* Vol. I, No. 2 (February, 1932).

————. "Defense of the Kansas Frontier, 1866–1867," *The Kansas Historical Quarterly,* Vol. I, No. 4 (August, 1932).

————. "Defense of the Kansas Frontier, 1868–1869," *The Kansas Historical Quarterly,* Vol. I, No. 5 (November, 1932).

Grant, Ben O. "Life in Old Fort Griffin," *West Texas Historical Association Yearbook,* Vol. X (October, 1934).

Haley, J. Evetts. "The Comanchero Trade," *Southwestern Historical Quarterly,* Vol. XXXVIII, No. 3 (January, 1935).

Hazen, General William B. "Some Corrections of *Life on the*

Plains," in *Chronicles of Oklahoma,* Vol. III, No. 4 (December, 1925).

Hinton, Harwood P., Jr. "John Simpson Chisum, 1877–1884," *New Mexico Historical Review,* Vol. XXXI, No. 3 and No. 4 (July, 1956).

Jacobs, Captain Richard T. "Military Reminiscences of Captain Richard T. Jacobs," *Chronicles of Oklahoma,* Vol. II (March, 1924).

Jenness, George B. "The Battle on Beaver Creek," *Transactions of the Kansas State Historical Society,* Vol. IX (Topeka, 1906).

Miles, Susan. "Fort Concho, in 1877," *West Texas Historical Association Yearbook,* Vol. XXXV (October, 1959).

Montgomery, Mrs. Frank C. "Fort Wallace and Its Relation to the Frontier," *Collections of the Kansas State Historical Society,* Vol. XVII (Topeka, 1928).

Nunn, Curtis W. "Eighty-six Hours Without Water on the Texas Plains," *Southwestern Historical Quarterly,* Vol. XLIII (January, 1940).

Ogle, Ralph. "Federal Control of the Western Apaches," *New Mexico Historical Review,* Vol. XIV, No. 4 (October, 1939); Vol. XV, No. 1 (January, 1940); Vol. XV, No. 2 (April, 1940); Vol. XV, No. 3 (July, 1940).

Opler, Morris E., and Catherine H. "Mescalero Apache History in the Southwest," *New Mexico Historical Review,* Vol. XXV, No. 1 (January, 1950).

Porter, Kenneth W. "The Seminole-Negro Indian Scouts, 1870–1881," *Southwestern Historical Quarterly,* Vol. LV (January, 1952).

————. "Negroes and Indians on the Texas Frontier," *Southwestern Historical Quarterly,* Vol. LIII (October, 1949).

Reddick, L. D. "The Negro Policy of the United States Army, 1775–1945," *The Journal of Negro History,* Vol. XXXIV, No. 1 (January, 1949).

Rister, Carl C. "Fort Griffin," *West Texas Historical Association Yearbook,* Vol. I (June, 1925).

————. "Colonel A. W. Evans' Christmas Day Indian Fight (1868)," *Chronicles of Oklahoma,* Vol. XVI (September, 1938).

Savage, W. Sherman. "The Role of Negro Soldiers in Protecting the Indian Frontier From Intruders," *The Journal of Negro History,* Vol. XXXVI, No. 1 (January, 1951).

Sutton, Mary. "Glimpses of Fort Concho Through Military Telegraph," *West Texas Historical Association Yearbook,* Vol. XXXII (October, 1956).

Taylor, Alfred A. "Medicine Lodge Peace Council," *Chronicles of Oklahoma,* Vol. II (March, 1924).

Temple, Frank M. "Colonel B. H. Grierson's Victorio Campaign," *West Texas Historical Association Yearbook,* Vol. XXXV (October, 1959).

————. "Federal Military Defense of the Trans-Pecos Region, 1850–1880," *West Texas Historical Association Yearbook,* Vol. XXX (October, 1954).

Wallace, Edward S. "General John Lapham Bullis, Thunderbolt of Texas Frontier," *Southwestern Historical Quarterly,* Vol. LV, No. 1 (July, 1951).

Whisenhunt, Donald W. "Fort Richardson," *West Texas Historical Association Yearbook,* Vol. XXXIX (October, 1963).

"Publishing a Newspaper in a 'Boomer' Camp," *Chronicles of Oklahoma,* Vol. V, No. 4 (December, 1927).

"Tribute to Captain Payne," *Chronicles of Oklahoma,* Vol. VIII, No. 1 (March, 1930).

IV. *Periodicals*

A. Special Articles

Davis, Theodore R. "A Summer on the Plains," *Harper's Monthly Magazine,* Vol. XXXVI (February, 1868).

Dorst, Captain Joseph. "Ranald Slidell Mackenzie," *Cavalry Journal,* Vol. X (December, 1897).

Forsyth, George A. "A Frontier Fight," *Harper's Monthly Magazine,* Vol. XCI (June, 1895).

Godfrey, Brigadier General E. S. "Some Reminiscences, Including an Account of General Sully's Expedition Against the Southern Plains Indians, 1868," *Cavalry Journal,* Vol. XXXVI (July, 1927).

————. "Some Reminiscences, Including the Washita Battle, November 29, 1868," *Cavalry Journal,* Vol. XXXVII, No. 153 (October, 1928).

Merritt, Wesley. "Three Indian Campaigns," *Harper's New Monthly Magazine* (April, 1890).

Pratt, Richard H. "Some Indian Experiences," *Cavalry Journal,* Vol. XVI (December, 1906).

Thompson, Major W. A. "Scouting With Mackenzie," *Cavalry Journal,* Vol. X (December, 1897).

B. Newspapers and Magazines

Army and Navy Journal.
Daily Express (San Antonio, Texas).
Daily Herald (Dallas, Texas).
Daily Herald (San Antonio, Texas).
Daily Journal (Austin, Texas).
Daily News (Galveston, Texas).
Daily State Journal (Austin, Texas).
Echo (Fort Griffin, Texas).
Flake's Daily Bulletin (Galveston, Texas).
Harper's Weekly Magazine.
Independent (Mesilla, New Mexico).
News (Galveston, Texas).
News (San Saba, Texas).
Standard (San Angelo, Texas).
Times (Dodge City, Kansas).
Tribune (New York, New York).
Winners of the West (St. Joseph, Missouri).

V. BOOKS

Armes, Colonel George A. *Ups and Downs of an Army Officer.* Washington, D.C., 1900.

Athearn, Robert C. *William Tecumseh Sherman and the Settle-*

ment of the West. Norman, University of Oklahoma Press, 1956.

Battles and Leaders of the Civil War. 4 vols. New York, Thomas Yoselof, Inc., 1956.

Beck, Warren A. *New Mexico: A History of Four Centuries.* Norman, University of Oklahoma Press, 1962.

Berthrong, Donald J. *The Southern Cheyennes.* Norman, University of Oklahoma Press, 1963.

Beyer, Walter F., and Oscar F. Keydel (eds.). *Deeds of Valor.* Detroit, Perrien-Keydel Co., 1903.

Boatner, Mark Mayo III. *The Civil War Dictionary.* New York, David McKay Co., 1959.

Bourke, John G. *An Apache Campaign in the Sierra Madre.* New York, Charles Scribner's Sons, 1886.

————. *On the Border With Crook.* New York, Charles Scribner's Sons, 1896.

Brady, Cyrus T. *Indian Fights and Fighters.* New York, McClure, Phillips and Co., 1904.

Brown, D. Alexander. *Grierson's Raid.* Urbana, University of Illinois Press, 1954.

Carter, Robert G. *On the Border With Mackenzie.* Washington, D.C., Eynon Printing Co., 1935.

Casey, Robert J. *The Texas Border and Some Borderliners.* New York, Bobbs-Merrill Co., Inc., 1950.

Cashin, Herschel V. and others. *Under Fire With the Tenth Cavalry.* Chicago, American Publishing House, n.d.

Catton, Bruce. *A Stillness at Appomattox.* Garden City, New York, Doubleday and Co., Inc., 1954.

————. *This Hallowed Ground: The Story of the Union Side of the Civil War.* Garden City, New York, Doubleday and Co., Inc., 1956.

Clum, Woodworth. *Apache Agent.* Boston, Houghton Mifflin Co., 1936.

Cook, John R. *The Border and the Buffalo.* Topeka, Kansas, Crane and Co., 1907.

Cornish, Dudley T. *The Sable Arm.* New York, Longman's, 1956.

Crawford, Samuel J. *Kansas in the Sixties*. Chicago, A. C. Mc-Clurg and Co., 1911.

Cullum, George W. *Biographical Register of Officers and Graduates of the United States Military Academy at West Point, New York, 1802–1867*. New York, D. Van Nostrand, 1868.

Custer, Elizabeth B. *Following the Guidon*. New York, Harper and Brothers, 1890.

—————. *Tenting on the Plains*. New York, C. L. Webster and Co., 1887.

Dale, Edward E. *The Indians of the Southwest*. Norman, University of Oklahoma Press, 1949.

Davis, Britton. *The Truth About Geronimo*. New Haven, Yale University Press, 1929.

Dunn, J. P., Jr. *Massacres of the Mountains*. New York, Archer House, Inc., 1886.

Dupuy, R. Ernest and Trevor N. *Military Heritage of America*. New York, McGraw-Hill Book Co., Inc., 1956.

Eastman, Elaine G. *Pratt, the Red Man's Moses,* Norman, University of Oklahoma Press, 1935.

Emmett, Chris. *Fort Union and the Winning of the Southwest*. Norman, University of Oklahoma Press, 1965.

Emmitt, Robert. *The Last War Trail: The Utes and the Settlement of Colorado*. Norman, University of Oklahoma Press, 1954.

Flipper, Henry O. *Negro Frontiersman*. El Paso, Texas Western College Press, 1963.

Foreman, Grant. *Fort Gibson: A Brief History*. Norman, University of Oklahoma Press, 1936.

Frazer, Robert W. *Forts of the West*. Norman, University of Oklahoma Press, 1965.

Ganoe, William A. *The History of the United States Army*. New York, D. Appleton and Co., 1924.

Gard, Wayne. *Frontier Justice*. Norman, University of Oklahoma Press, 1949.

Garrett, Pat F. *The Authentic Life of Billy the Kid*. Norman, University of Oklahoma Press, 1954.

272

Gibson, A. M. *The Kickapoos*. Norman, University of Oklahoma Press, 1963.

Glass, Major E. N. *History of the Tenth Cavalry*. Tucson, Acme Printing Company, 1921.

Grinnell, George B. *The Fighting Cheyennes*. Norman, University of Oklahoma Press, 1956.

Haley, J. Evetts. *Fort Concho and the Texas Frontier*. San Angelo, Texas, San Angelo Standard-Times, 1952.

Hamlin, William Lee. *The True Story of Billy the Kid*. Caldwell, Idaho, Caxton Printers, 1959.

Herr, John K., and Edward S. Wallace. *The Story of the United States Cavalry, 1775–1942*. Boston, Little, Brown and Co., 1953.

Higginson, Thomas Wentworth. *Army Life in a Black Regiment*. East Lansing, Michigan State University Press, 1960.

Hyde, George E. *A Sioux Chronicle*. Norman, University of Oklahoma Press, 1956.

Keim, De Benneville R. *Sheridan's Troopers on the Borders: A Winter Campaign on the Plains*. Philadelphia, D. McKay, 1885.

Keleher, William A. *Violence in Lincoln County*. Albuquerque, University of New Mexico Press, 1957.

King, James T. *War Eagle: A Life of General Eugene A. Carr*. Lincoln, University of Nebraska Press, 1963.

Knapp, Frank Averill, Jr. *The Life of Sebastián Lerdo de Tejada, 1823–1889*. Austin, University of Texas Press, 1951.

Koller, Larry. *The Fireside Book of Guns*. New York, Simon and Schuster, 1959.

Leckie, William H. *The Military Conquest of the Southern Plains*. Norman, University of Oklahoma Press, 1963.

Litton, Gaston. *History of Oklahoma*. 4 vols. New York, Lesis Historical Publishing Co., Inc., 1957.

Lockwood, Frank E. *The Apache Indians*. New York, Macmillan Co., 1938.

McCracken, Harold (ed.). *Frederic Remington's Own West*. New York, Dial Press, 1960.

McReynolds, Edwin C. *Oklahoma: A History of the Sooner State*. Norman, University of Oklahoma Press, 1954.

Mayhall, Mildred. *The Kiowas*. Norman, University of Oklahoma Press, 1962.

Miles, General Nelson A. *Personal Recollections of General Nelson A. Miles*. Chicago, Werner Co., 1896.

Nolan, Frederick W. *The Life and Death of John Henry Tunstall*. Albuquerque, University of New Mexico Press, 1965.

Nye, W. S. *Carbine and Lance: The Story of Old Fort Sill*. Norman, University of Oklahoma Press, 1943.

Phisterer, Frederick. *Statistical Record of the Armies of the United States*. New York, Charles Scribner's Sons. 1883.

Pratt, Richard Henry (Robert M. Utley, ed.). *Battlefield and Classroom: Four Decades With the American Indian, 1867–1904*. New Haven, Yale University Press, 1964.

Price, George F. *Across the Continent With the Fifth Cavalry*. New York, D. Van Nostrand Publishers, 1883.

Quarles, Benjamin. *The Negro in the Civil War*. Boston, Little, Brown and Company, 1953.

Raht, Carlysle G. *The Romance of Davis Mountains and Big Bend Country*. Odessa, Texas, Rahtbooks Co., 1963.

Randall, James G. *The Civil War and Reconstruction*. Boston, D. C. Heath and Co., 1937.

Richardson, Rupert N. *The Comanche Barrier to South Plains Settlement*. Glendale, Arthur H. Clark Co., 1933.

Rickey, Don, Jr. *Forty Miles a Day on Beans and Hay*. Norman, University of Oklahoma Press, 1963.

Rister, Carl C. *Land Hunger: David L. Payne and the Oklahoma Boomers*. Norman, University of Oklahoma Press, 1956.

―――. *The Southwestern Frontier, 1865–1881* Cleveland, Arthur H. Clark Co., 1928.

Roberts, Dan W. *Rangers and Sovereignty*. San Antonio, Wood Printing and Engraving Co., 1914.

Rodenbough, Theo. F., and William L. Haskin (eds.). *The Army of the United States*. New York, Maynard, Merrill, and Co., 1896.

274

Scobee, Barry. *Old Fort Davis*. San Antonio, Naylor Co., 1947.

Sheridan, Philip H. *Personal Memoirs*. 2 vols. New York, Charles L. Webster and Co., 1888.

Sherman, General W. T. *Memoirs of General W. T. Sherman*. 2 vols. New York, Charles L. Webster and Co., 1892.

Sonnichsen, C. L. *The Mescalero Apaches*. Norman, University of Oklahoma Press, 1958.

————. *Tularosa: Last of the Frontier West*. New York, Devin-Adair Co., 1960.

Tatum, Lawrie. *Our Red Brothers and the Peace Policy of President Ulysses S. Grant*. Philadelphia. J. C. Winston and Co., 1879.

Toulouse, Joseph H. and James R. *Pioneer Posts of Texas*. San Antonio, Naylor Co., 1936.

Twitchell, Ralph E. *The Leading Facts of New Mexican History*. Cedar Rapids, Iowa, Torch Press, 1912.

Utley, Robert M. *The Last Days of the Sioux Nation*. New Haven, Yale University Press, 1963.

Webb, Walter P. *The Texas Rangers: A Century of Frontier Defense*. Boston, Houghton Mifflin Co., 1935.

Wellman, Paul I. *Death on Horseback*. Philadelphia, J. B. Lippincott Co., 1934.

Wheeler, Homer W. *Buffalo Days*. New York, Bobbs-Merrill Co., 1925.

Whitman, S. E. *The Troopers*. New York, Hastings House, Publishers, 1962.

Wilbarger, J. W. *Indian Depredations in Texas*. Austin, Hutchings Printing House, 1889.

Williams, George W. *A History of the Negro Troops in the War of the Rebellion, 1861–1865*. New York, Harper and Brothers, 1888.

VI. Unpublished Materials

Kubela, Marguerite E. "History of Fort Concho, Texas." Unpublished Master's thesis, Department of History, University of Texas, 1936.

Rickey, Don, Jr., "The Negro Regulars: A Combat Record, 1866–1891." Unpublished paper delivered at the Western History Association meeting at Helena, Montana, October, 1965.

Big Sandy Creek: 33, 43

Big Spring: 146–47, 157, 167

Big Tree: 59, 61–63, 67, 70, 74, 76–77, 120n., 135n.

Big Wichita River: 115

Billy the Kid: 195n., 196–97, 201–202, 204

Bird Chief: 135n.

Black Bear: 167

Black Beaver: 122

Black Horse: 136, 155, 168

Black Range Mountains: 214, 241

Blackstone, Private Charley: 108, 109n.

Blair, Captain Thomas: 188, 190

Blanco Cañon: 167

Blanco River: 207

Blazer's Mill: 197

Blue River Cañon: 170

Bluff Creek: 52

Board of Indian Commissioners: 173

Bodamer, Lieutenant J. A.: 53, 63–64

Bond, Private John: 162

"Boomers": 245–52

Boone, A. G.: 46

Borajo, Antonio: 186–87

Borden County, Texas: 157

Boston, Massachusetts: 12–13, 20

Boudinot, Colonel Elias C.: 246

Bowie Station, Arizona: 239

Boyer, Private Eli: 85 & n.

Brady, William: 193, 195–97

Brazeale, Thomas: 58

Brazos River: 125; Double Mountain Fork, 80, 146; Fresh Fork, 143–44, 148; Salt Fork, 88

Brewer, Richard: 196–97

Brooke, Brigadier General John R.: 253, 255; battle of Wounded Knee, 256–57

Brown, Private John L.: 164

Brown, Mrs. Lydia: 98

Brownsville, Texas: 11, 86, 111, 115

Buchanan, William: 134

Buck Antelope: 135

Buell, Lieutenant Colonel George: commanding at Fort Griffin, 74, 78–80, 114, 118, 124; search expedition, 125ff.; Victorio campaign, 227ff.

Buffalo soldiers: 46, 51, 53–54, 65, 67, 69, 73, 76, 78, 80–81, 84–85, 87–90, 93, 97–98, 105, 107, 111, 114, 121, 133, 135, 148–52, 163–64, 166–70, 176, 178, 187, 190, 192, 202, 204, 208, 231–34,

241, 244–46, 260; title origin, 26 & n.; rescue of Forsyth, 34–36; commended by Sheridan, 38; Penrose campaign, 40–43; arrest of Satanta, Satank, and Big Tree, 59–63; battle of Anadarko, 123–24; Buell's campaign, 128–30; battle of Sand Hill, 138–40; Shafter's expedition, 143–44; campaign in Mexico, 154–55; Victorio War, 210ff.; trouble at Fort Concho, 237–38; expelling "Boomers," 249–51; fight at Drexel Mission, 257–58

Buffalo Tank: 37, 38n.

Bull Creek: 157, 162

Bullis, Lieutenant John L.: 97–98, 143, 146 & n., 150, 152, 154

Burnett, Lieutenant George (Medal of Honor winner): 232–33

Burnett County, Texas: 87

Burns, Private Carter: 230

Burnside, General Ambrose: 5

Byrne, Captain Edward: 15, 44, 56

Cache Creek: 30, 46, 56–57, 63–64, 118, 247

Caddo Indians: 121

Caldwell, Kansas: 249

California Springs: 104

Camp Alice, Indian Territory: 248

Camp Grant, Arizona: 173

Camp Hudson, Texas: 85

Camp McDowell, Arizona: 173, 181n.

Camp Supply, Indian Territory: 45 & n., 47, 51–54, 64, 68–69

Camp Verde, Arizona: 173–74

Camp Wichita, Indian Territory: 46, 47n., 51n.

Camp Wood, Texas: 153

Campbell's Camp: 22

Canadian River: 29, 117, 124–25, 127–28, 134; North Fork, 136

Candelaria Mountains: 214, 227

Cañon de los Embudos: 242

Cardis, Luis: 187–88

Carleton, Captain Caleb: 131

Carleton, Brigadier General James H.: 172

Carpenter, "Colonel" Charles C.: 246

Carpenter, Captain Louis H.: 12, 33–34, 43, 51, 53, 65, 74, 131, 149n., 169–70, 217; rescue of Forsyth, 35 & n.–36 & n.; wins Medal of Honor, 37–38; arrest of Satanta, Satank, and Big Tree, 60–62;

279